Additions to clay bodies

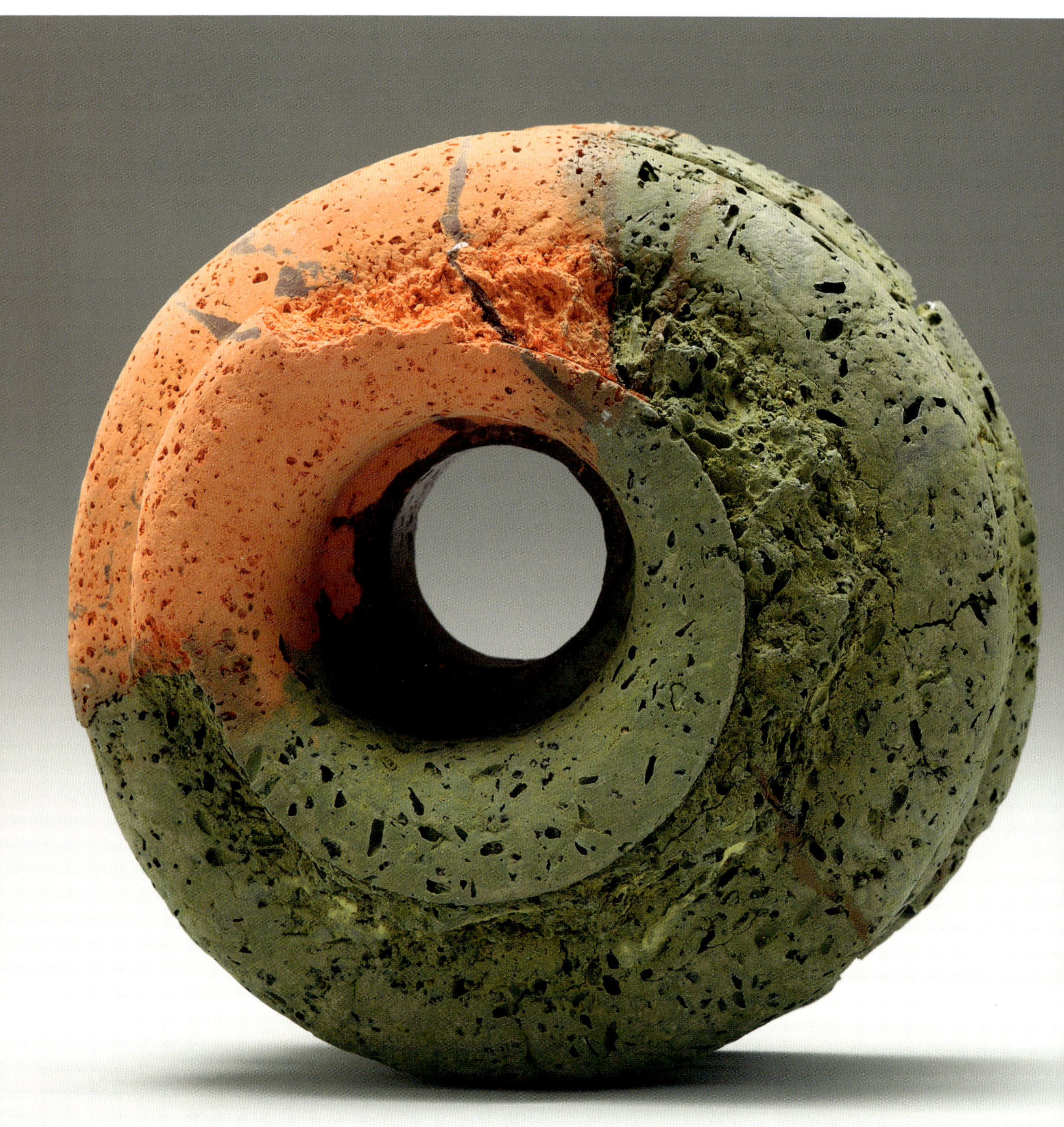

Additions to clay bodies

Kathleen Standen

HERBERT PRESS
LONDON • OXFORD • NEW YORK • NEW DELHI • SYDNEY

HERBERT PRESS
Bloomsbury Publishing Plc
50 Bedford Square, London, WC1B 3DP, UK
29 Earlsfort Terrace, Dublin 2, Ireland

BLOOMSBURY, HERBERT PRESS and the Herbert Press logo are trademarks of Bloomsbury Publishing Plc

First published in 2013 by Bloomsbury Publishing Plc
This edition published in 2017

A catalogue record for this book is available from the British Library
Library of Congress Cataloguing-in-Publication data has been applied for

ISBN: PB: 978-1-912217-13-7

6 8 10 9 7

Series: New Ceramics

Typeset in 10 on 13pt Rotis Semi Sans
Book design by Susan McIntyre
Cover design by Sutchinda Thompson
Edited by Kate Sherington

Printed and bound in India by Replika Press

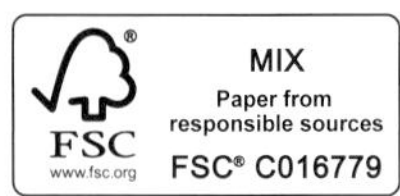

To find out more about our authors and books visit www.bloomsbury.com

FRONT COVER: Top: Kathleen Standen, *Haze II*, 2011. Porcelain clay body, organic additions, body stains and oxides, glaze, 40 x 22 cm (15¾ x 8¾ in). *Photo: Roland Paschhoff.* Bottom, left: Fred Gatley, *Erosion*, 2009. Pinch-formed and polished bone china bowl, with inclusions of iron oxide, fired to 1220°C (2228°F), diameter: 4 cm (1½ in), with slabbed base, white St Thomas clay with additions of river silts, sand and brick grogs, 1020°C (1868°F) sawdust-fired, 6 x 15 cm (2½ x 6 in). Silver feet attached. *Photo: by the artist.* Bottom, centre: Dominique Bivar Segurado, Calcium Bowl, 2004. Porcelain clay, press-moulded and hand-cut, unglazed, fired to 1240°C (2264°F). *Photo: Dougal Waters.* Bottom, right: Kathleen Standen, *Green Rock Pool* (detail), 2009. Porcelain clay body, organic additions, body stains and oxides, glaze. *Photo: Roland Paschhoff.*

BACK COVER: Jim Turner, *Black and White Bottles*, 2009. Thrown and extruded altered forms, fibre slip on top of glaze with fibre, once-fired to 1300°C (2372°F), height: 65 and 55 cm (25½ and 21¾ in). *Photo: Roland Paschhoff.*

FRONTISPIECE: Kathleen Standen, *Landmarks II*, 2009. Porcelain clay body, organic additions, oxides, 26 x 15 cm (10¼ x 6 in). *Photo: Roland Paschhoff.*

RIGHT: Kathleen Standen, *White Rock Pools*, 2009. Porcelain clay body, organic additions, body stains and oxides, glaze, 10 x 11 cm (4 x 4¼ in). *Photo: Roland Paschhoff.*

Contents

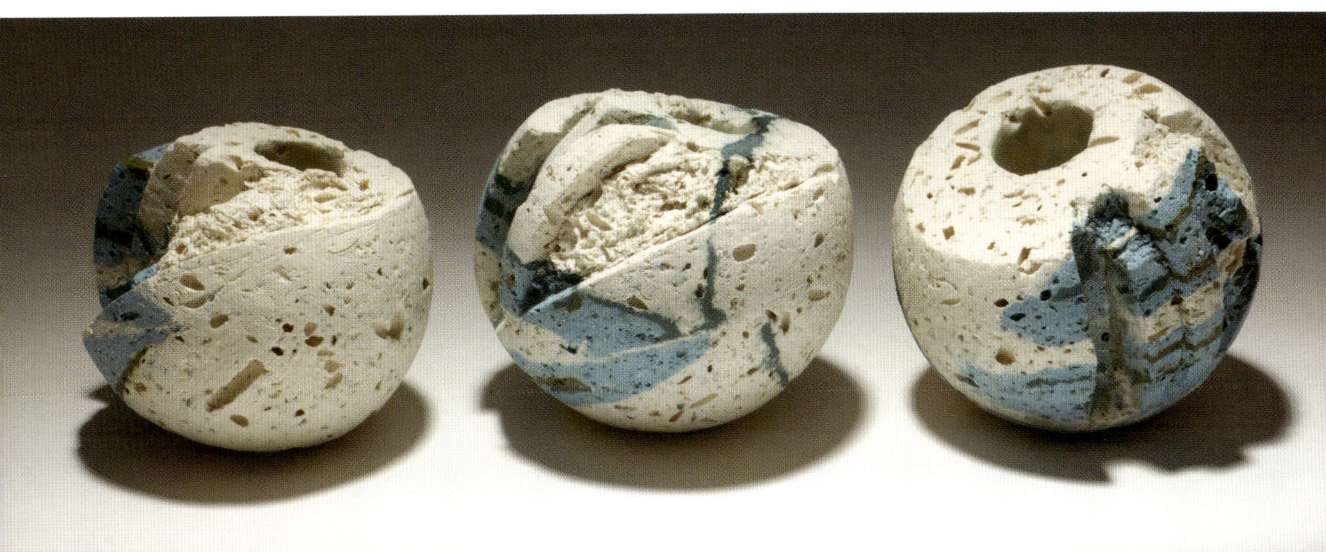

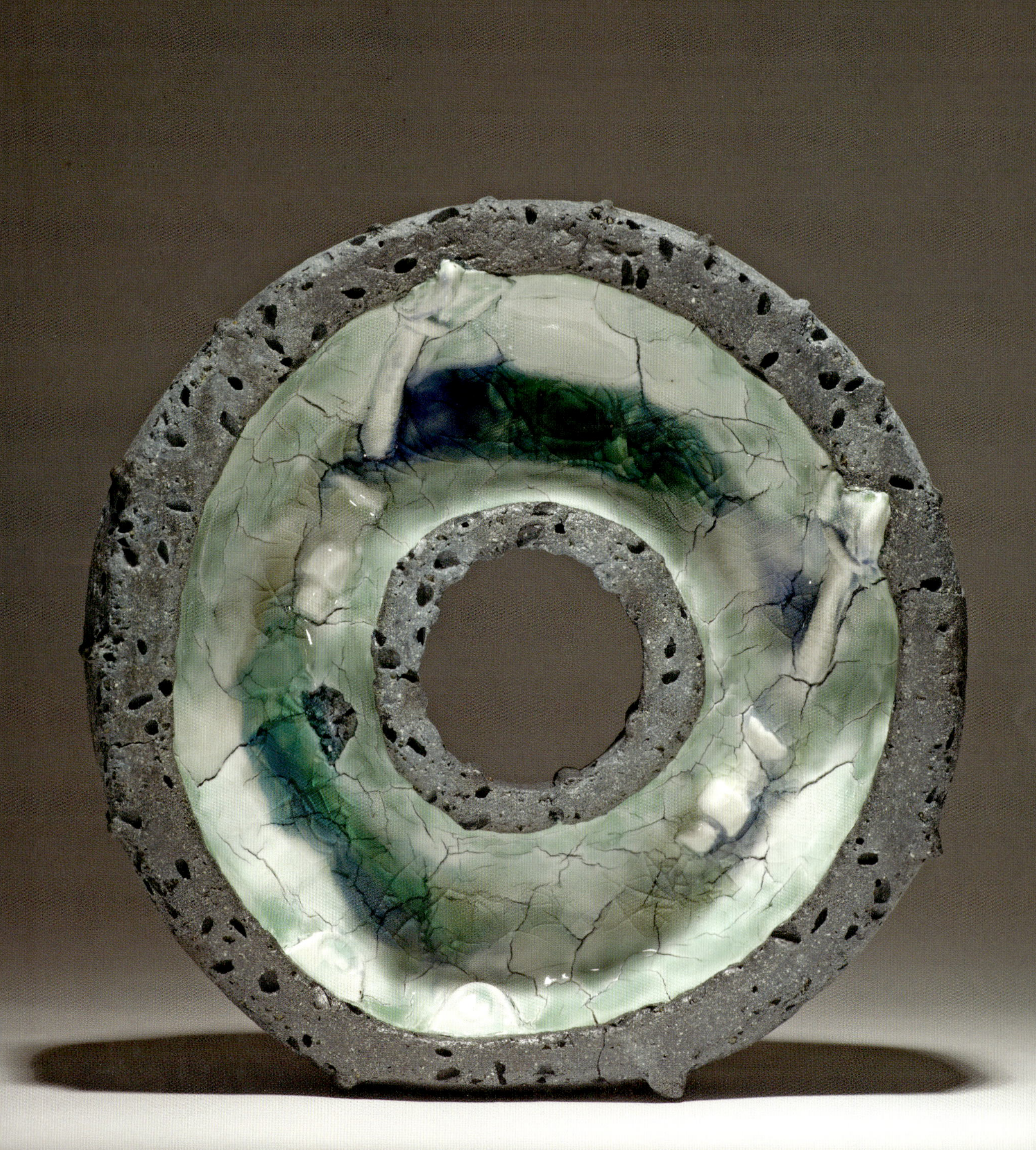

Acknowledgements

I wish to thank all the artists who generously gave their time to send me information about themselves and images of their work, and in many instances making and photographing work for this book. I have learnt so much from you all.

Bill Jones and Jessica Knapp, of *Pottery Making Illustrated* and *Ceramics Monthly*, gave me a huge helping hand by pointing me in the right direction to approach American artists.

Thanks also to Carol and Kazumi, who lent me their expertise by reading through the manuscript and making suggestions, and thanks also to Laura who volunteered to proof-read the text. I am grateful to Alison Stace and the editorial team at Bloomsbury for giving me this opportunity, which I have thoroughly enjoyed.

And to my husband John, for giving me encouragement and keeping me on track, thank you so much.

LEFT: Kathleen Standen, *Horizon III (view 2)*, 2011. Porcelain clay body, porcelain paperclay impressions, organic additions, oxides, 27 x 27 x 10 cm (10½ x 10½ x 4 in). *Photo: Roland Paschhoff.*

RIGHT: Kathleen Standen, *Haze I*, 2011. Porcelain clay body, organic additions, body stains and oxides, glaze, 40 x 36 cm (15¾ x 14¼ in). *Photo: Roland Paschhoff.*

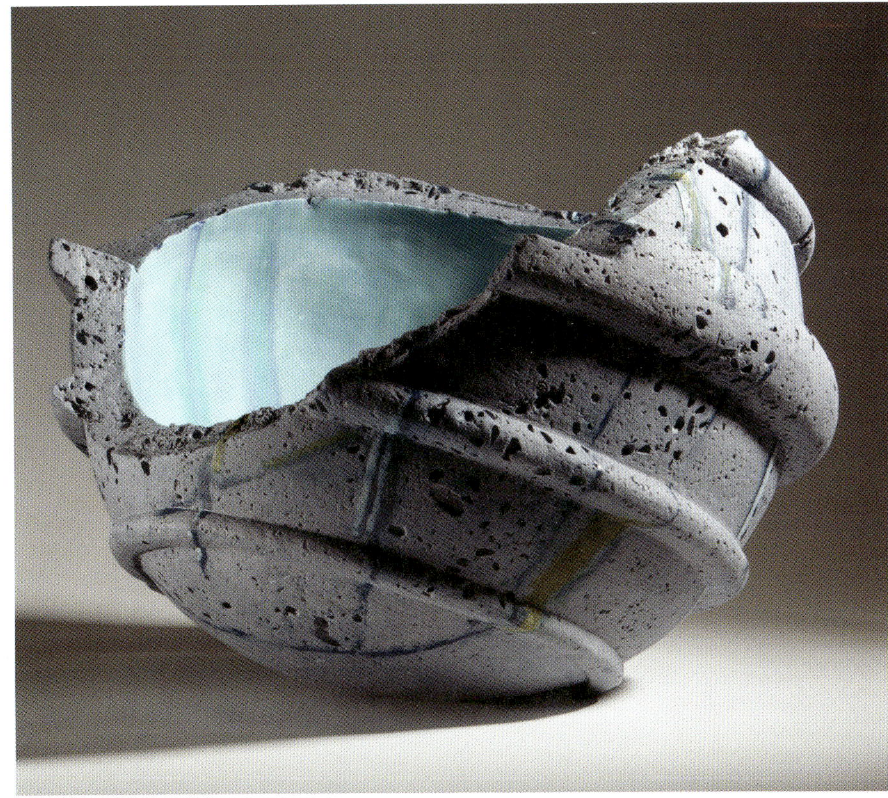

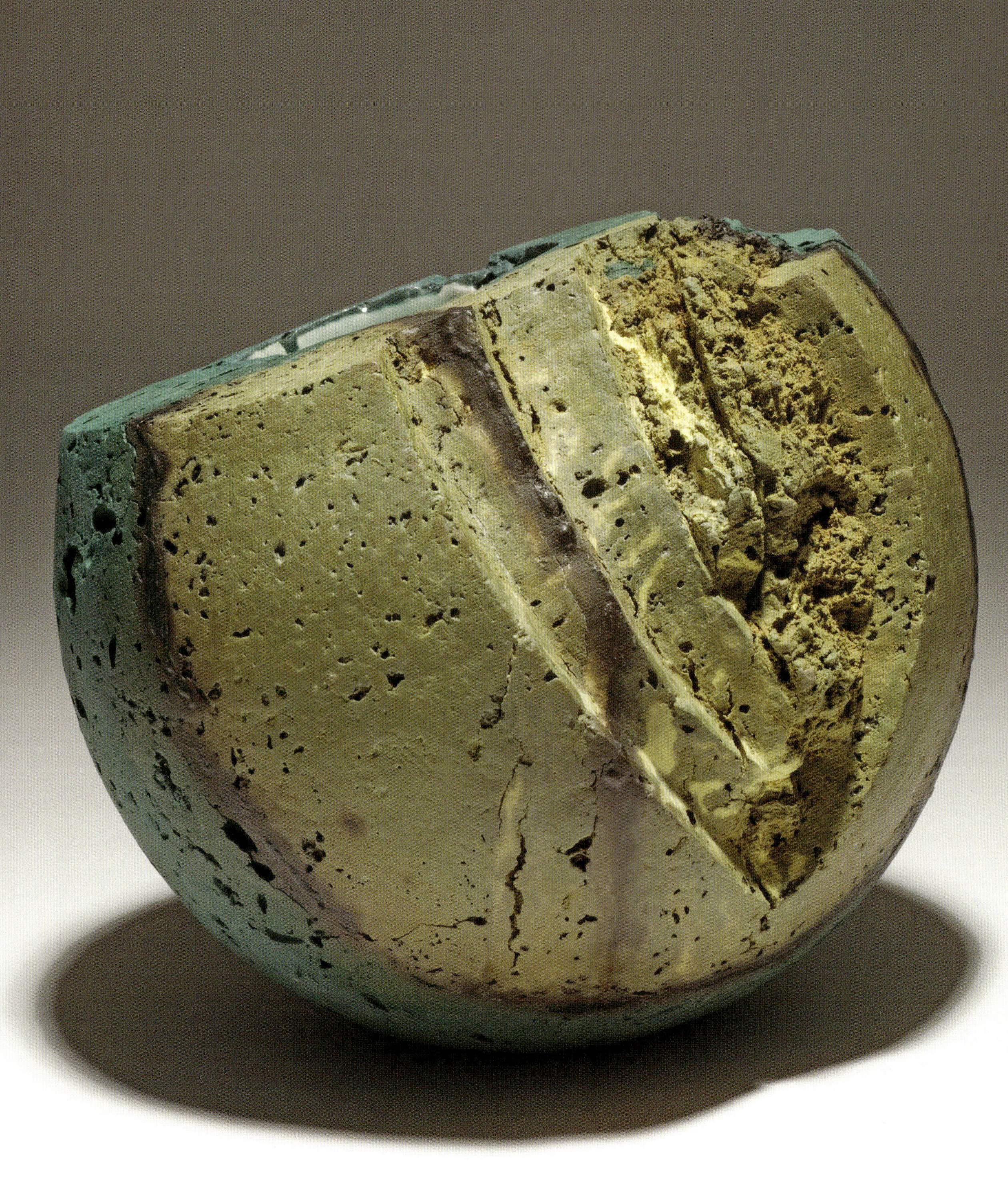

Introduction

LEFT: Kathleen Standen, *Green Rock Pool*, 2009. Porcelain clay body, organic additions, body stains and oxides, glaze, 15 x 16 cm (6 x 6¼ in). *Photo: Roland Paschhoff.*

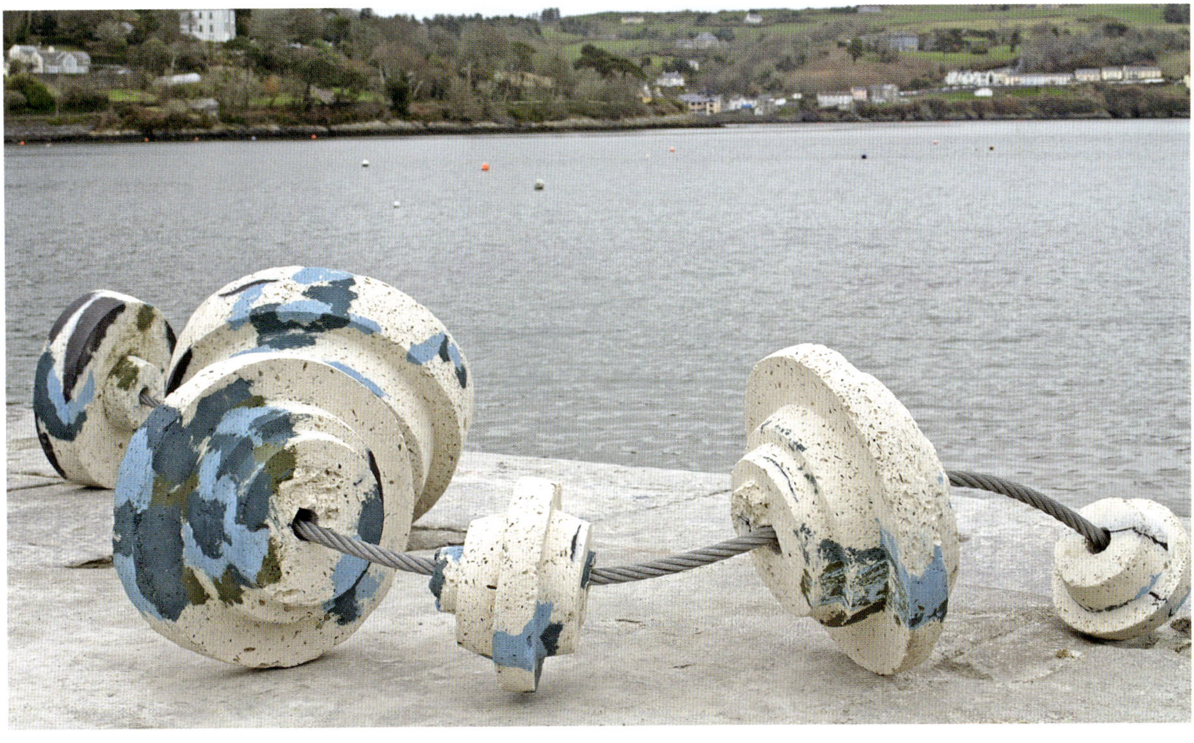

BELOW: Kathleen Standen, *Cascade group*, 2008. Coloured porcelain clay 1220°C (2228°F), metal marine rope and clamps, 300 x 45 x 45 cm (118 x 17¾ x 17¾ in). Pictured on the old pier in Union Hall, West Cork. *Photo: John Standen.*

Rice, dog biscuits, coffee beans, cereal grains, nuts, bark chippings, glass beads, pebbles, nails, perlite and bits of broken pots: all lying on the studio bench, waiting to be used in some combination or other. But what conceivable difference can these materials make if I add them to a clay body? That was the challenge I was set one day in my studies.

That trigger set me off on a journey, exploring and embracing the difference additions can make to clay making. This journey has been eventful and wonderful and I hope this book brings some of that wonder to a wider audience.

Additions can make clay making more challenging, visually stunning and unique. In researching additions to clay, I have come across a number of leading ceramicists exploring the possibilities that additions can offer. Examples include Fiona Byrne-Sutton, who collects clay from a farmer in Clackmannanshire in Scotland; Helen Gilmour, who knits cotton teapots for her pieces; Todd Leech, who applies glazes on kiln elements, causing them to foam; Emma Rodgers' animal sculptures, from which broken saucers and nails emerge; and the candy-coloured flowers of Deborah Sigel.

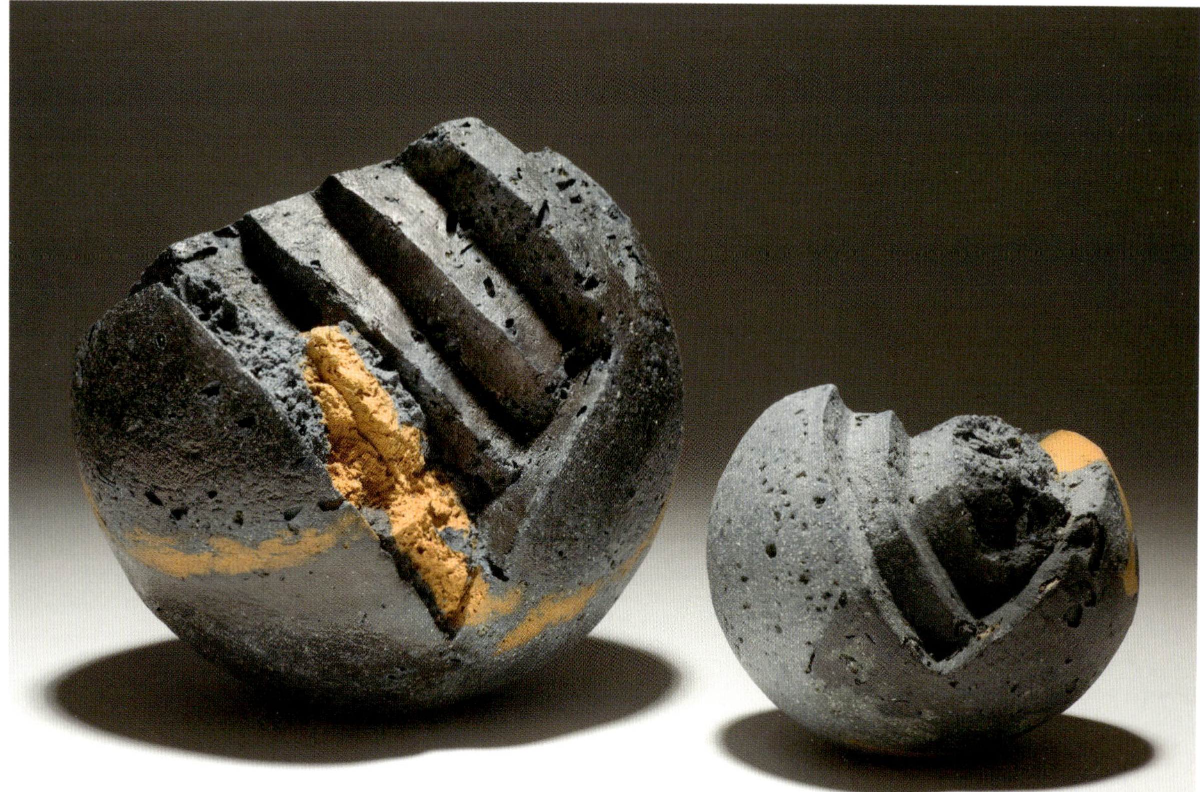

Kathleen Standen, *Blue Rock Pools*, 2009. Porcelain clay body, organic additions, body stains and oxides, glaze, 15 x 16 and 10 x 11 cm (6 x 6¼ and 4 x 4¼ in). *Photo: Roland Paschhoff.*

This book is about encouraging the reader to experiment and take informed risks with the clay body, opening up the imagination for the many possibilities that additions provide:

- What if I dipped a piece of lace into slip and fired it?
- What if I added crushed monkey-nut shells to the clay before filling my mould?
- What if I increased the grog by 25% and then made my form 10 cm (4 in) thick?
- What if I inserted metal pins into my thrown form?
- What if I brushed clay onto fibreglass and then constructed a form of unimaginable thinness?
- What if I rolled grasses into my porcelain paperclay slabs?

These opportunities to expand the horizons of clay, and many more, have been tried by successful artists and their experiences will be shared with you in this book.

Please note that the chapter headings I have used are for generalised purposes, to draw the reader to a theme. Many of the techniques and applications cross chapter boundaries. This book encourages an open-minded approach to making ceramic forms.

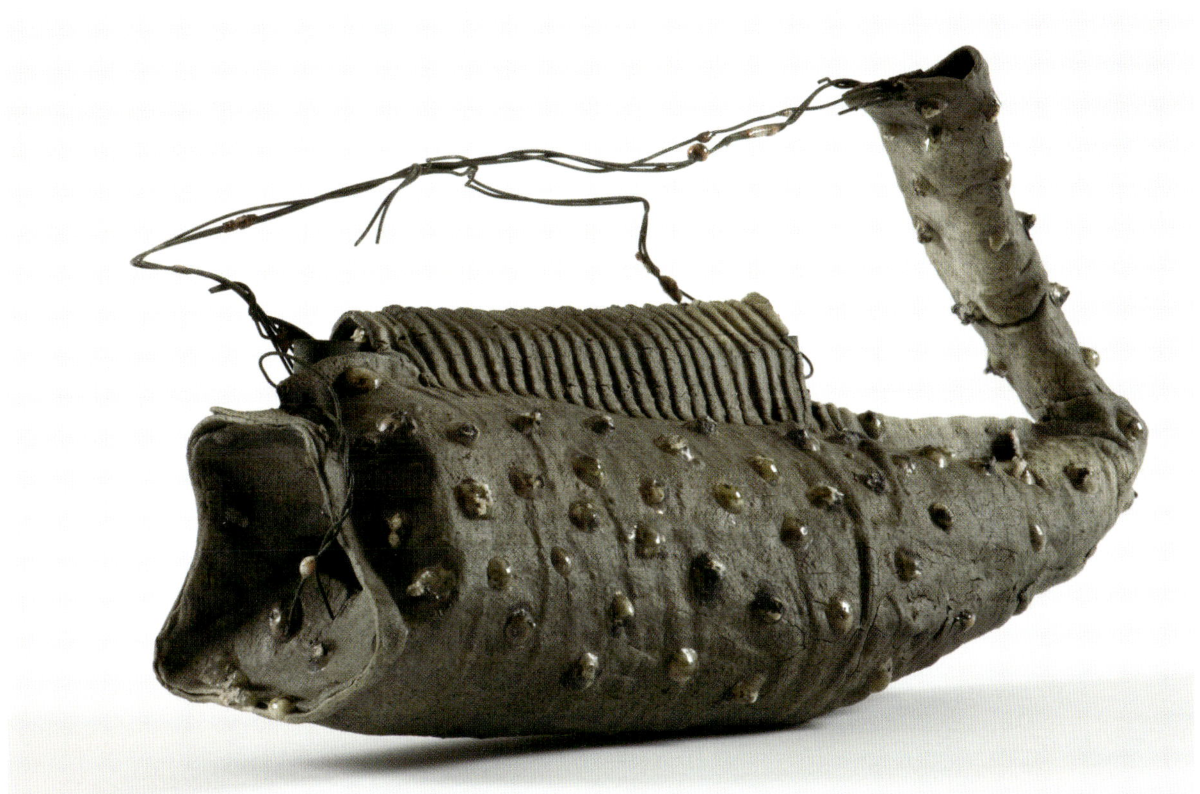

Gillian Lowndes, *Tail of the Dog*, 1983. Part of a series of work based on the 'kuba cloth' from the Congo; clay slip on fibreglass, nichrome wire, granite chippings, Egyptian paste, fired to 1280°C (2336°F), 30 x 21 cm (11¾ x 8¼ in). *Photo: supplied by the Craft Council, UK.*

Challenging conventional practice: Gillian Lowndes

One of the first potters to break away from the convention of using only clay and glaze in her ceramic practice was Gillian Lowndes. In the late 1970s, Lowndes made the breakthrough that has come to define her work, when she started to incorporate non-conventional materials into her objects, most notably fibreglass tissue dipped in porcelain slip. Her intention was to capture the appearance of bark cloth, a material that has ceremonial uses in Samoa and Fiji. She continued to experiment with a broad range of additions, which included Egyptian paste, 18th-century brick, nichrome wire, bits of broken crockery, granite chips, bulldog clips, curled bus tickets and wire mesh. She redefined the role of clay in her pieces, using it as a 'glue' to hold the form together.

One series was based on American Indian quivers, the shapes of horns, and a motif she called *Tail of the Dog*, derived from a pattern seen on an appliqué wrapper from the Congo.

Today, many ceramicists explore the potential of adding something to their clay, and their reasons for doing this are as varied as the additions themselves. In the following chapters you will find a range of additions and ways of using them. I am very grateful to the many artists who have generously shared their knowledge, enabling you to have an insight into their techniques and ideas.

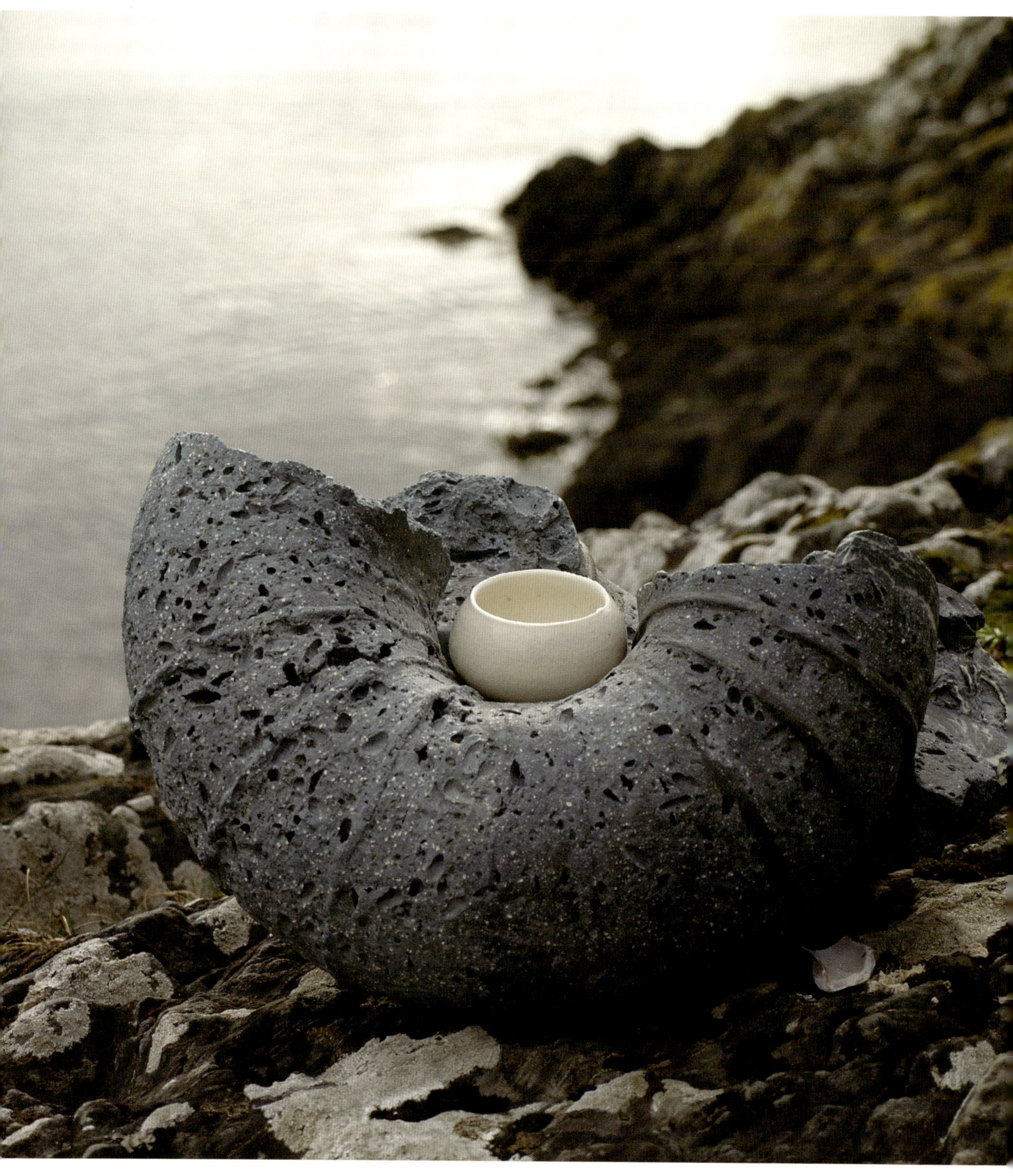

1

Clays

One of the first decisions that a ceramicist will make concerns choice of clay. Most artists find something to suit them from commercial clays sold in bulk by pottery suppliers. But there are alternatives and this chapter introduces artists who want something different that is not just 'off the shelf'. Examples of artists who work in this way include Fiona Byrne-Sutton, who digs her own clay; David Binns, who collects granular materials from around the world to add to clay; and myself, Kathleen Standen, making clay from scratch using dry, raw materials.

Digging up your clay

Fiona Byrne-Sutton makes large press-moulded vessels, which explore the heritage of Central Scotland. She travels from her Glasgow studio to Clackmannanshire in the Forth River Valley area, where farmer Ian MacFarlane digs up orange firing clay for Fiona, on his own land.

Preparation

Byrne-Sutton does not process this clay in terms of 'washing' and 'sieving', and only removes large pebbles to prevent her pots 'blowing' in the kiln. There are risks in this, but she welcomes blisters appearing in the clay due to bits of coal or silica. The

LEFT: Kathleen Standen, *Horizon with vessel*, 2011. Photographed in the scenic village of Glandore, West Cork, Ireland, coloured porcelain clay fired to 1220°C (2228°F), 18 x 34 cm (7 x 13½ in). *Photo: by the artist.*

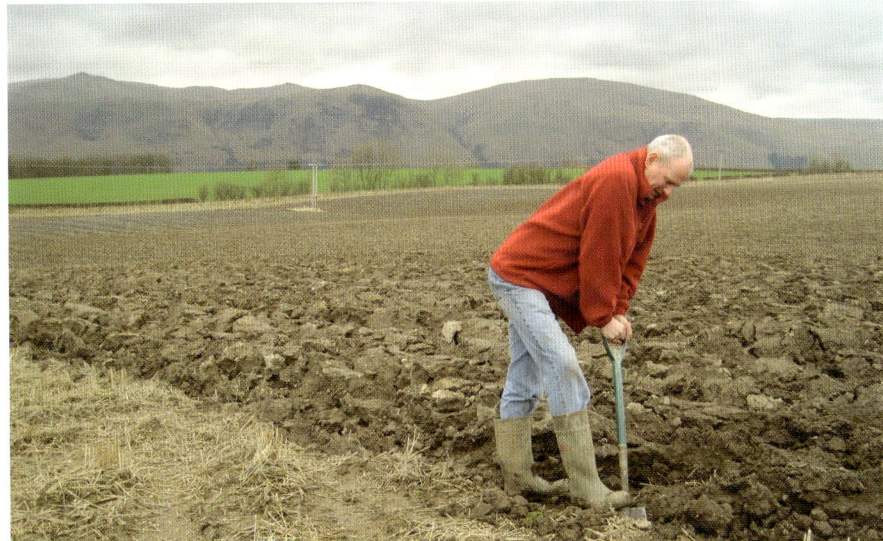

RIGHT: Ian MacFarlane digging up clay at Gartenkeir Farm, Coalshaughton, Clackmannanshire, Scotland. *Photo: Fiona Byrne-Sutton.*

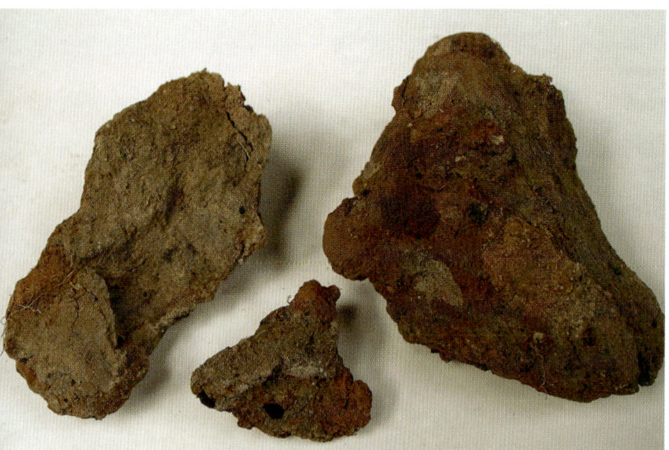

Unfired Clackmannanshire clay, straight from the ground, is marbled grey and brown with iron ochre. *Photo: Helen Gilmour.*

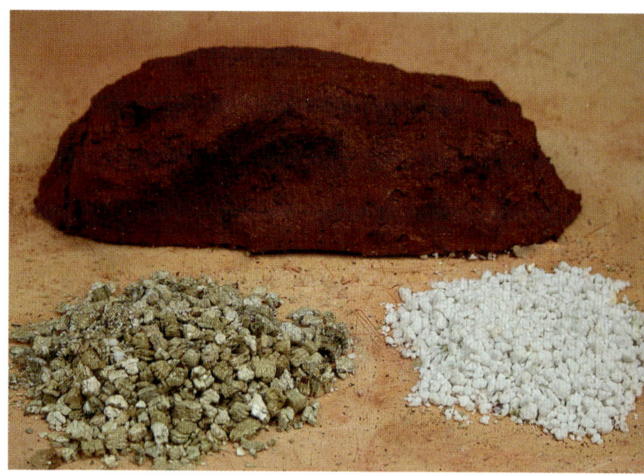

Black Scarva Earthstone, vermiculite on left, perlite on right. *Photo: Helen Gilmour.*

boulders or fragments of clay are pressed into the surface of her large vessels, just as they have been dug up, to the extent that you can see the line of the shovel and the naturally occurring strata of secondary iron ochre and white clay.

Byrne-Sutton describes her Clackmannanshire vessels as 'rural pots embedded with ferns, Scots pine, boulders of clay from a farm; an embedded biodiversity echoing a local human population with strong communal links.'

The Clyde River area near Glasgow is another of her favoured locations for collecting clay samples and this **strath** clay is a deeper red than Clackmannanshire clay, due to a higher percentage of iron oxide. Her Glasgow vessels are 'urban, painted with topsoil slip. They are pressed with "weeds" that have arrived on the wind, growing out of roadside crevices, opportunist, seeking out their chances like migrant city residents.'

All these elements represent the personality of the material and the place.

Process

Byrne-Sutton's forms start off in a plaster mould lined with black Scarva Earthstone clay. Sometimes she presses **vermiculite** into the clay before filling the mould, which helps the thick walls dry evenly and reduces the overall weight, an important consideration in large forms. She advises that care be taken with vermiculite, as it can cause the clay to blister. It should be pressed, rather than wedged, into the clay.

Vermiculite in the black Earthstone clay gives a warm, toasty speckle to the ceramic body, which Byrne-Sutton says makes the black clay 'sing'. She then partially paints the interior of the form with white **slip**, before pressing in lumps of found clay. This allows the orange tones of the dug clay to stand out from the black base. Seasonal plants are pressed in and painted over with Clackmannanshire slip, dug from the ground. The slip will fire white or different shades of orange depending on which clay strata it was dug from. White slip is sometimes mixed with found clay to give a greater range of colour tones. Red iron oxide, manganese dioxide and copper

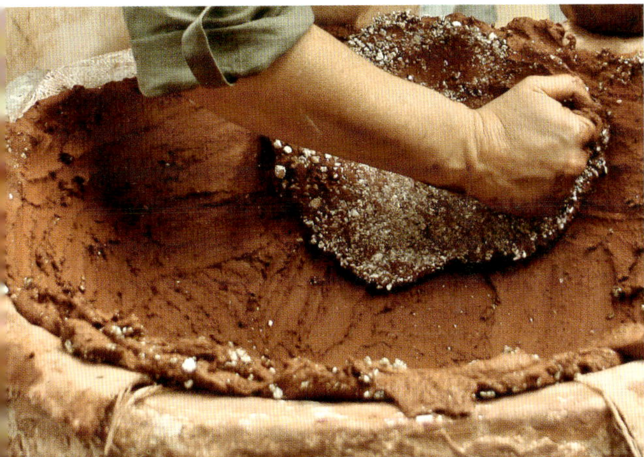

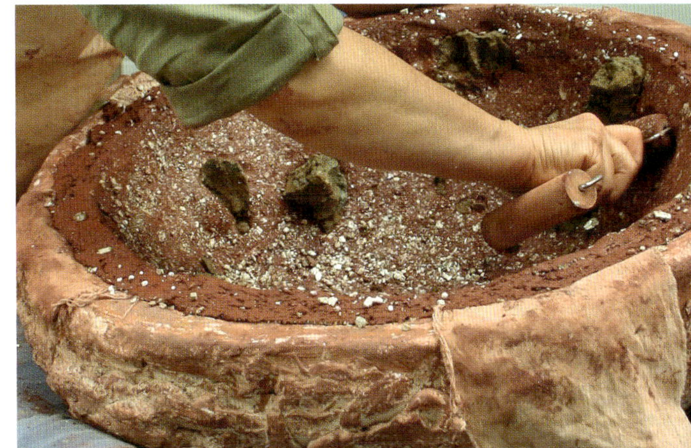

ABOVE LEFT: Fiona Byrne-Sutton building up the wall of the vessel: Pressing and not wedging vermiculite into the clay body avoids creating air pockets, helps the thick walls dry evenly and makes the bowl lighter after firing. *Photo: Helen Gilmour.*

ABOVE RIGHT: Surface decoration: boulders of marbled Clackmannanshire clay are inserted into black-firing Earthstone. The grey clay fires white while the iron ochre in the clay body reverts to red iron oxide when fired; the boulders show the sedimentation patterns of the clay in the ground. Vermiculite is rolled into the surface and the golden speckle makes the black clay come to life. Unlike perlite, it doesn't disappear during firing. *Photo: Richard Campbell.*

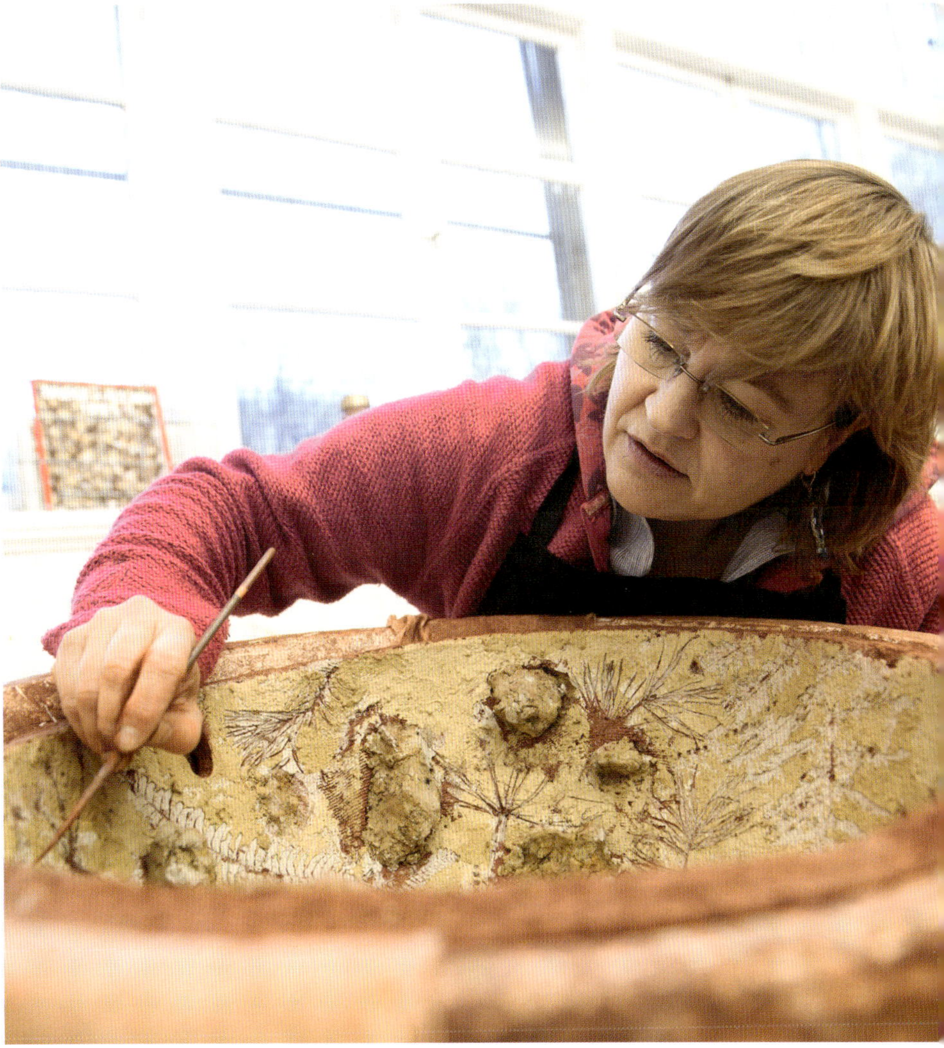

RIGHT: Surface decoration: seasonal plants are pressed in and painted over with Clackmannanshire slip. The slip will fire white, or different shades of orange, depending on the clay strata from which it has been dug. *Photo: Helen Gilmour.*

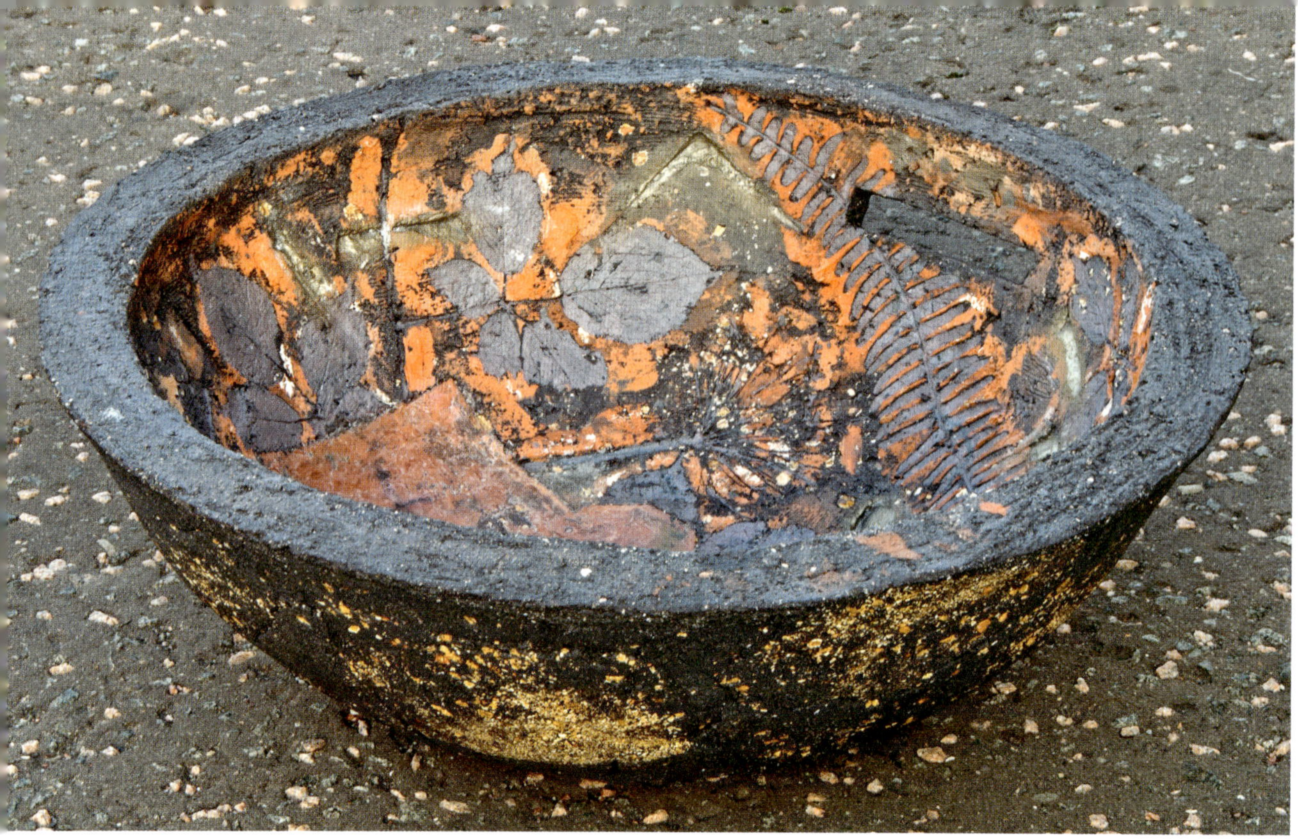

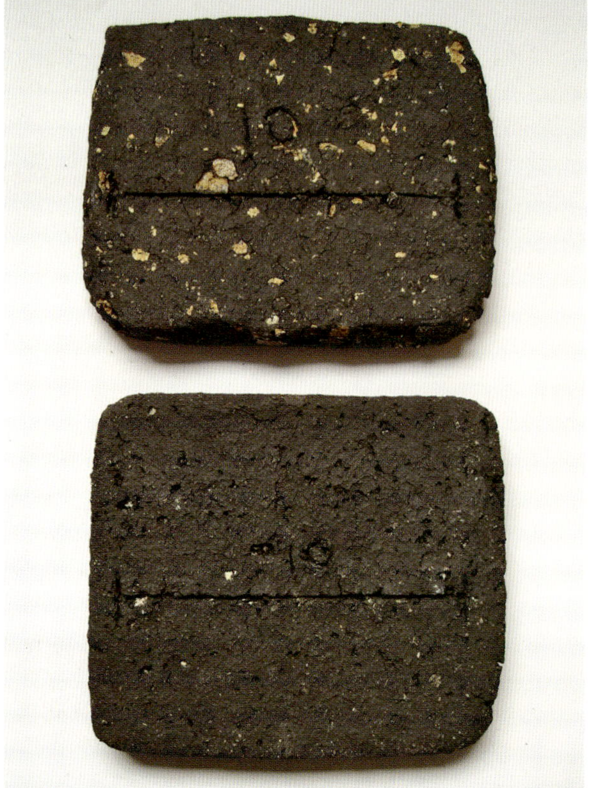

ABOVE: Fiona Byrne-Sutton, *Clackmannanshire Roadside*, 2011. Black Earthstone clay, press-moulded, with vermiculite, Clackmannanshire clay slips from the ground, red iron oxide painted on Earthstone, copper wire, manganese and copper dioxide mixed to give gold, shoe polish, beeswax. Once-fired to 1160°C (2120°F), 19 x 53 cm (7½ x 21 in). *Photo: Michael Wolchover.*

LEFT: Top tile is black Earthstone clay and vermiculite, showing brown husks of vermiculite remaining; bottom tile is Earthstone and perlite, of which only pock marks or small cavities remain. Both tiles were fired by Fiona Byrne-Sutton to 1180°C (2156°F). *Photo: Fiona Byrne-Sutton.*

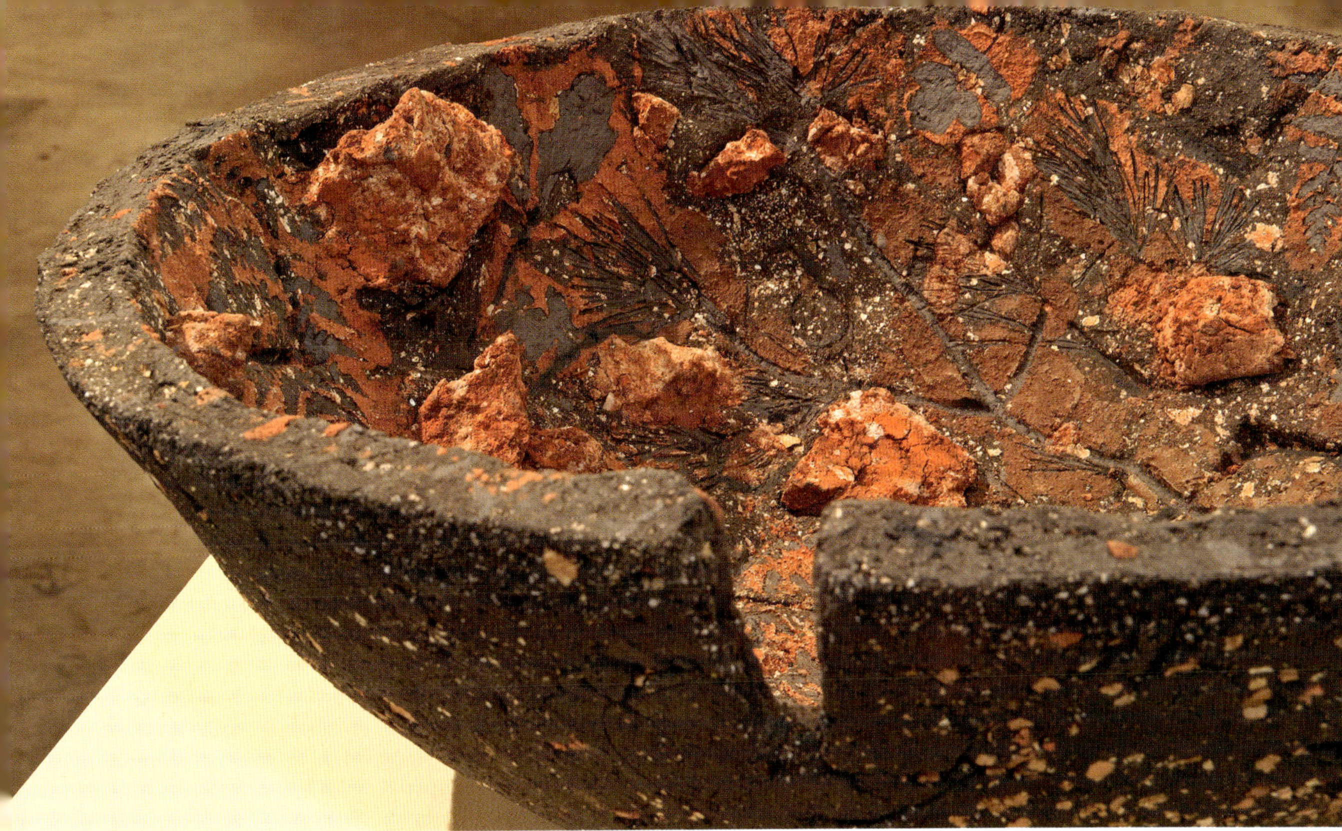

Fiona Byrne-Sutton, *Rhapsody in Orange and Black Clackmannanshire*, 2010. Press-moulded black Earthstone clay, vermiculite, Clackmannanshire boulders and slip from the ground, red iron oxide painted on Earthstone, copper wire. Once-fired to 1160°C (2120°F), 19 x 53 cm (7½ x 21 in). *Photo: Michael Wolchover.*

wire all give different blacks when painted and fired onto black Earthstone, building up a painterly surface. She works intuitively and very quickly at this stage to create pattern, colour and texture.

A long **soak** partway through firing, before taking the temperature up high to 1160°C (2120°F), helps to set the colour in this once-fired work.

Collecting china clay and plants

The most southern region of the UK is where most businesses involved in the extraction and processing of high-quality **china clay** for the ceramics industry are based. It is also the home of **Jenny Beavan**, a ceramicist who has spent more than a decade making work here, and who has important links to this area. The industries have undergone much change in recent decades, including decommissioning, and in 2001 Imerys Minerals granted Beavan permission to study all aspects of their work at the Fal Valley China Clay Pits in Cornwall.

She has observed the important role of water in all stages of the extraction and processing of china clay and kept a diary of her observations. Her frequent visits to the pits were also recorded using photography, drawing and words, and this was the genesis for a new body of work.

When I first saw Jenny Beavan's ceramics, the words 'frozen movement' came to mind. And that was before I had read the titles: *Beach Erosion*, *Oscillation*, *Upsurge* and *Energised Water*.

What interests Beavan is movement in relation to natural change, such as decay, disintegration, relocation and reformation, and in particular the role water plays in this action. She has collected materials from the pits, both combustible and non-combustible, which become part of the fabric of her unusual compositions. The series of four photographs below shows stages in the making of *Beach Erosion*. Beavan has arranged curved slabs of clay into a walled mould and then poured and placed a range of additions including **molochite**, sand, plants and china clay slip.

She continues to visit china clay pits in Cornwall and to create work that reflects her observations. Her ceramic works are held in public and private collections in the UK and abroad.

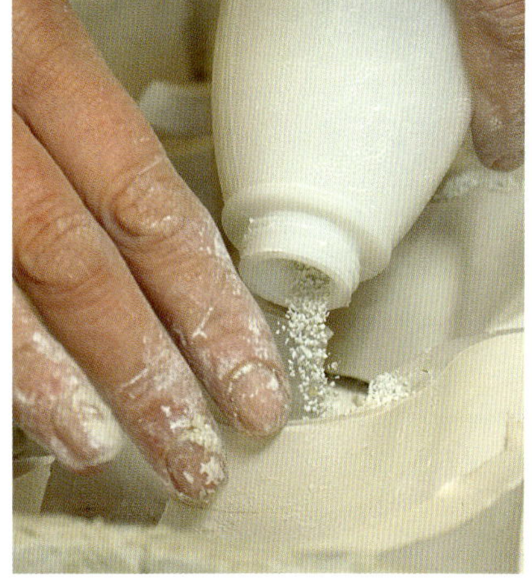

Adding molochite to the clay in the mould.

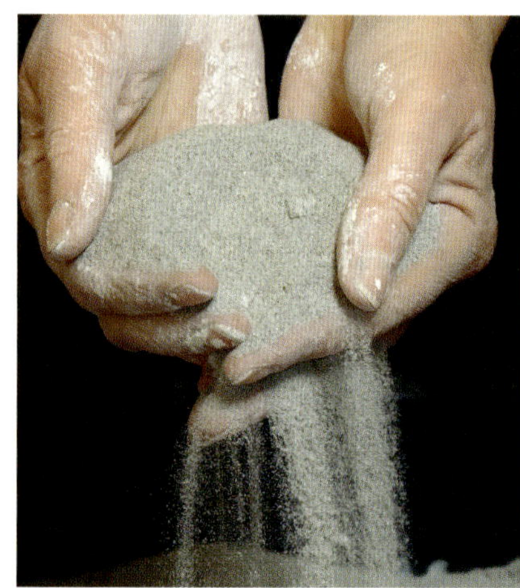

Adding sands.

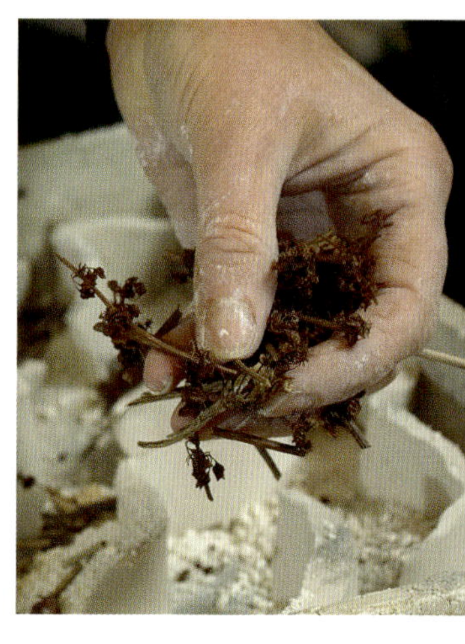

Adding plants.

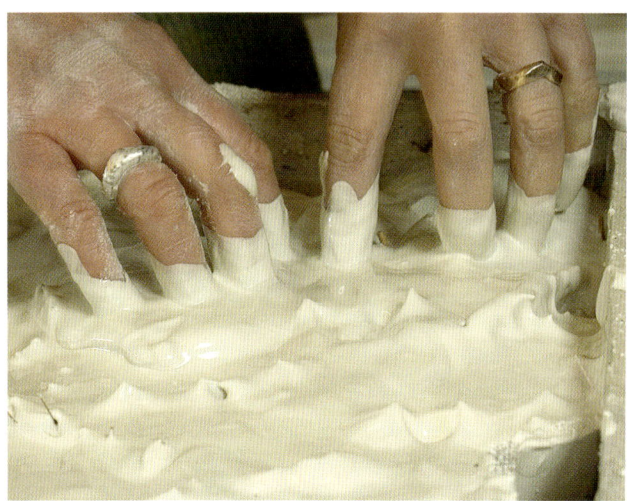

Adding china clay slip over the top of the slabs and additions.

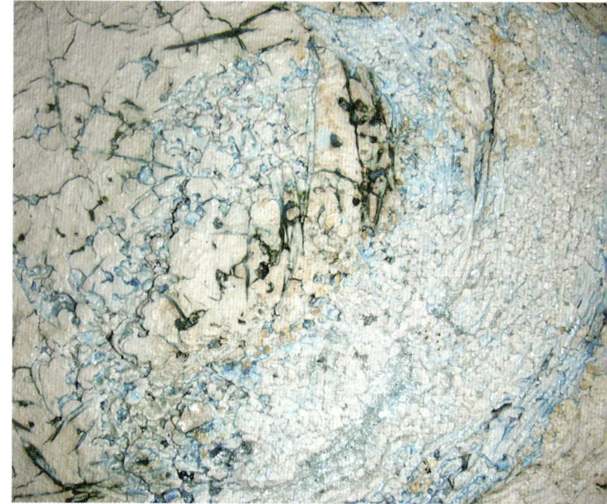

Jenny Beavan, *Upsurge* (detail), 2001. China clay matrix with processed china clay, glazes and glass, 1260°C (2300°F), 55 x 55 cm (21½ x 21½ in). *Photos: by the artist.*

Jenny Beavan, *Beach Erosion*, 2011. Porcelain with china clay, combustible material, beach sands and pebbles, glazes and glass, fired to 1260°C (2300°F), 40 x 40 cm (15¾ x 15¾ in). *Photo: by the artist.*

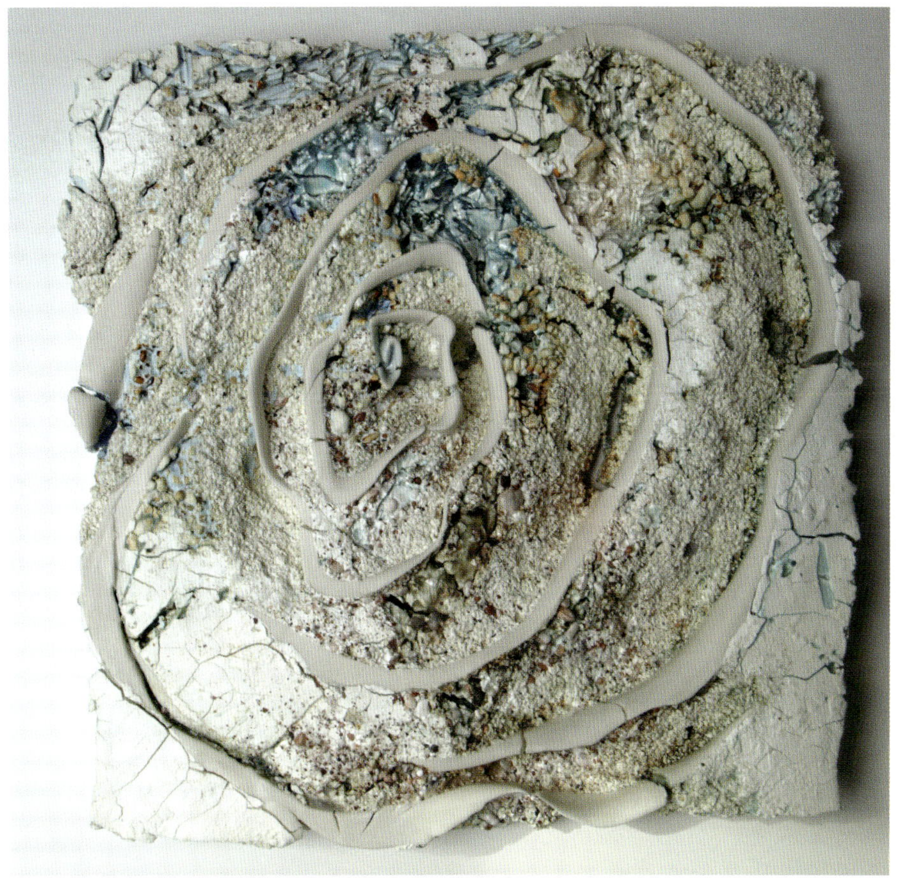

Collecting granular material

A brief introduction to the ceramicist **David Binns** is relevant here because, despite not digging up his clay, he does collect granular material from particular locations, which bestow each of his works with a specific sense of place.

His research and testing of found materials has yielded interesting results, with grey granite from the mountains of North Wales, beach shingle from the east coast of England, and pink granite gathered during a visit to Tasmania. He always travels with collecting bags, looking for the opportunity to gather interesting granular material.

Binns, however, tells a cautionary tale concerning the addition of found materials in ceramic work. In his enthusiasm to develop new surfaces, he collected and mixed beach shingle into porcelain clay, having picked out obvious pieces of seaweed and shell, and created a boat form. This was promptly exhibited, but fortunately failed to sell. Within a few weeks, the form had disintegrated. Binns concluded that the shingle must have included fragments of calcium-bearing rock, such as limestone. The stones had calcined and then slowly absorbed atmospheric moisture, creating a monumental case of lime spit. As a result Binns advises washing and pre-firing all found material. Any calcium

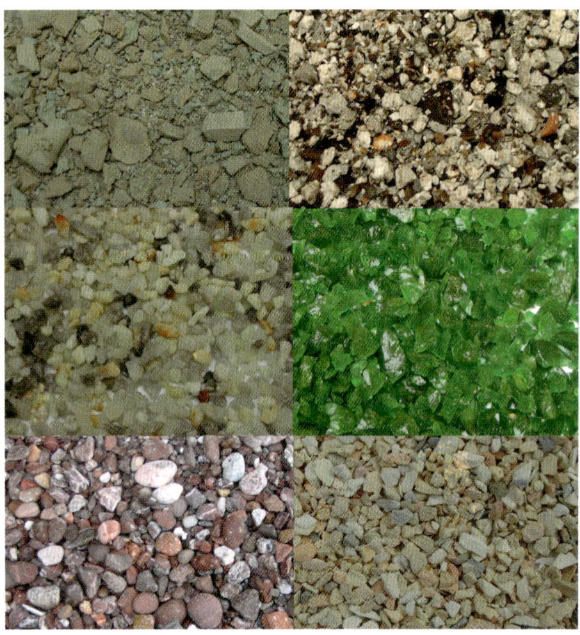

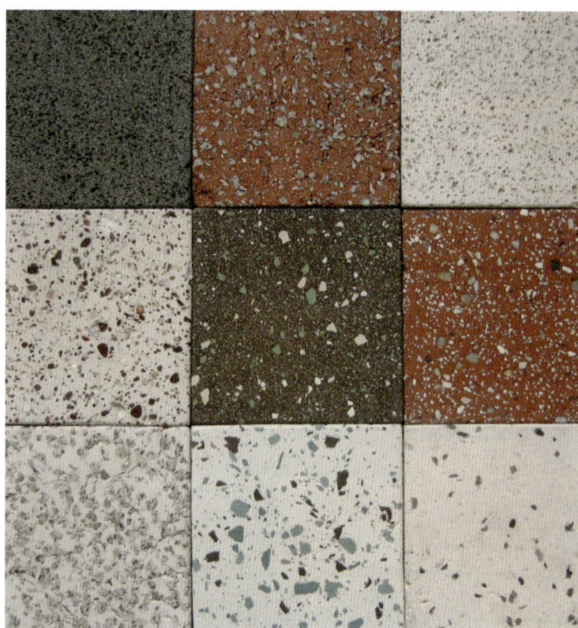

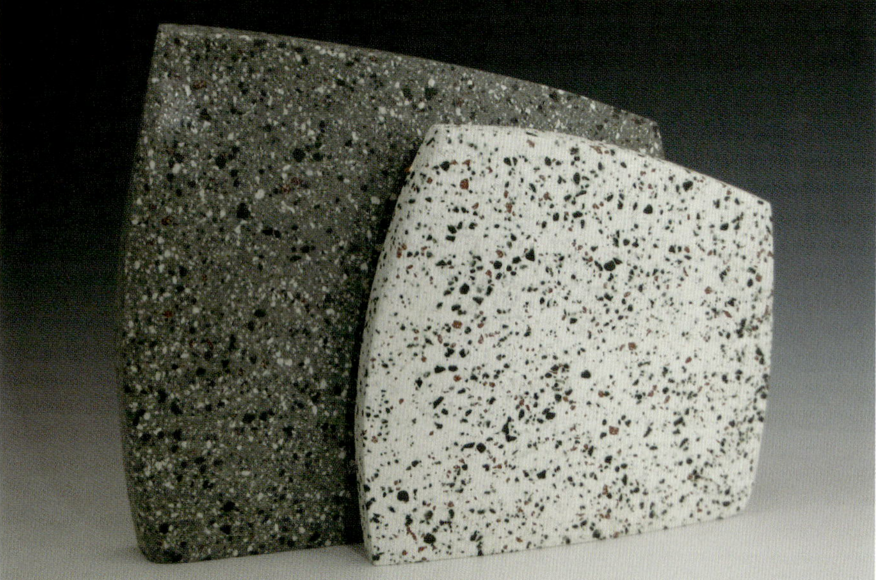

ABOVE LEFT: Examples of made, found and industrial aggregates, added in varying amounts to clay bodies. Clockwise from top left: copper-stained porcelain (5%), granular flint, recycled bottle glass, fused zircon, beach shingle, dense, fused mullite.

ABOVE RIGHT: Test samples of porcelain and terracotta, with additions of found and made aggregate materials in varying percentages.

LEFT: David Binns, *Two Piece Standing Form*, 2008. Porcelain with copper and terracotta aggregates, copper-stained porcelain with molochite aggregate, fired 1160–1220°C (2120–2228°F), ground and polished, 42 x 53 x 24 cm (16½ x 21 x 9½ in). *Photos: by the artist.*

material will turn to soluble quick lime, leaving the remainder stable and inert.

The Thames and Deptford Creek in London is where artist **Fred Gatley** collects mud, pebbles and other hard debris, as well as organic material, for his work. The creek also provides much of the inspiration for his sculptural work, which explores the vessel arranged on a base.

Chapter 2 will look at both Binns' and Gatley's work in more detail (pp. 28–31 and 32–35, respectively).

Making your own clay

An alternative to using commercial clay or blends is to make your own clay from scratch, using the dry, raw minerals. I measure and mix the dry ingredients, add them to water, sieve this mixture and finally spread it out to firm up on plaster slabs.

Why do I go to all this trouble to make a clay body? The answer lies partly in where I live and work, as well as my background. My studio is in a coastal village in south-west Ireland and this place has a strong influence on my ceramic work. My work has a painterly quality, exploring the colours and textures of the location, influenced in part by my father, an artist who captured his impressions of the world using oils on canvas. The extra work of making my own clay allows me to add accurate amounts of colour (oxides and body stains) to the body, and to choose **grog** and other additions to mix in at any stage of the making process. This flexibility allows me to capture the spirit of my home.

I make my clay in quantities ranging from 1 to 50 kg (2¼ to 110¼ lbs) depending on the project I am working on, but the process is the same each time. I always work in a well-ventilated area and wear a face mask. If adding colour, I protect my hands with vinyl gloves.

Various grog materials collected from the Thames at low tide. As these are found materials, the artist has identified them as closely as possible. *Photo: Fred Gatley.*

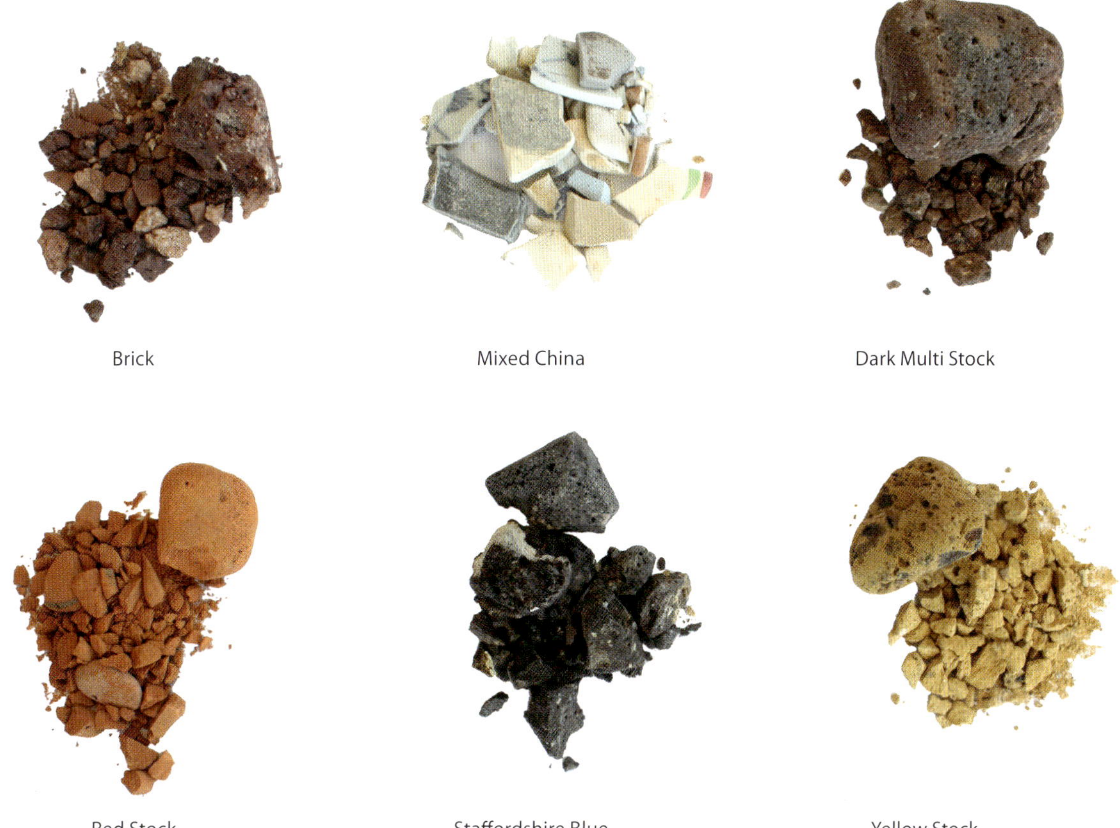

Brick

Mixed China

Dark Multi Stock

Red Stock

Staffordshire Blue

Yellow Stock

Recipe for porcelain clay

Provided by the technician at The City Lit Institute, Holborn, London

(Firing range of porcelain body: 1240–1280°C/2264–2336°F)

China clay	21
Flint	23
Potash Feldspar	18
Black ball clay	18
Silica sand	10
Molochite (Fine, medium or coarse)	10

If I want to make 10 kg (22 lbs), for example, then each item should be multiplied by 100. I always write down the exact measurements, as I need to weigh in batches of 500g (1 lb), and tick off as I go along. It is very easy to lose track. I fire slowly to 1220°C (2228°F) with a 20 minute soak, so the heat work is sufficient to vitrify the clay, but is excellent for colour and also reduces the risk of slumping of the curved forms.)

Preparing clay with additions of cotton linter and perlite

I always wear a mask and gloves and work in a well-ventilated area.

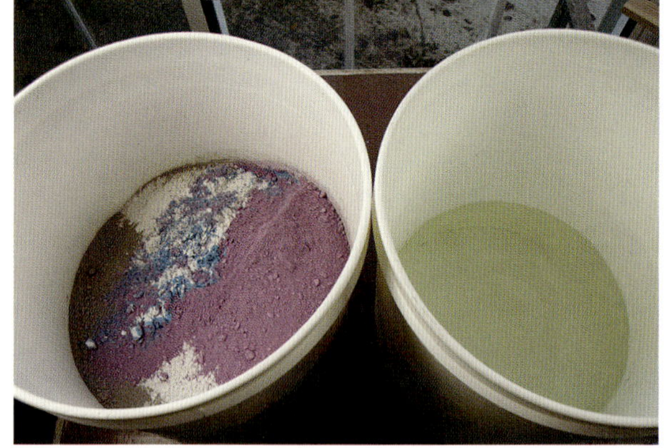

RIGHT: Measure out the dry materials and the water into two separate buckets.

BELOW LEFT: Mix the dry materials together, then add them in scoops to the water. Allow each scoop to dissolve before adding the next. (This is a similar process to making plaster.)

BELOW RIGHT: Leave the wet mixture for about 20 minutes and then sieve through a 60-mesh sieve. Stir in any remaining dry materials that you did not want to sieve, such as molochite and silica. If this is the end of your process, the completed clay can be spread out on plaster to firm up, then wedged and stored, wrapped in plastic, for up to a week before using. If you wish to add fibres and perlite, the process continues on the opposite page. *Photos: Kathleen Standen.*

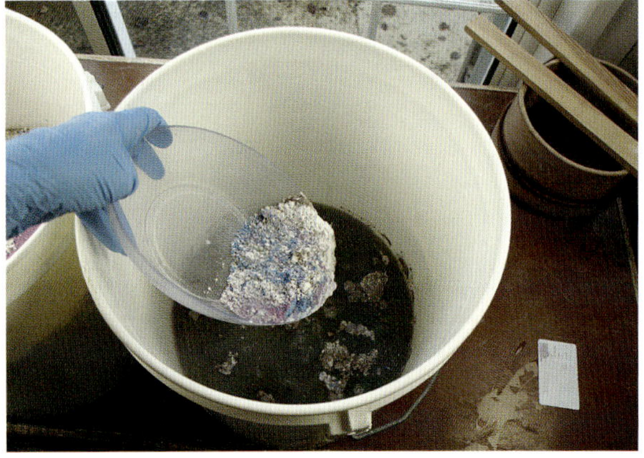

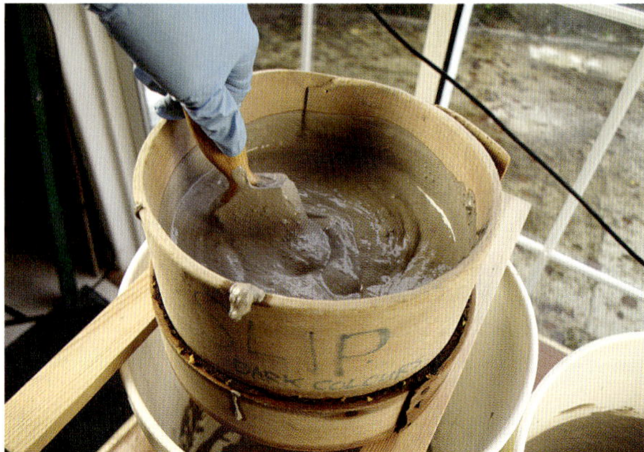

RIGHT: Soak strips of **cotton linter** in water and then break up into a mushy mixture.

BELOW LEFT: Squeeze out as much water as possible from the cotton linter.

BELOW RIGHT: Add the cotton linter to the wet clay and blend with an electric mixer, to give an even, smooth mixture. You have now mixed up your own paperclay.

BOTTOM LEFT: Add the measured perlite to the paperclay.

BOTTOM RIGHT: Spread out onto plaster to firm up a little and then put into a labelled bucket until ready to use.
Photos: Kathleen Standen.

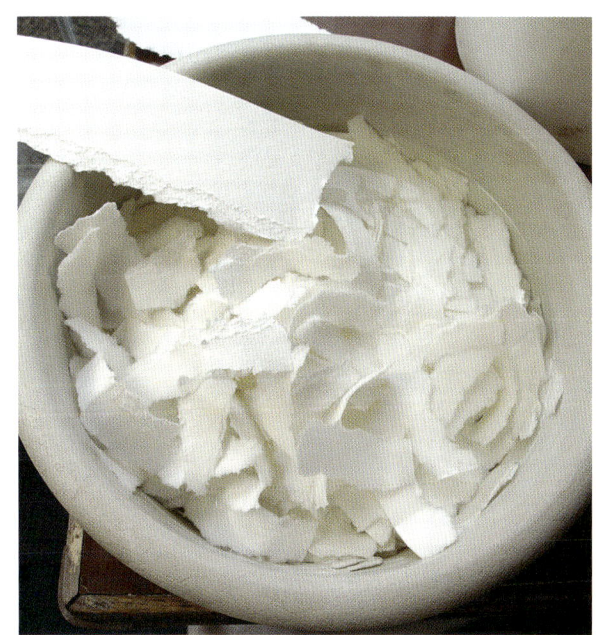

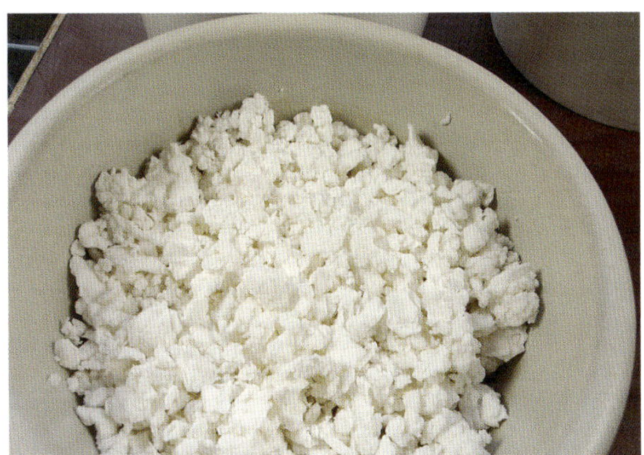

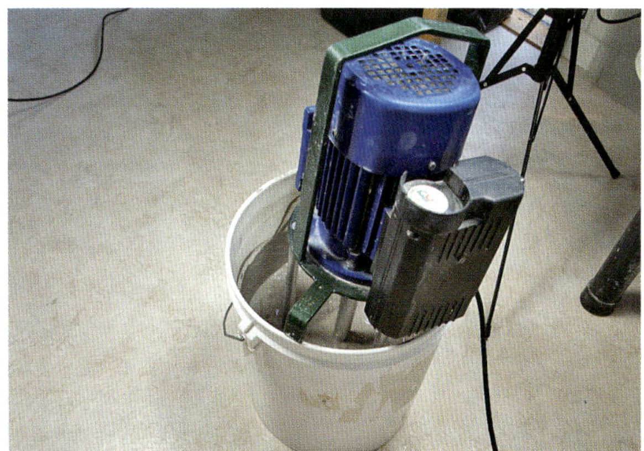

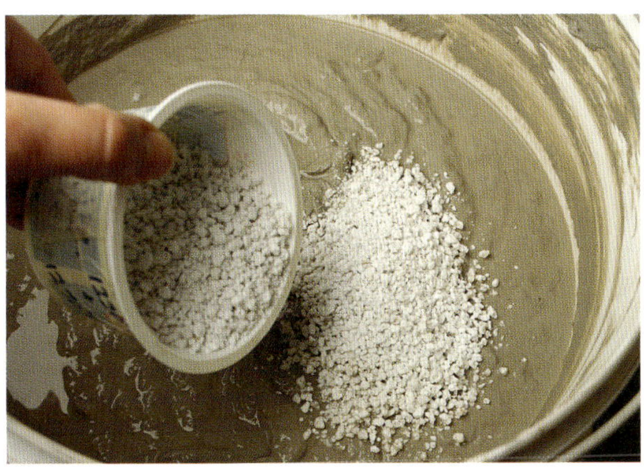

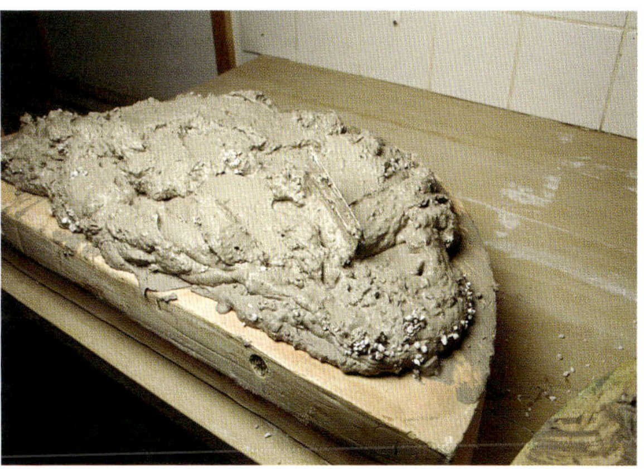

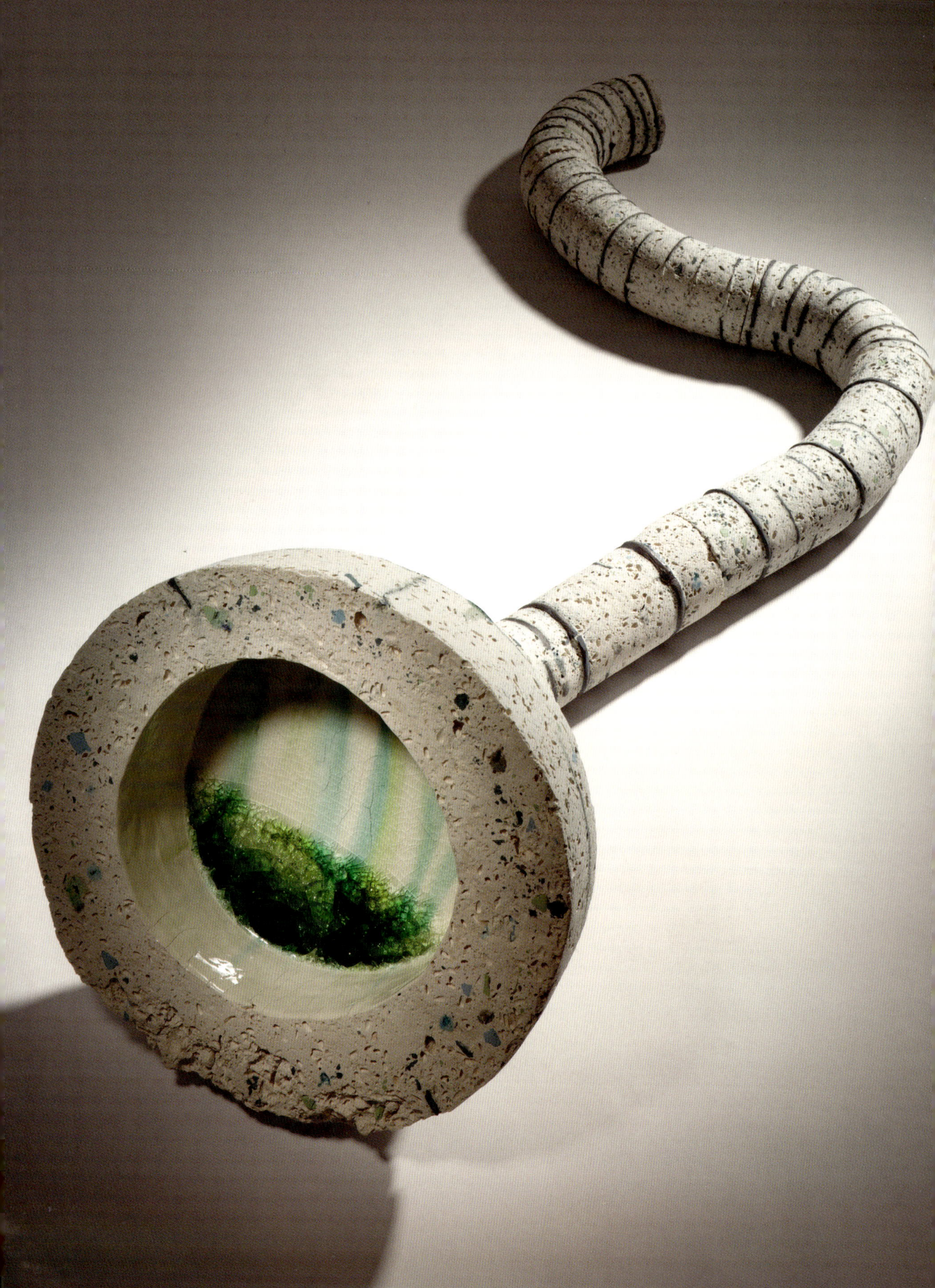

2

Hard materials

Additions of hard, non-combustible materials to a clay body 'open up' the body and reduce shrinkage. Most commercial clays contain tiny particles of hard, non-combustible materials in the form of grog or **corderite**, made from crushed, unused kiln shelves. This grog is a buff colour, so is a good choice for adding to buff-firing clays. Alternatively, white molochite, made from calcined china clay, can be added to white-firing clays. Both of these can be purchased in a range of grades from fine (200) to coarse (16–30).

Some bodies, such as crank, contain as much as 40% grog, which makes it the clay of choice for artists working on a large scale, when walls may be reasonably thick. There is less danger of warping and cracking when such a clay body is used. **Saggars** and work for raku firing should also be made with clay that has a high sand or grog content, to enable the clay to cope with sudden changes in temperature (**thermal shock**) and repeat firings.

Hard additions can also be used to enhance the surface of forms, such as when clay is scraped with a metal kidney, exposing rough, hard grog particles on the surface. But you don't need to confine your use of hard materials to just commercially sold varieties. Some of the ceramics featured in this chapter include coloured grog made by the makers themselves, as well as inclusions of coloured glass. Other artists source their own hard materials in the environment to add to their clay bodies.

Coloured grog and recycled glass

Meander 1 and *2* were made for an installation at the West Cork Art Centre in Ireland and comprised two large, glazed, 'winch'-inspired forms connected to curved tubes, which extended three or more metres. The tubes were made by casting domestic soil pipe in plaster and then forming in clay.

In this work, I aimed to question the impact of our activities on marine and freshwater ecosystems: machine-inspired forms were combined with the colours, patterns and textures of the unspoilt environment. Additions to the clay body provided the colours, patterns and textures that I was seeking.

LEFT: Kathleen Standen, *Meander 2*, 2011. Coloured and glazed porcelain clay fired to 1220°C (2228°F), 300 x 52 cm (118 x 20½ in). *Photo: Roland Paschhoff.*

Coloured grog

For this project, I made my own grog from coloured clays. In my search for a range of blue-greys, I carried out tests on several black clay recipes. The black was blended with white, in equal proportions, and this was repeated several times. When all the test tiles were fired to 1220°C (2228°F), one black recipe provided me with a range of colours from black to metallic grey, dark blue and pale blue.

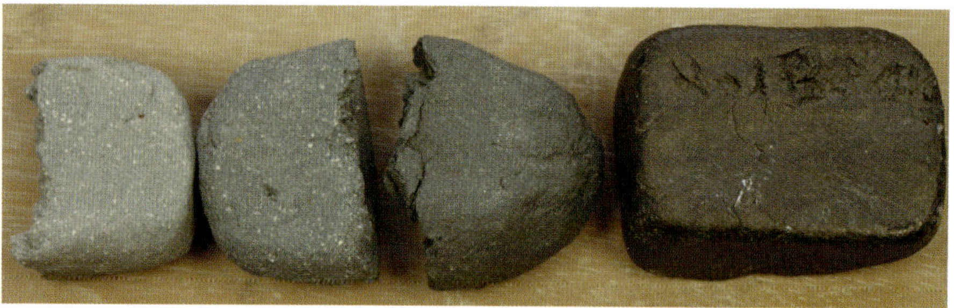

Fired to 1220°C (2228°F), this recipe gave a range of colours: pale blue, mid-blue, grey and black.

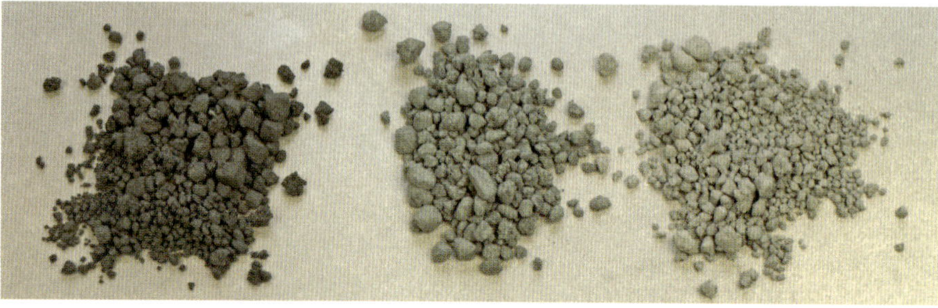

Grog made from the shades of blue clay above.
Photos: Kathleen Standen.

Using these same proportions, it is possible to make a series of grogs of different sizes. The coloured clay is rolled out into slabs of different thicknesses and allowed to dry. I then crush the clay with a rolling pin (always wearing a mask and ensuring good ventilation). The particles are spread onto a kiln shelf and fired to 1220°C (2228°F). They are then sieved and sorted by particle size and stored in labelled containers for later use.

Process

All the components of *The Meander Series* were firstly cast in plaster either using ready-made shapes (waste domestic pipe) or forms made by me (winches). As the winch forms were 50 to 60 cm (19¾ to 23¾ in) in diameter, with walls of 10 cm (4 in) thickness, I needed to use an 'open clay' for strength and to reduce cracking. The basic clay was made by me, using coarse molochite; this is described in the previous chapter (p. 22). To this I added coloured grog, recycled glass fragments, and 10% perlite and cotton linter. These additions not only give strength, but also colour, pattern and texture.

The cotton linter was blended with the wet clay slurry (p. 23) and then the perlite was stirred in afterwards. After drying on plaster slabs, this clay mixture was arranged in a plaster mould, together with sheets of coloured clay, according to a predetermined design. In places, sunflower seeds and monkey-nut shells were added to the clay in the mould to give a different pattern and texture. In this way I was able to create forms with the visual and tactile appeal I was looking for.

After allowing the work to dry gradually over several weeks, it was slowly fired in a well-ventilated electric kiln to 950°C (1742°F). Using a vacuum cleaner and brush, all particles of carbon dust, created from the burning of organic matter, were removed from the bisque forms, which were then glazed and refired at 1220°C (2228°F), with a 20-minute soak. Finally, the flat and curved surfaces on the large end pieces were polished using an electric stone polisher to expose the 'grain' of the clay colours.

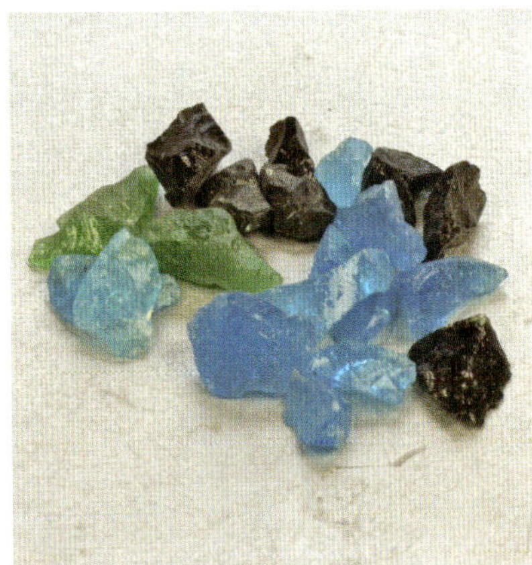

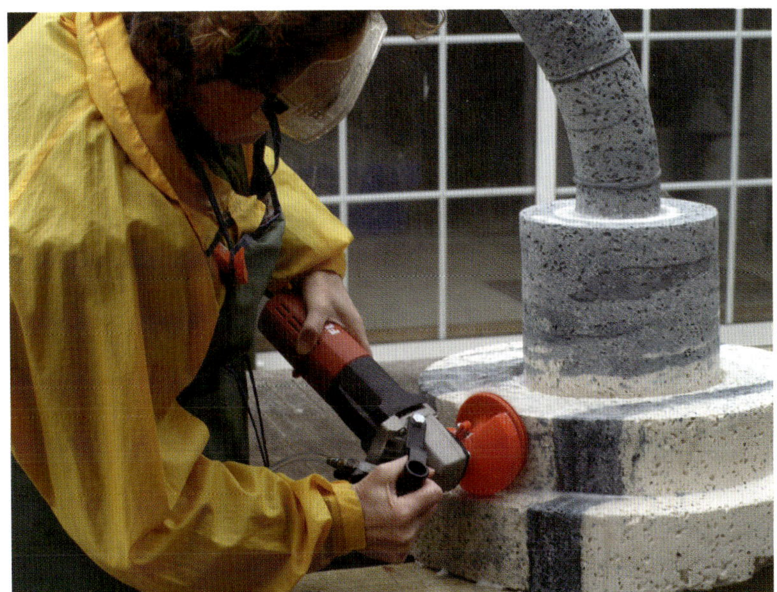

ABOVE: Recycled glass fragments supplied by a funeral parlour.

RIGHT: Grinding and polishing the surface of the clay.
Photos: Kathleen Standen.

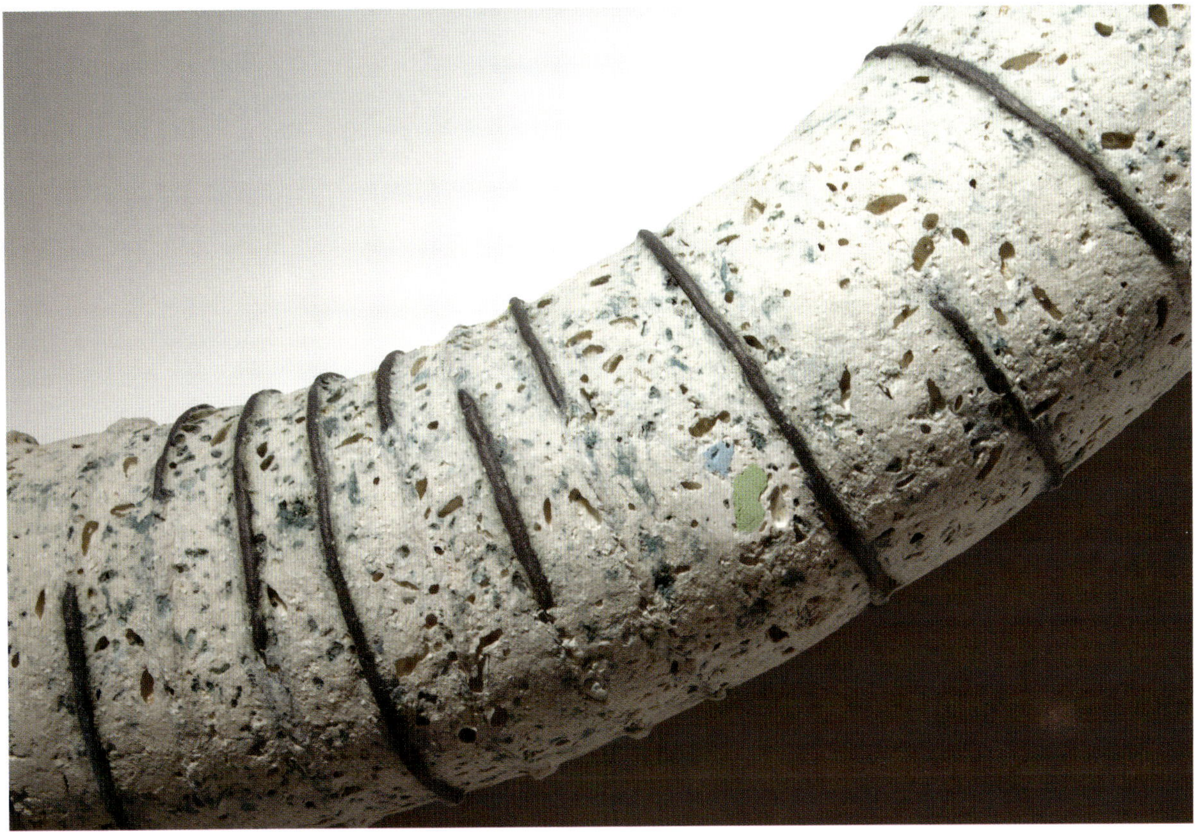

Kathleen Standen, *Meander 1* (detail), 2011. Coloured, glazed porcelain clay fired to 1220°C (2228°F), 170 x 45 cm (67 x 17¾ in).
Photo: Roland Paschhoff.

Found pebbles, coloured grog and other hard additions

The UK artist synonymous with coloured grog and other hard additions is **David Binns**. Binns is a Reader in Contemporary Ceramics at the University of Central Lancashire and he also lectures and exhibits widely. From his studio in North Wales, he draws inspiration from forms and textures found in engineering, architecture and the natural landscape. He says, 'My work is rooted in materials and involvement in the making process. I enjoy the challenge of striving for new aesthetic qualities through researching new techniques and alternative use of materials.'

Binns has certainly lived up to this statement; the article he wrote about aggregates in ceramic bodies, published in *Ceramics Technical* in 2006, is a revealing testament to this. He describes the challenge of creating work with 'a visual richness whilst conveying a sense of quietness and simplicity – the exclusion of the inessential'.

Binns' work is made through a variety of forming processes: free hand-building, rolling thick slabs, which are sometimes draped into or over wooden or fabric formers, and press-moulding clay into wooden or plaster moulds. A single unique batch of clay is made for each piece and in virtually every case, pieces are made solid, meaning that what is seen on the surface of the form passes through the core of the piece, thus integrating form and surface. He explains that 'this aspect is important to the intent of my work, rather than the aesthetic qualities of the piece relying on a thin skin of applied decorative treatment, such as glaze or slip.'

Process

The starting point is a porcelain or terracotta base clay. Into this, Binns wedges damp paper pulp (milled newsprint), in the following proportions: ½ bucket dry pulp per 12 kg (26½ lbs) plastic clay. Pulp is added to aid drying and help prevent cracking, which is an increased risk when firing very thick forms. It also opens up the body, creating pores that allow moisture to escape more easily.

Varying amounts of aggregate material are then added to the plastic clay, determining the overall aesthetic appearance of the finished piece: molochite, crushed recycled sanitary ware and tableware, found, washed granular materials such as beach pebbles and granite dust, and made coloured grog are just some of the hard additions he uses.

Binns achieves a wide palette of coloured grogs by adding between 1% and 10% of oxide or stains to porcelain. Initially, he thought of adding small, broken pieces of stained, unfired clay to the base-clay body, but then realised they would re-soften and the colour would merge into the base clay during preparation, rather than giving him the distinct suspended particles of colour he desired. Instead, he fires small lumps of coloured porcelain to around 900°C (1652°F), then crushes them easily to whatever grain size is required.

Binns' 'signature' grog is stained with copper oxide, which bleeds a halo of colour into the surrounding parent clay of the finished form.

After slow drying, the work is fired extremely slowly in an **electric kiln**. A biscuit firing is not necessary, so the work is fired straight through to top temperature – between 1150 and 1220°C (2102 and 2228°F).

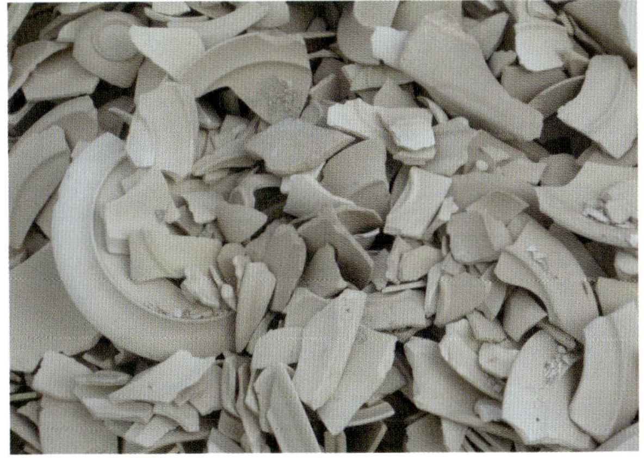

Recycled tableware waste from the ceramic industry, crushed and used as aggregate within many pieces of my work.

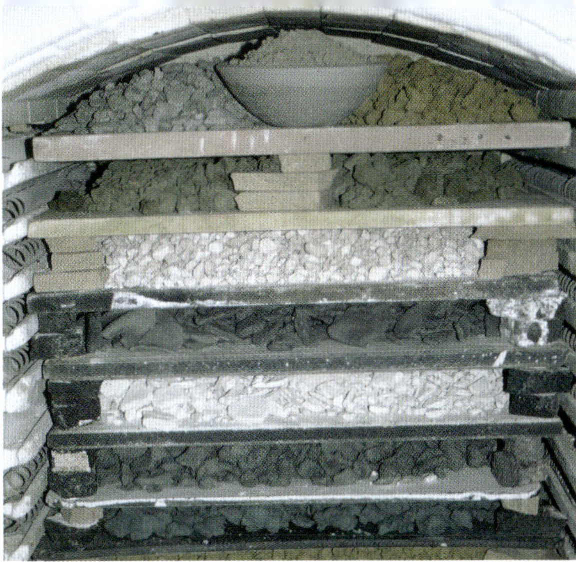

Firing stained clay in order to make grog.

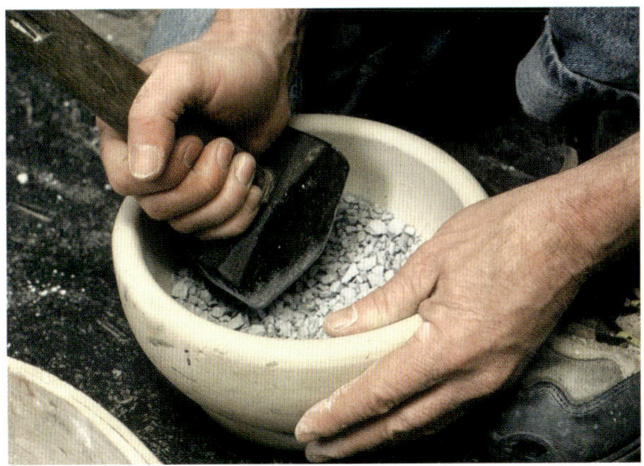

Crushing stained and fired clay using a pestle and mortar.

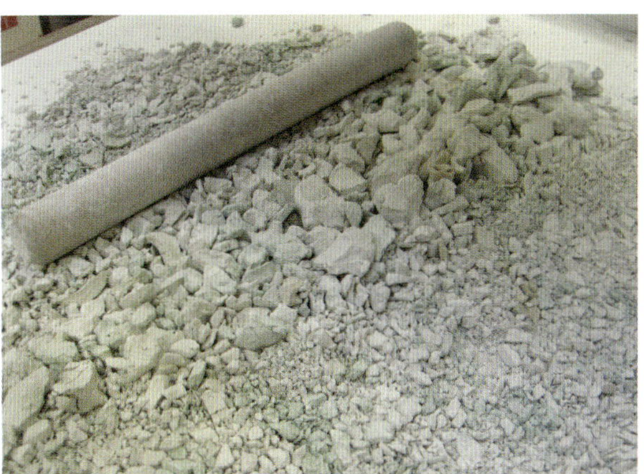

Crushing stained and fired clay with a rolling pin.

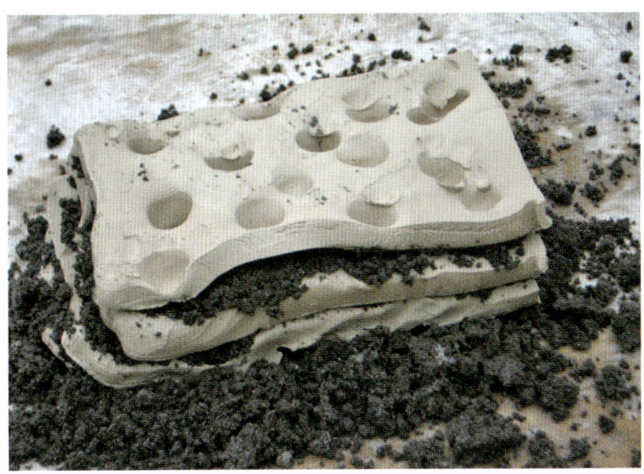

Adding milled newsprint (paper pulp) to plastic porcelain – creating a 'sandwich' of clay and pulp prior to wedging.

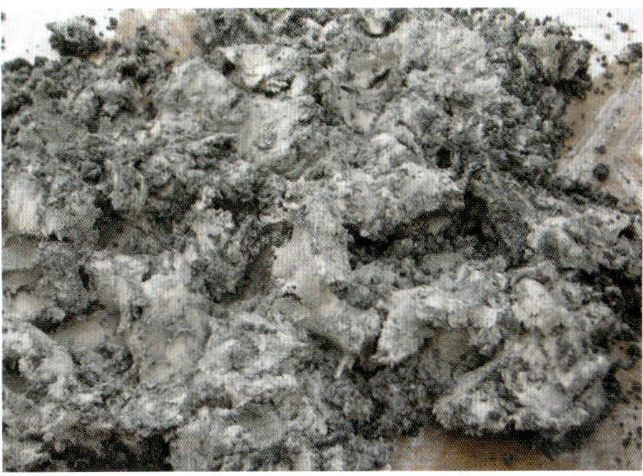

Wedging milled newsprint into plastic porcelain.
Photos: David Binns.

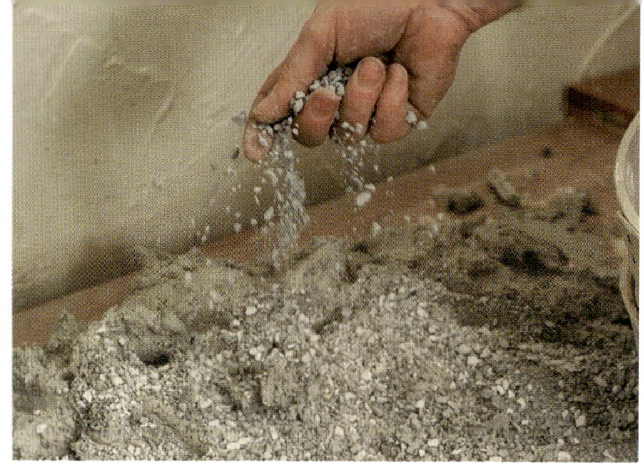

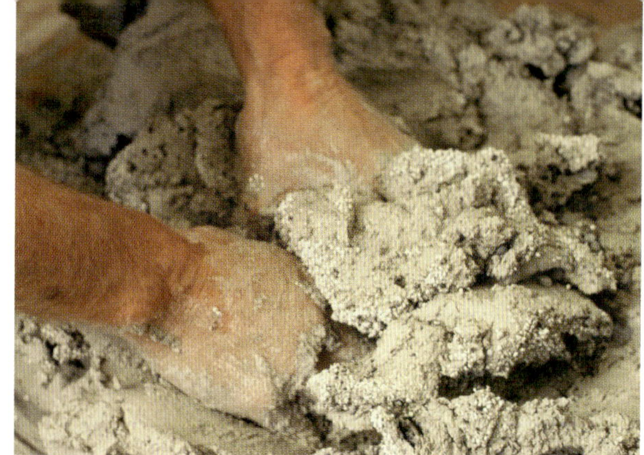

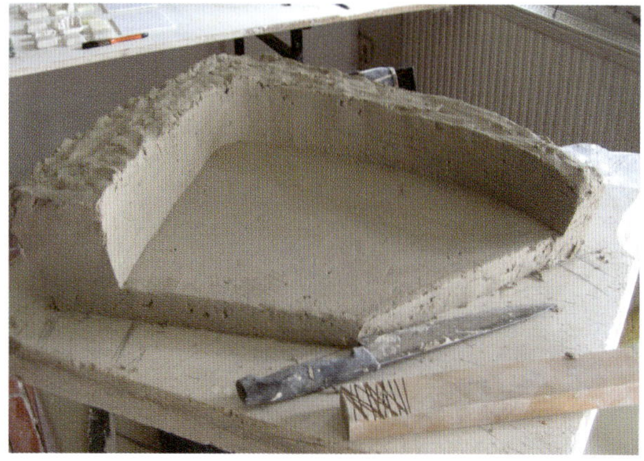

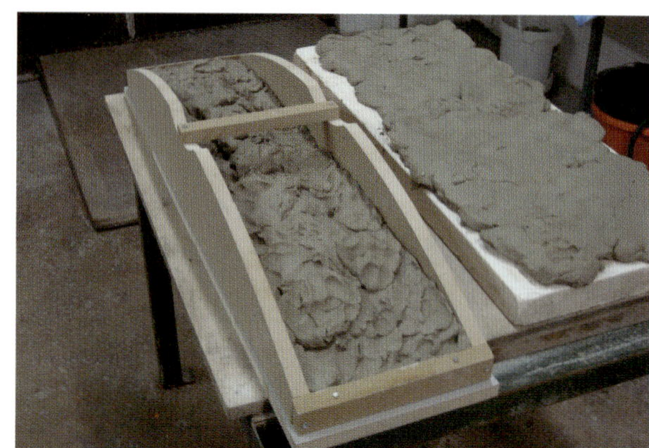

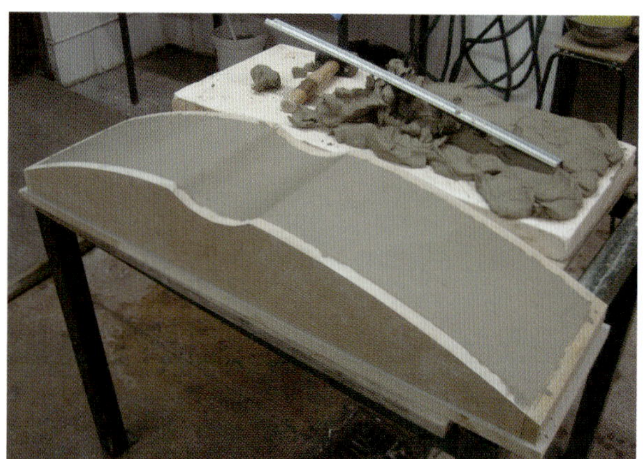

TOP, LEFT TO RIGHT: Adding graded (sieved) grog to porcelain, and wedging grog (aggregates) into plastic, porcelain clay.

ABOVE, LEFT TO RIGHT: Hand-building a 3D 'fragment' form from heavily grogged porcelain. Close-up of press-moulding grogged stoneware clay into wooden former.

RIGHT: Complete, press-moulded *Boat Form*. When the work comes out of the kiln, there is little evidence of the full extent of the visual qualities of the added aggregates. They are hidden under a thin layer of clay that will be removed by mechanical grinding of the surface. *Photos: David Binns.*

The additions of both paper pulp and large amounts of granular material open up the body considerably, allowing very thick pieces of clay to be fired. Once fired, all Binns' work undergoes a process of grinding and polishing, done using a hand-held, water-fed angle grinder combined with a series of Velcro-backed diamond pads. The water helps to minimise dust. He starts with a very coarse pad that cuts aggressively through the fired clay, both removing the top layer of material and refining the shape of the form, then attaches finer pads and uses these until a polish is achieved.

Finally the pieces are allowed to dry, after which they are waxed, both to seal the surface and to bring out the full colour of the work.

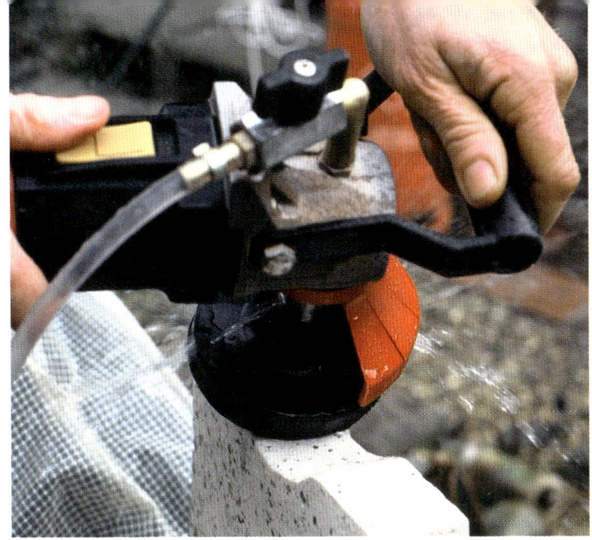

Close-up of Electro-Flex angle grinder, refining shape and polishing fired ceramic form.

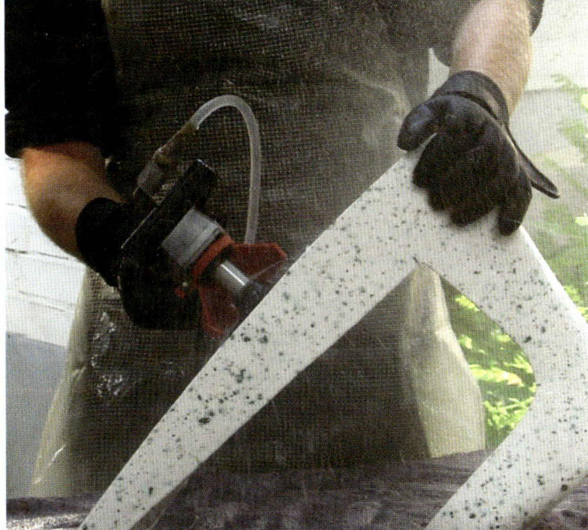

David Binns operating the water-fed angle grinder.

BELOW: David Binns, *Two Piece Standing Form*, 2010. Porcelain with copper and molochite aggregates, combined with kiln-cast recycled ceramic and glass aggregates, 1160–1220°C (2120–2228°F), ground and polished, 40 x 33 x 7 cm (15¾ x 13 x 2¾ in). *Photos: David Binns.*

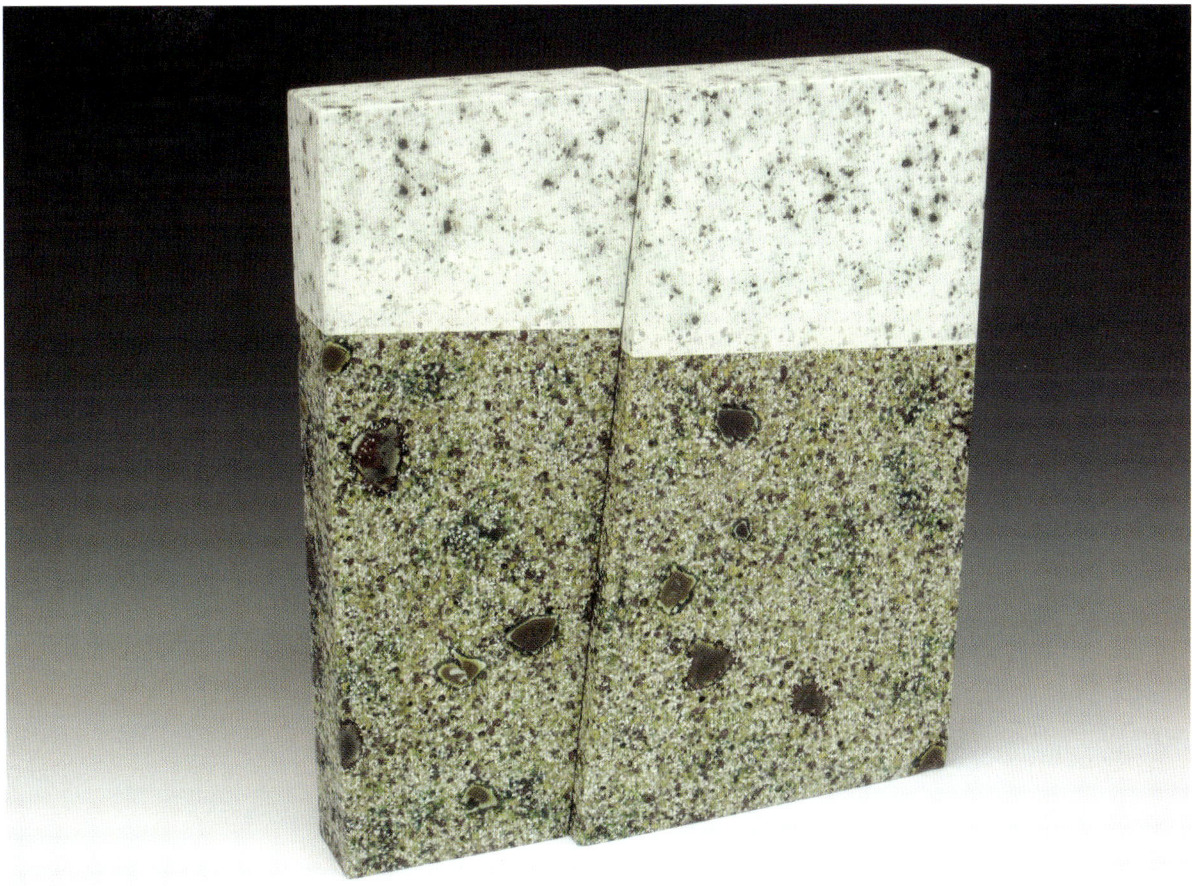

Found materials – crushed brick and crockery, rust scrapings from metal

Fred Gatley lives and works in London, where he also teaches at the London Metropolitan University. His work frequently consists of two contrasting but complementary forms: the bowl and the base. He draws a parallel with ceremonial artefacts: the chalice and the altar, the offering of an object for contemplation. Surface texture, balance and proportion are vital in his pieces.

Gatley uses Potclays bone china and Limoges porcelain, to which he adds a variety of materials, including coloured porcelain grogs (made by him), crude flakes of rust scraped from found metal objects, and grogs made from shards of pottery or crushed brick. Recent work also includes additions of sand, gravel, silt, iron oxide, mud and organic material, collected on walks by the Thames and Deptford Creek.

He makes his own coloured grogs, which are low-fired at around 850–900°C (1562–1652°F) before being crushed.

Note: It is essential to take precautions against inhaling dust during the crushing, sieving and handling of grogs. Wear a face mask.

Polishing tools

Gatley's use of additions developed alongside his interest in polishing ceramics. For over thirty years, he has been researching and developing techniques to refine methods for surface polishing his ceramics. He has designed and made a range of over seventy bespoke tools that screw onto his grinder, allowing him to work most surfaces, and even complex interior shapes!

Fred Gatley, *Erosion*, 2009. Pinch-formed and polished bone china bowl, with inclusions of iron oxide, fired to 1220°C (2228°F), diameter: 4 cm (1½ in); slabbed base of white St Thomas clay with additions of river silts, sand and brick grogs, smoke-fired to 1020°C (1868°F), silver feet attached, 6 x 15 cm (2¼ x 6 in). *Photo: by the artist.*

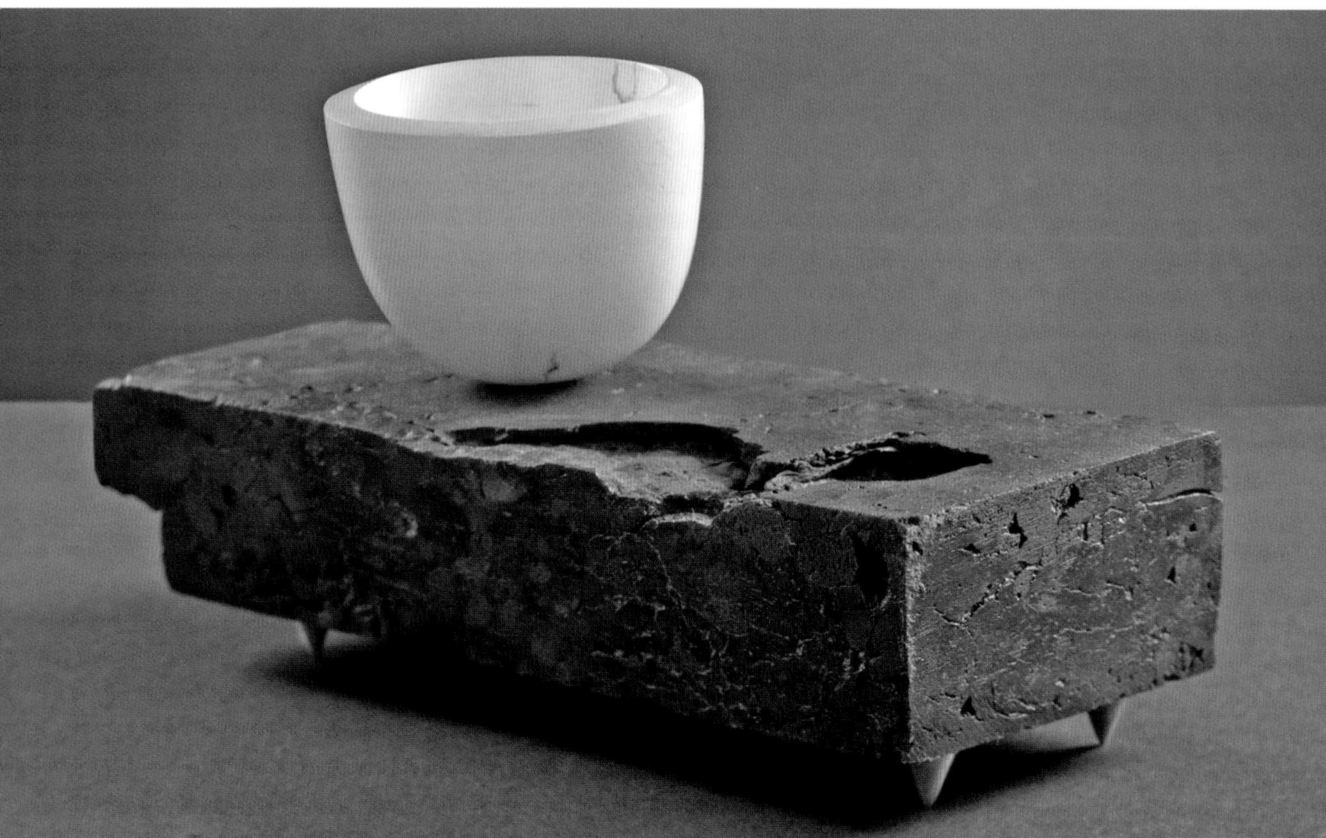

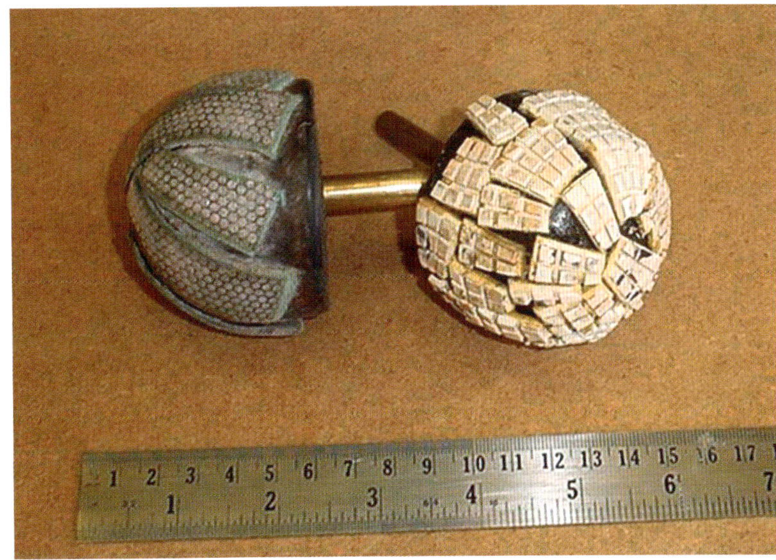

Tools made by Fred Gatley for use in a pillar drill. They were turned from solid rubber with a central brass spindle, which fits into a drill chuck. Various diamond abrasives are cut and glued onto the surface and water is trickled onto work while it is being ground. *Photo: Fred Gatley.*

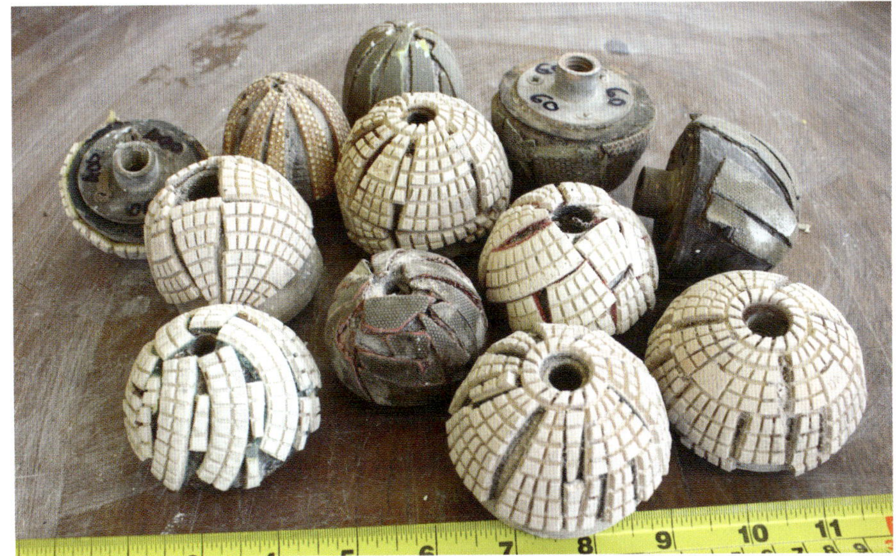

Grinding and polishing pieces made for use on the air-tool. Fred made bespoke fitments to fix onto the solid rubber so they would fit the air-tool. These connectors allow water through the centre of the tool itself and onto the surfaces being ground. *Photo: Fred Gatley.*

These tools, made from solid rubber, are faced with diamond abrasive compounds and he says they have never 'failed', although frequently used tools require 'resurfacing'.

He has constructed a jig in a sink, to secure his air-powered polishing machine in such a way that the grinding tool can be held upright, enabling both his hands to hold and manipulate pieces onto the tool during working. This device has a water-feed, which passes through the main grinding tool and so onto the work during polishing. This flow of water is crucial for many reasons: to avoid the creation of dangerous dust; to lubricate the surfaces of the tools to prevent them overheating; and to sluice away the discarded material. This whole assembly has a Perspex 'splash-guard' built around it to contain most of the spray, but even so, it can prove to be an extremely wet process!

Process

A variety of techniques are employed in the forming of Gatley's work, from slabbing and pinch-pots, to press-moulding and **jolleying**. After the first firing at around 850–900°C (1562–1652°F), he starts to grind the forms to reveal the matrix of contrasting additions within each piece. He then selects the most interesting ones: attractive 'seam' lines, rich grog textures and interesting cavities, which are returned to the kiln for a higher firing – 1000–1020°C (1832–1868°F) if they are to be sawdust-fired, otherwise 1040–1120°C (1904–2048°F), followed by a second grinding.

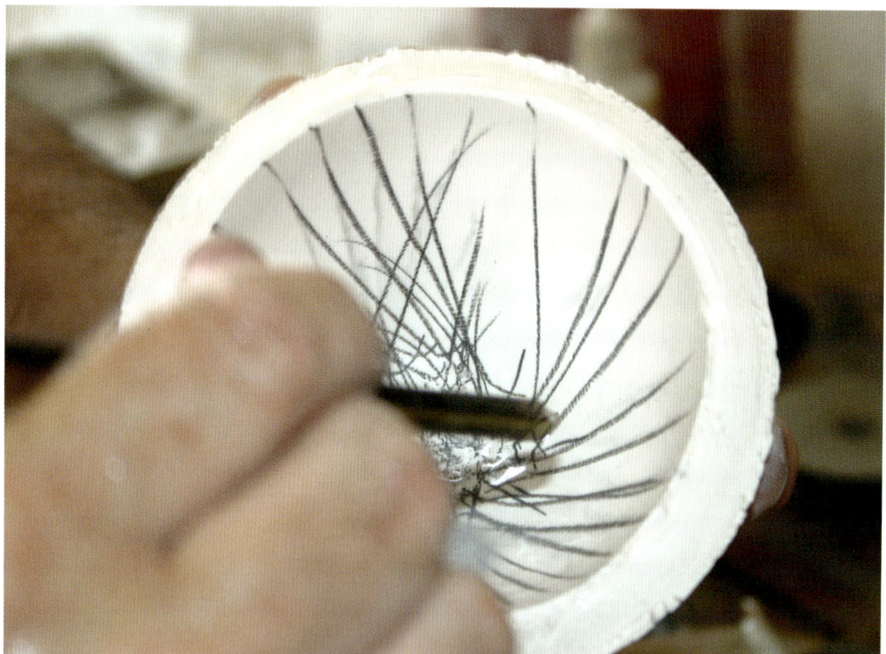

Marking bowls for grinding. The removal of these pencil lines indicates how the grinding process is working. This process of surface marking is repeated at each grinding stage and the surface is worked until all the lines are removed. *Photo: Fred Gatley.*

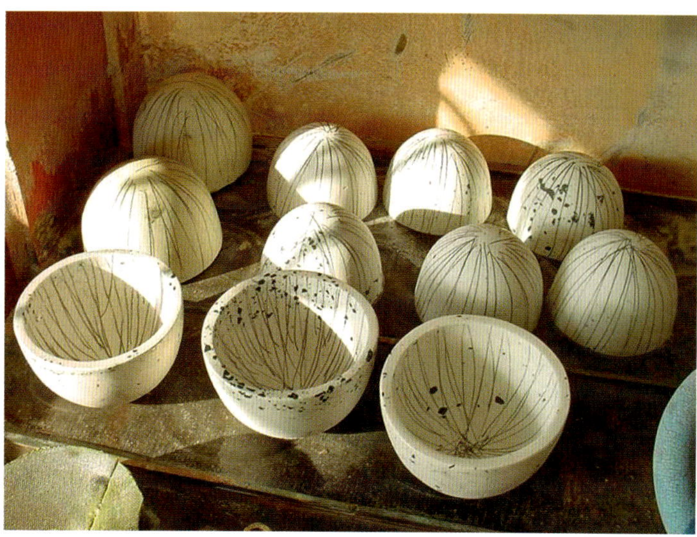

Some bowls marked for grinding, both interior and exterior. Various distributions, amounts and sizes of black grog are visible. *Photo: Fred Gatley.*

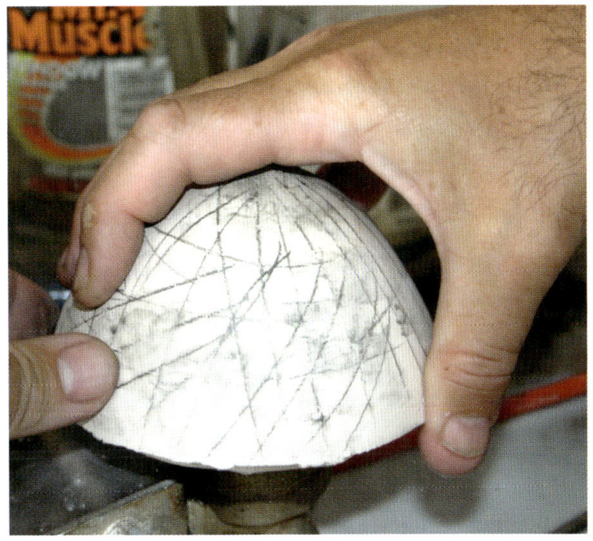

Grinding the interior of a bowl on the air-tool. Due to the tool being clamped in place, both hands are free to hold and present the form being ground. The exterior surface markings can be seen.

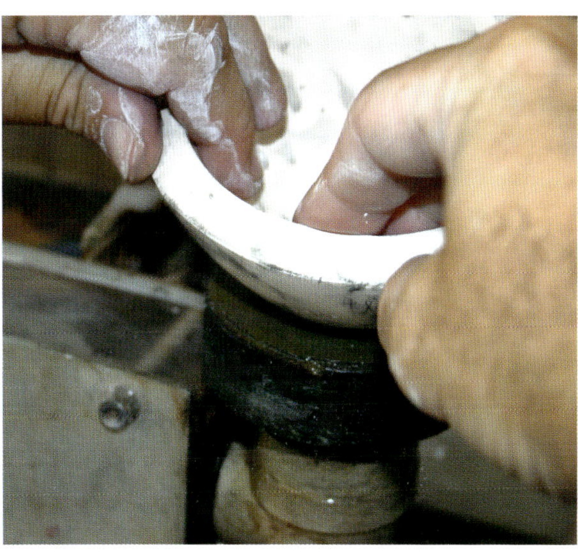

Working on the air-tool. This is a concave tool for polishing exterior curved forms. Again, due to the tool being clamped in place, both hands are free to work the form.

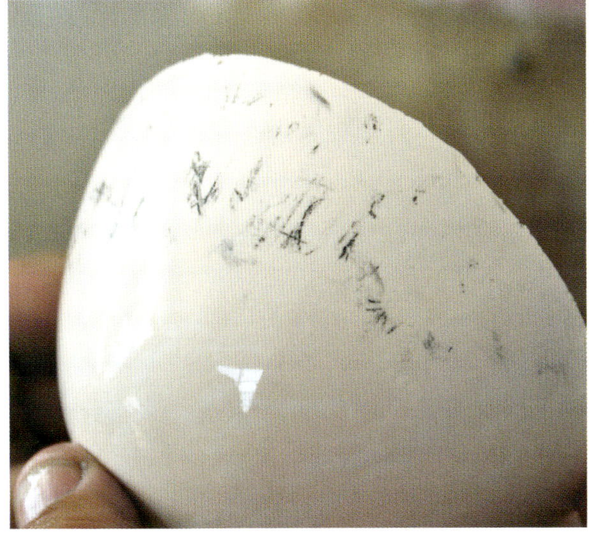

Some exterior lines remain after initial surface working.

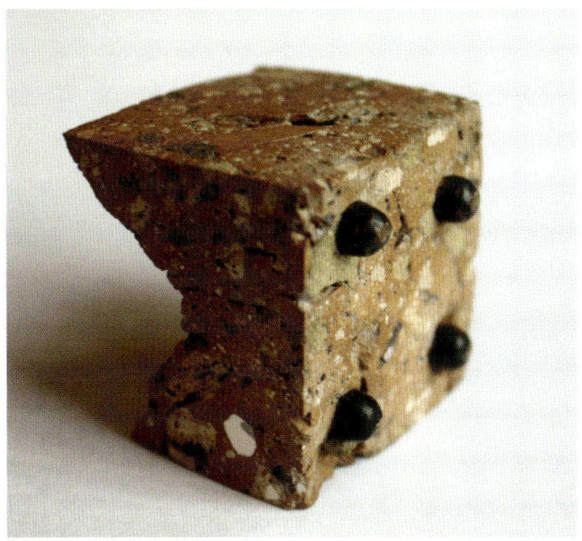

A small base piece with copper feet. *Photos: Fred Gatley.*

Pieces are reworked with finer abrasive tools and some are fired again to an even higher temperature. Pieces that are selected after the final high firing are polished with finer and finer diamond abrasives until their surfaces gleam like marble.

Years of dedication to this method of working have enabled Gatley to develop a body of work that demonstrates his deep understanding of process and aesthetics.

Volcanic rock

The unusual sculptural forms of the Polish ceramicist **Aneta Regal Deleu** combine 'the rigidity of rock with the malleability of clay, naturally occurring elements with man-made ones, rough textures and smooth'.

She builds her forms by hand, using clay into which volcanic rock has been added. Multiple firings follow, at temperatures between 1000 and 1260°C (1832 and 2300°F). Basalt rock, collected from stonemason's skips, is crushed with a hammer and incorporated into the clay during the making process. She aims to instil 'a sense of life' in her forms, creating what others have described as 'invented living creatures'.

Recycled vitrified clay

Camille Virot divides his time between teaching, working as a consultant to art schools, and his own studio practice in Provence, France. The clay bodies of his Japanese-inspired raku vessels have a range of hard additions in them, including crushed, recycled clay, pâte de verre (glass paste), vitreous concrete (glass and concrete), cement and pieces of metal.

Virot describes his techniques as complex and difficult, having taken many years to develop. The pieces are built in layers, alternating building and firing, and this process may be repeated several times.

Camille writes about his *Bol-genèse* as follows:

The genesis of a bowl
Firstly it is the idea of a bowl,
maybe a hollow in the rock where water collects.
It is a ceramic object made from geological substances.
It is the minerals that inform the shape of the object.
It is the reunification by fire that, after multiple failures, a new object is born.
It is recycling material.

Feldspar

Feldspar is another hard material that can be added to clay to give texture and pattern to the form and is used by the American artist **Gillian Parke** in the making of her wheel-thrown vessels. She describes the effect of feldspar as 'pearl-like eruptions covering the surface of the vessel'.

Parke works from her studio in Durham, North Carolina, where she has developed her own style of vessels combining rough textured and refined smooth surfaces. The roughness is embodied in the Japanese aesthetic of *wabi-sabi*, which finds beauty in the natural imperfections that arise in thrown and fired stoneware; this contrasts with the smooth, decorated porcelain, commonly seen in manufactured ware.

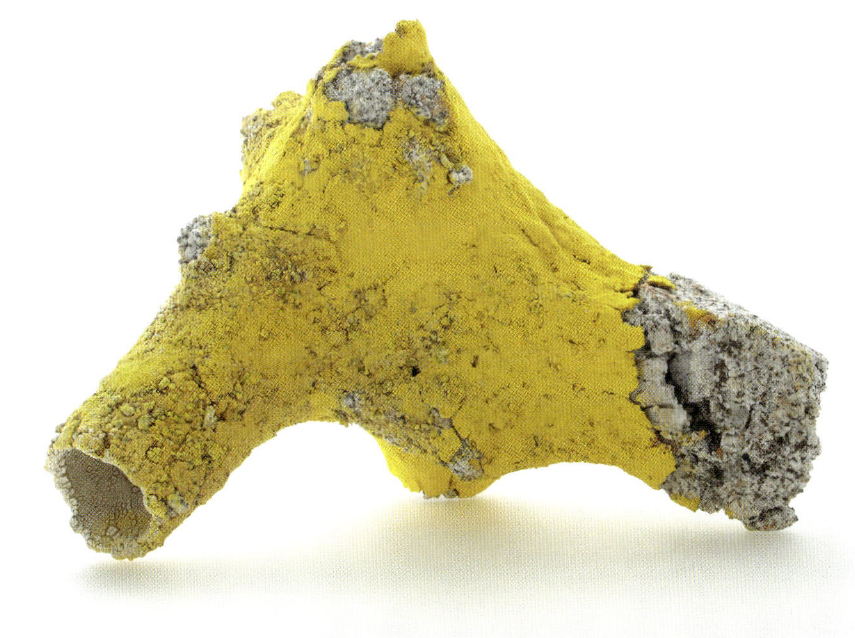

Aneta Regel Deleu, *Metamorphosis 2*, 2011. Hand-built and multiple-fired to various temperatures, 65 x 56 x 42 cm (25½ x 22 x 16½ in). *Photo: Sylvian Deleu.*

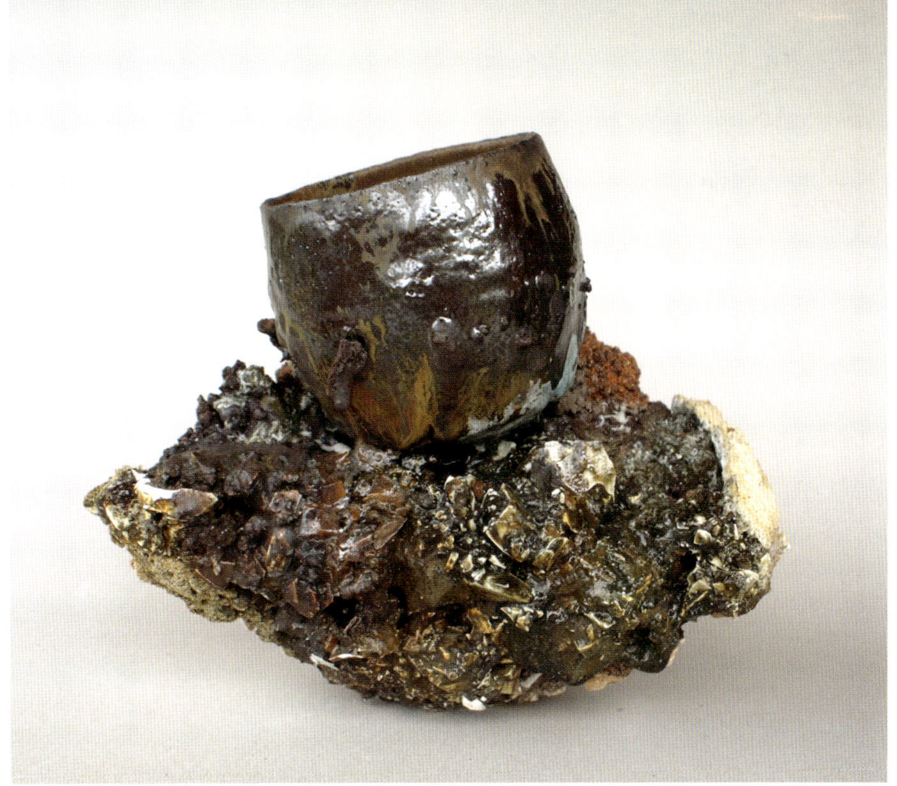

Camille Virot, *Bol-genèse*, 2010. Raku-fired with additions of crushed recycled clay, 24 x 27 cm (9½ x 10½ in). *Photo: Camille Virot.*

She wedges coarse cluster feldspar (1–10 mesh), together with 50–80 mesh molochite, into a porcelain body (Highwater Helios Porcelain). Parke advises that throwing with these inclusions requires a substantial amount of water to provide sufficient slip for lubrication. A word of caution should be added here, as too much water can cause the porcelain to lose strength and collapse, due to its low plasticity. Each section is thrown on the wheel, and surfaces scraped down to expose the feldspar and molochite matrix.

After assembling the piece, it is completely dried and **wax resist** is painted onto areas that will eventually be glazed. Underglaze is then applied to the unwaxed clay areas. This is removed from the surface with a damp sponge, leaving an underglaze patina that accentuates the feldspar and throwing lines. Wax resist and underglaze are sometimes applied again before bisque firing at 998°C (1828°F). Glazes are poured, dipped and/or brushed, and the piece is then fired in a gas reduction kiln to 1285°C (2345°F). Lustre firings (post-reduction) are at 738°C (1360°F). Multiple firings are common, as each colour is fired on separately, in addition to a separate decal firing.

Richard Burkett also adds feldspar for surface interest and texture in his wheel-thrown tea bowls. He uses a chunky feldspar (purchased as chicken grit 10–15 mesh stones) and fires to 1315°C (2399°F) in an **anagama** kiln. The feldspar chunks melt out of the surface as glassy spots, adding to the effects of the natural wood ash that glazes the anagama-fired tea bowls. Burkett's work is also featured in Chapter 3 (pp. 51–52).

Nic Collins epitomises the stereotype of the rural rustic potter. When I visited him twelve years ago, his kitchen, bedroom and potter's wheel shared the same floor space. Since then he has moved into a converted barn in Moretonhampstead, on the edge of Dartmoor National Park. After nearly 30 years of clay work, he has established himself as a specialist in anagama kiln-building in the UK, and the making of large, thrown wood-fired pots (p. 40).

Collins is included in this section of the book because he adds chunks of feldspar to the clay he throws. I marvel that he can throw such rough, textured clay and keep control of the form (not to mention the damage to his hands!). His pieces demonstrate the balance between the skill of the maker and the risks of the fire.

Limestone chips

Most artists go to great lengths to make sure their clay is not contaminated with plaster or limestone, but in his exhibition *Points in Time*, **Andy Glass** included work that was deliberately made with this addition.

He sourced limestone chips from a building supplies outlet. The slabbed vessels were made with inexpensive School Clay body, mixed with approximately 20% limestone chips, then fired to around 1120°C (2048°F). During the exhibition, he sprayed the vessels with water and within half an hour they started to disintegrate as the calcium carbonate in the limestone chips rehydrated (absorbed water).

Glass called this work *Deconstruction vessels* and they formed part of this exhibition *Points in Time* about performance art. There is another example of Glass's work from this exhibition in Chapter 6 (pp. 107–109).

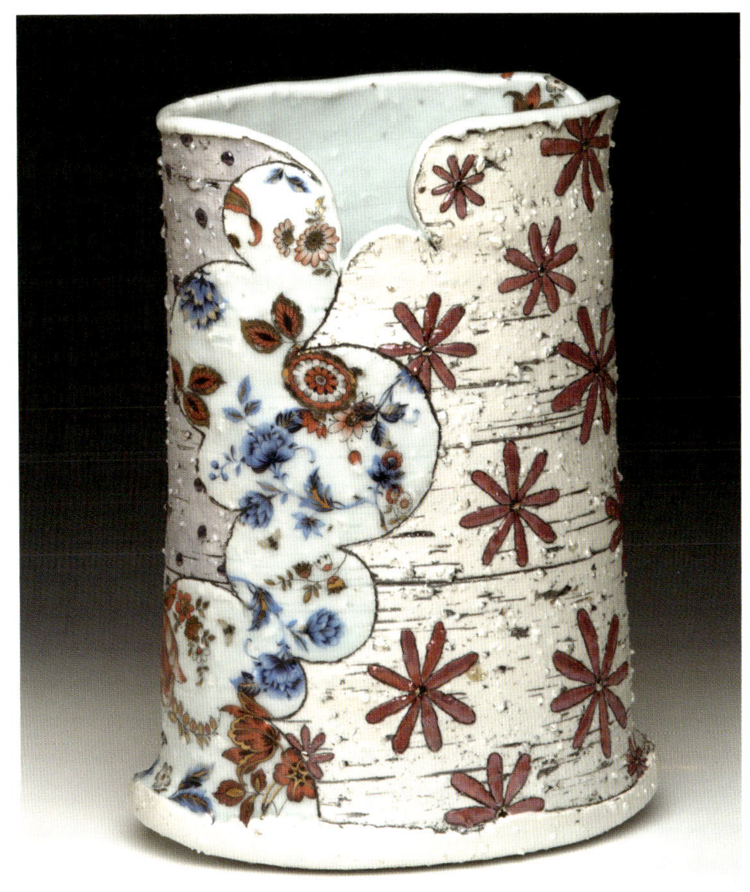

Gillian Parke, *Red, White and Blue*, 2009. Wheel-thrown and altered porcelain with feldspar and molochite inclusions, celadon glaze, fired to 1285°C (2345°F) in gas reduction kiln; open-stock decals and lustres, multiple firings of up to seven in this piece, 28 x 13.5 x 21.5 cm (11 x 15¼ x 8½ in). *Photo: Seth Tice-Lewis.*

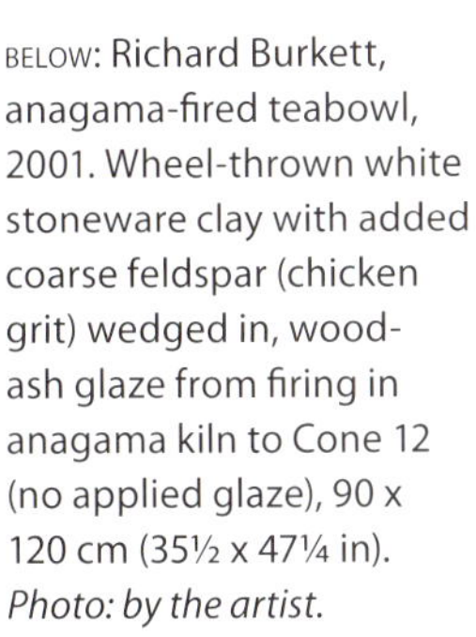

BELOW: Richard Burkett, anagama-fired teabowl, 2001. Wheel-thrown white stoneware clay with added coarse feldspar (chicken grit) wedged in, wood-ash glaze from firing in anagama kiln to Cone 12 (no applied glaze), 90 x 120 cm (35½ x 47¼ in). *Photo: by the artist.*

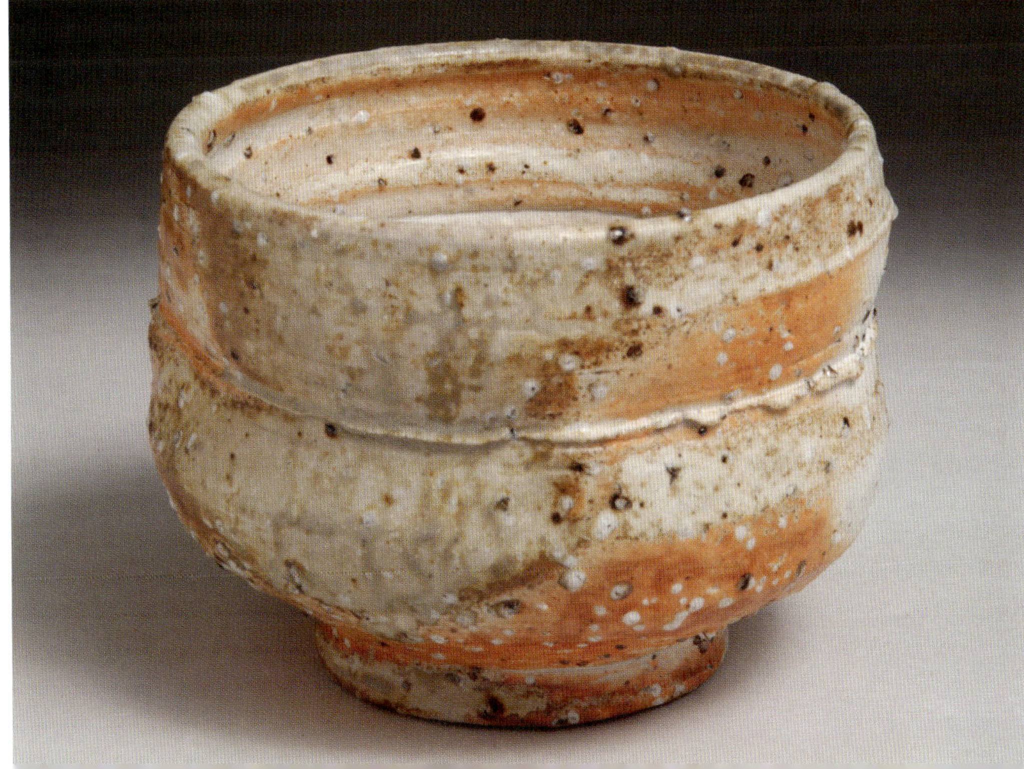

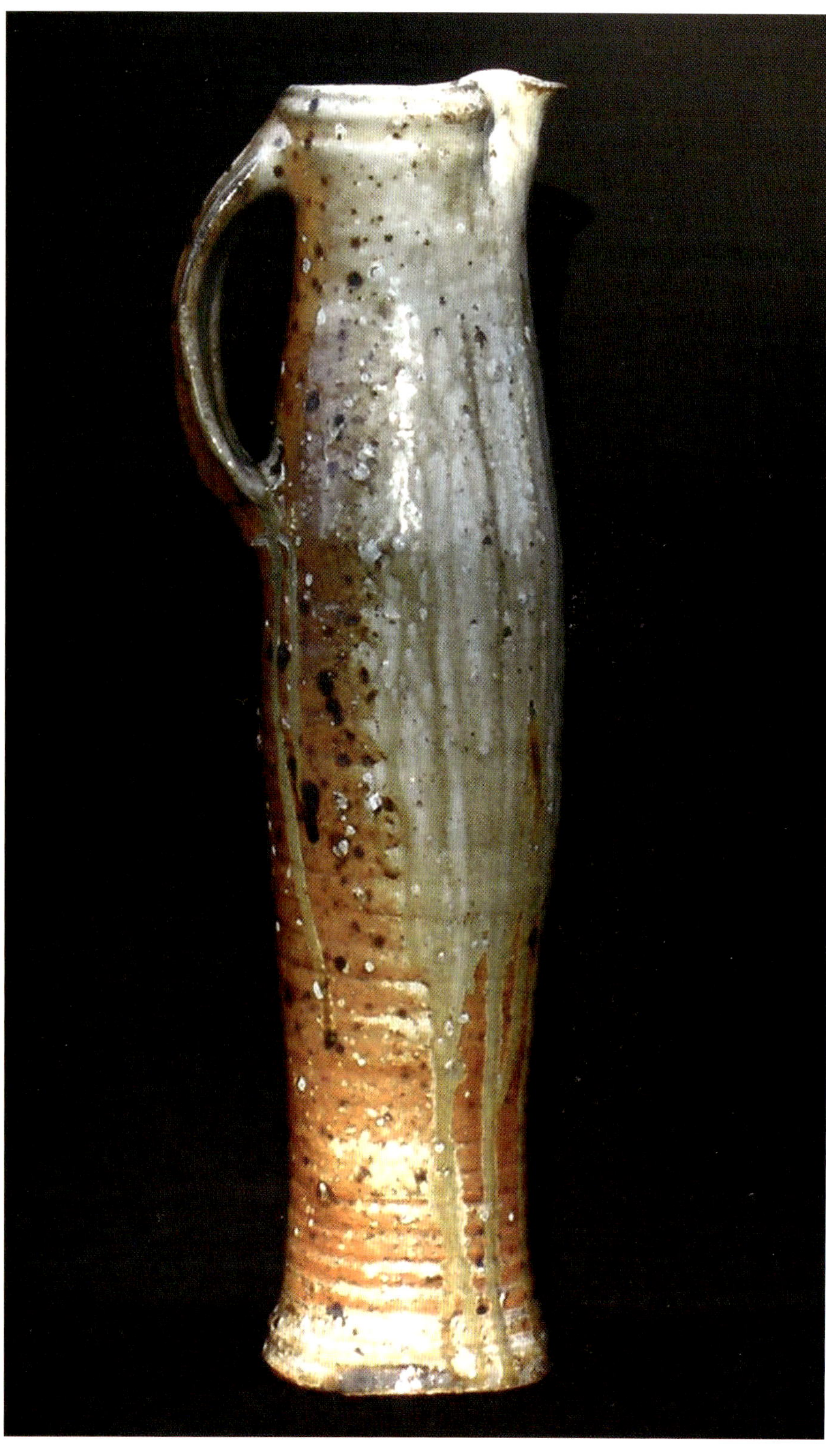

Nic Collins, *Tall jug*. Thrown using clay with feldspar additions, anagama-fired, height: 62 cm (24½ in). *Photo: courtesy of the author.*

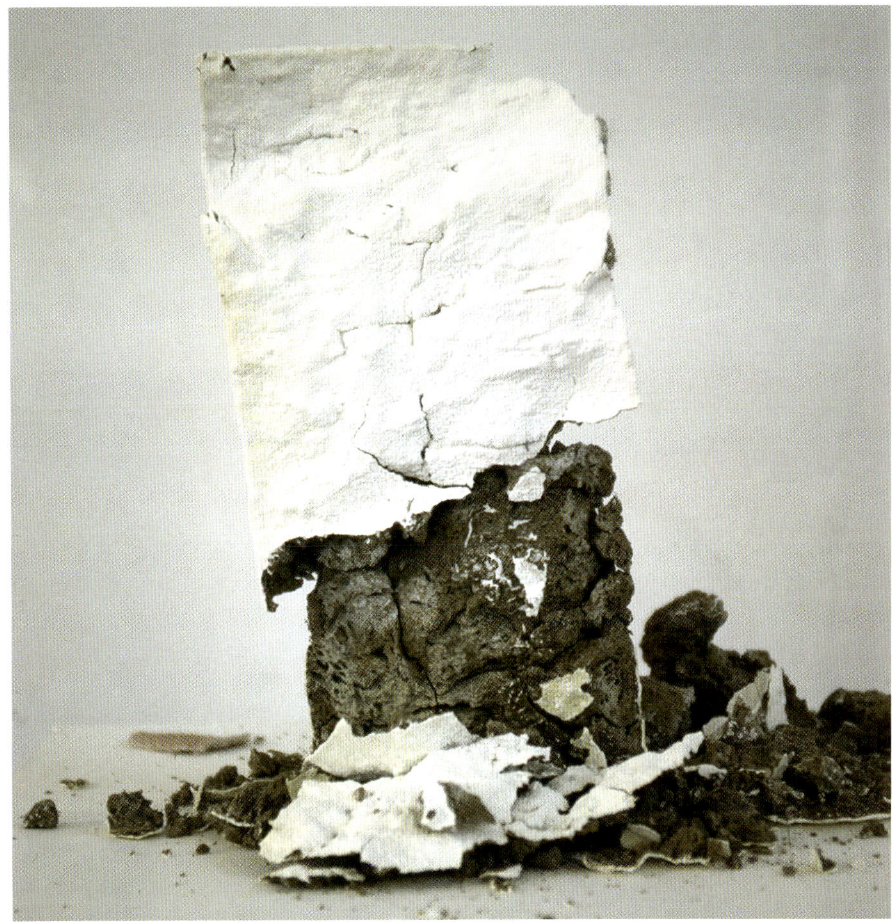

Andy Glass, *Deconstruction vessels*, 2004. Clay and limestone vessels, 80 x 50 cm (31½ x 19¾ in). *Photo: by the artist.*

Shards of crockery

'Idiosyncratic' is the word that springs to mind when I think back to the first time I saw **Henry Pim**'s ceramics in an exhibition. Attached to a wall at eye level, the work comprised complex amalgamations of shapes, many evoking memories from my own childhood. His work seeks to sift through evidence from the past, reinterpreting this in the context of how we live in the present.

Of his work *Conglomerate*, Pim says, 'Embedded within these small sculptures are the ruins of my mother's Spode dinner service. The pattern was of classical ruins populated by shepherds, suggesting a romantic co-existence between past and present. The good china, already chipped and depleted when I first ate from it as a small child, had been passed down from the grandparents, mute evidence of some hypothetical tradition, a bit of family history used on posh occasions and in the process gradually getting smashed.'

The work is biscuit-fired, followed by an application of matt transparent glaze, fired to 1100°C (2012°F) with a 15-minute soak. He says that glazing the forms makes them much less brittle.

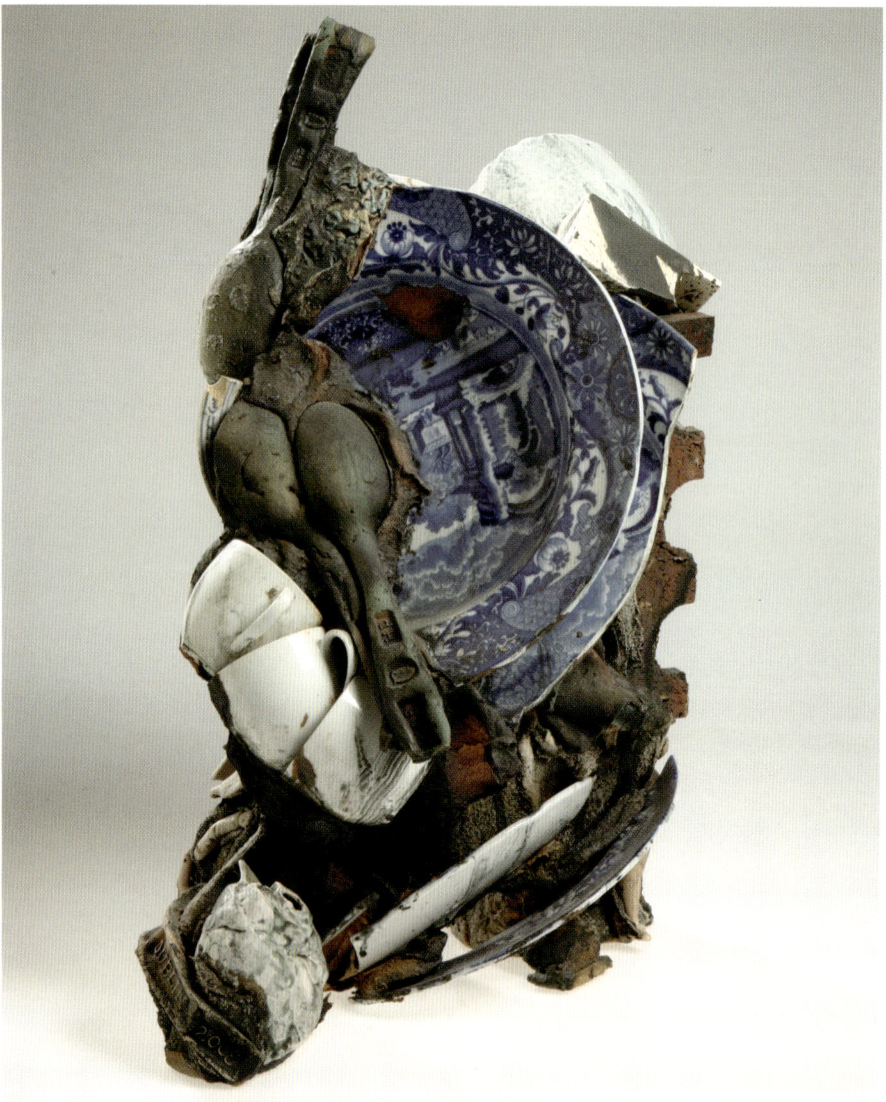

Henry Pim, *Conglomerate*, 2008. '*Conglomerate* incorporates broken pieces of my own work, the remains of a dinner service belonging to my mother and a slip-cast heart made by an ex-student, Fifi Cudmore (used with her permission)', height: 60 cm (23½ in). *Photo: by the artist.*

Pim has combined a career in teaching with his own studio practice. He says that by using pieces of students' work, he is able to pay tribute to the important part that teaching has played in his creative life.

Emma Rodgers also uses fragments of broken crockery for some of her sculptures, as in *Brace of Pheasants*, in which pieces of saucer have been inserted to represent bone or wings.

She looks for certain qualities in the materials she adds to her clay sculptures: saucers have hard, clean edges, moulded into a smooth curve, and it is this quality that dictates their suitability for the wings of her bird forms.

Rodgers' use of metal additions is discussed in Chapter 6 (pp. 102–103).

RIGHT: Emma Rodgers, *Brace of Pheasants*, 2010. With additions of broken crockery. Each bird is 50 x 22 cm (19½ x 8½ in). *Photo: Mills Media.*

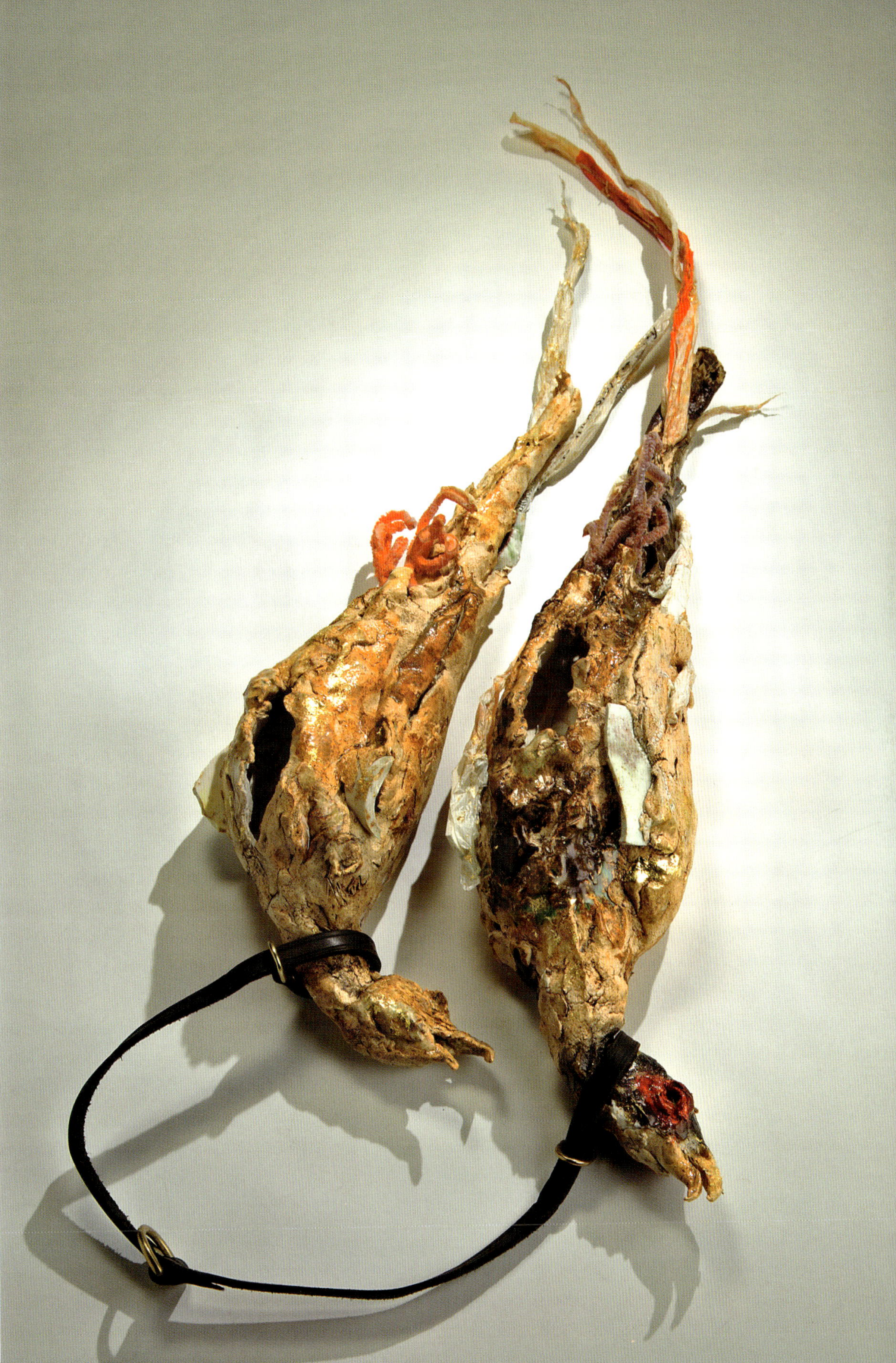

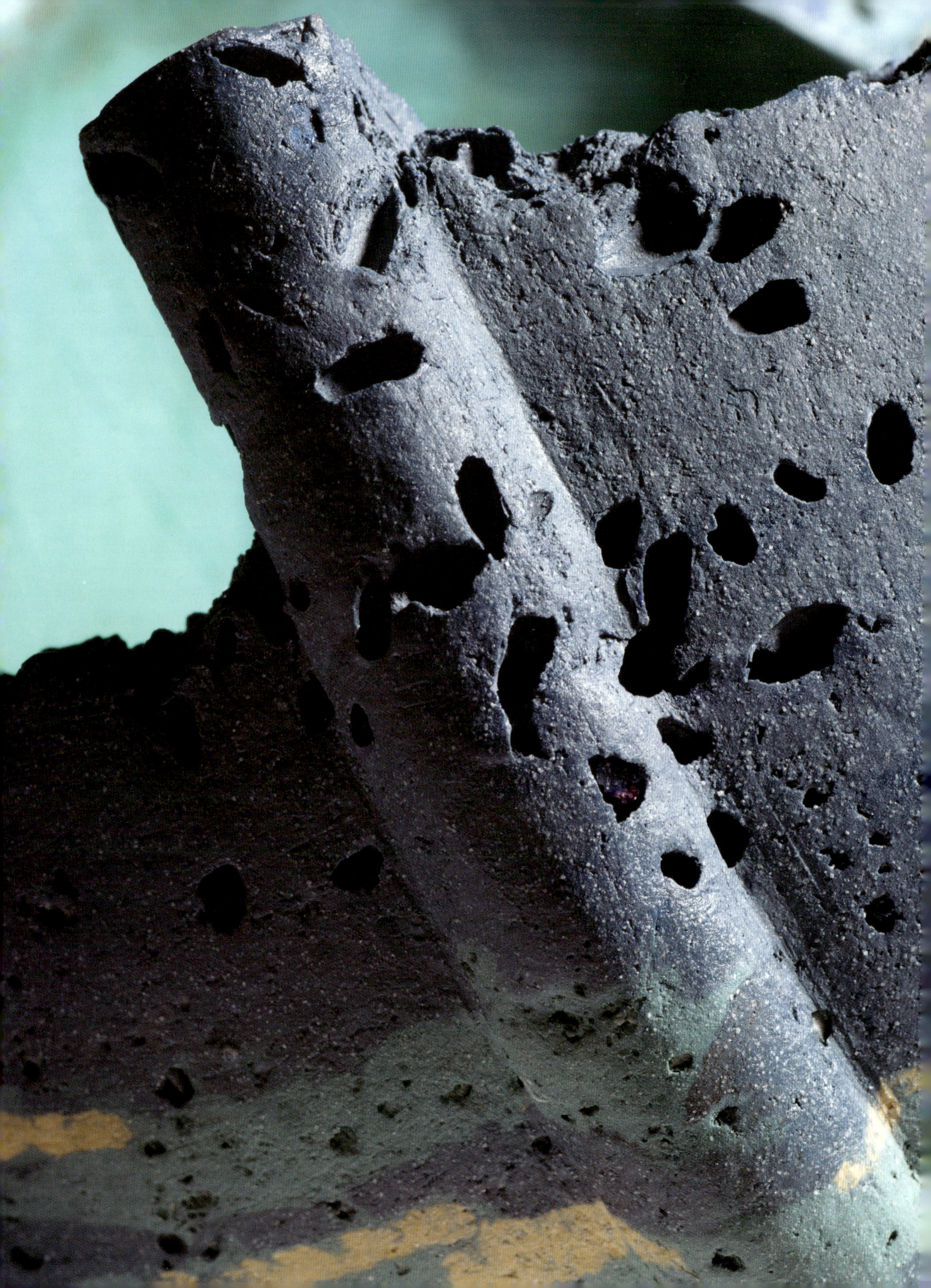

3 Combustible materials

All organic matter is combustible and this chapter deals with a range of organics, including plants and seeds, biscuits and bread, and wood shavings. Perlite should get a mention, too, as this naturally occurring siliceous rock, sold in garden centres in its expanded form, is also combustible. Perlite takes the form of lightweight irregular shapes, rather like small pieces of popcorn. When mixed into a clay body it will soak up some of the water, so make sure your mix is wet enough to allow for this absorption. When a perlite and clay mixture is fired to just over 1000°C (1832°F), the perlite burns out, leaving small pockmarks. It is a useful addition to thick-walled clay forms as it is very light and so reduces the overall weight; it also promotes even drying of the walls.

When organic matter is placed in an oven or kiln and heated above 300°C (572°F) it will smoulder and burn and then break down into carbon and water. What you will see is smoke issuing from the kiln (see safety precautions pp. 46–47); what will be left is an ash residue. If the organics are mixed with clay, all that is left after firing is a cavity where the organics have burnt out. This property is used by artists to provide interest and texture.

The resulting work is very different for each of the artists featured here, but there are a few common features in the use of organics in clay.

LEFT: Kathleen Standen, *Sea Foam* (detail), 2011. *Photo: Roland Paschhoff.*

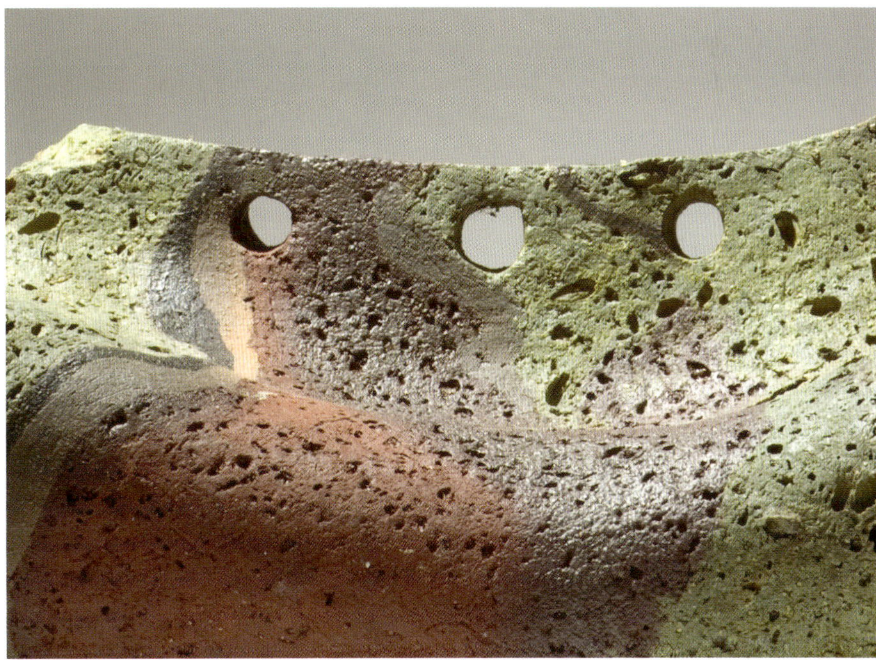

RIGHT: Kathleen Standen, *Landmarks* (detail), 2009. Showing the pockmarks left when perlite burns out. *Photo: Rory Moore.*

Safety issues concerning organic matter and clay

Organic matter decays in certain conditions, such as when it is added to damp clay. The decay frequently appears as mould, growing on and inside the material. When left undisturbed, spores are produced by the mould, which will be released into the air and are easily inhaled.

Here are some suggestions for limiting your exposure to this and other health hazards:

1. Prepare just enough of the clay mixture for your needs and dry leftover clay for storage, or wrap it up and dispose of it carefully in a bin outside.
2. Mould is likely to grow on clay work that has been wrapped in plastic for a few days or longer. If possible carry the work outside before unwrapping. Alternatively, unwrap in a well-ventilated area and wear a mask and disposable gloves.
3. Wearing protective clothing (mask and gloves), scrape off any visible mould and dispose of this carefully.
4. I frequently burn off the mould using a butane burner, then scrape off the burnt mould and throw it away as described above.
5. Before re-using plastic wrappings, wipe down with hot water with disinfectant mixed in and then hang up to dry.
6. Provide good ventilation when firing clay work containing organics, because between about 150°C (302°F) and 350°C (662°F), smoke will be produced from the burning additions. A hood and extractor fan is the best solution for a kiln placed inside a building, but otherwise ventilate well. If your kiln shares your

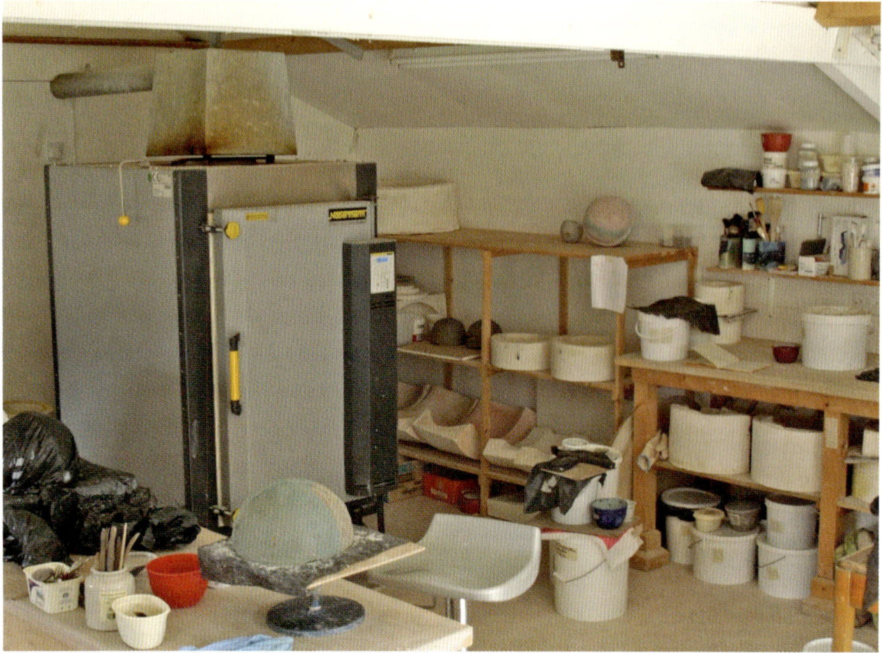

The electric kiln is fitted with a hood and extractor fan to remove most of the smoke from burning seeds, paper, etc. *Photo: Kathleen Standen.*

workspace (as mine does) avoid working there until all the organics have burnt off and dispersed.

7. A slow firing is recommended to allow combustibles to burn in a controlled manner.

Don't let these safety considerations deter you from using organic additions. You will see in the next few pages lots of exciting work using organics, which should encourage you to experiment yourself!

Organics that create deep fissures

When any organic material is incorporated into a clay form, it will burn out during the firing process. The work described below exhibits large holes or fissures in the form, planned by the maker. Some materials lend themselves more to this way of working; bread dough, dog biscuits and strammin board (see p.49) are the examples given here.

Claudi Casanovas has evolved a style of work that renders his ceramics immediately recognisable. Not only are his pieces unique, but his modus operandi is also unusual.

He has adopted the Japanese practice of *neriage* – the laminating together of different clay bodies – and puts into practice the belief that it is imperative to touch the clay as little as possible during the making process. He works alone, even on large-scale pieces, so relies on industrial machinery to manipulate the forms.

He often includes a variety of combustible materials into the making, including bread dough. During the firing process, the combustibles burn out, leaving deep fissures in the clay. Sandblasting is another process he uses to exploit the different properties of the many clay bodies used, often in one piece of work.

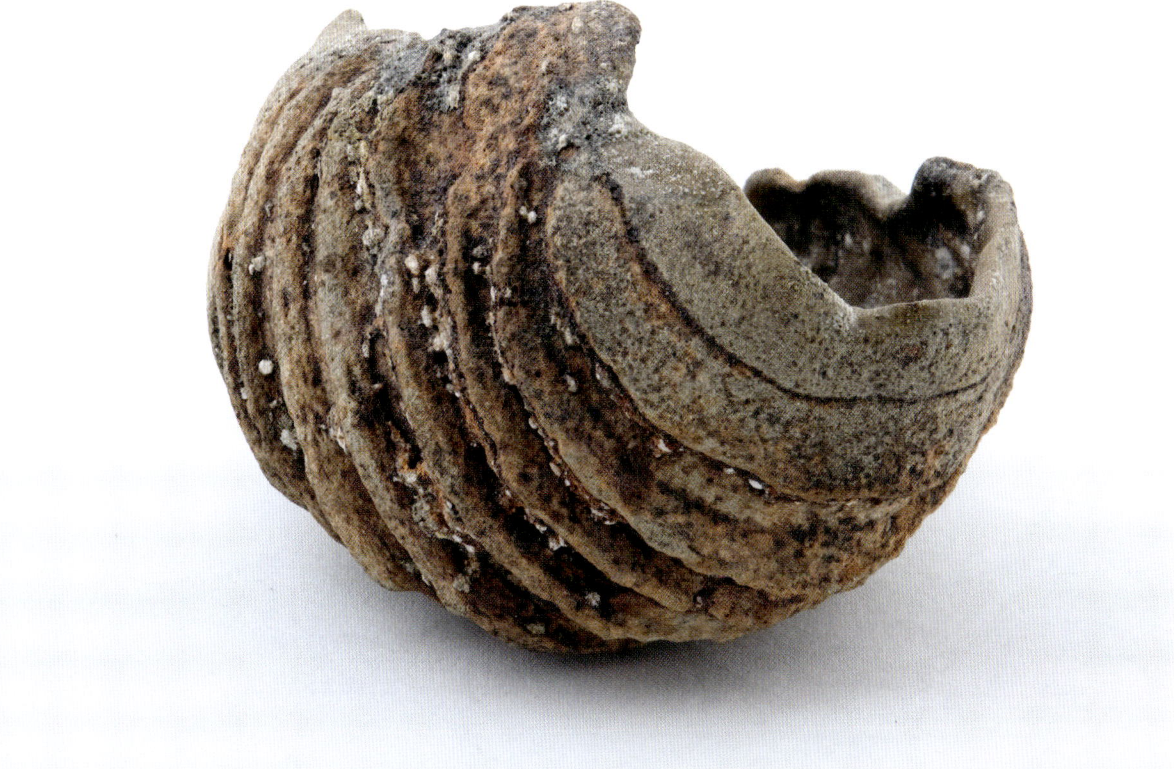

Claudi Casanovas, *Untitled*, 1991. 15 x 14 x 11 cm (6 x 5½ x 4¼ in). *Photo: Tom Gunn, provided by the Ceramics Collection, Aberystwyth University.*

Casanovas lives and works in Olat, Catalonia, a volcanic landscape from which he sources material for his ceramics. 'Nature in all its forms' is his inspiration and he is at pains to indicate that his work does not aim to emulate the landscape, but perhaps to mimic some of the processes that brought the landscape into being. Other influences are the Catalonian artist Antonio Tapies, the American abstract expressionists, and the Japanese ceramicist Royoji Koie, who encouraged Casanovas to find his own voice.

Natural Evolution is the name that **Dominique Bivar Segurado** has chosen for her Norwich-based studio and website, and this term encapsulates the key influences on the sculpted ceramic pieces she makes – namely the evolutionary effects of erosion and weathering on the natural landscape.

There are similarities with the ceramics of Casanovas, in the use of internal spaces or openings within bowl or platter forms, but the methods adopted by Segurado could not be more different. She painstakingly hand-forms her sculptures, bowls and wall pieces.

The first stage of making is to wedge coarse grog and molochite into stoneware clay, which gives the clay texture and strength. She starts bowls and platters by rolling out thick slabs onto a sawdust-covered surface. The slabs are then placed in plaster moulds. The sawdust creates a textural surface underneath the pieces. Some forms are then hand-carved and others have organic material, in the form of dog biscuits, pushed into the slightly firm clay.

A slow biscuit firing to 1015°C (1859°F) is followed by the removal of any loose ash from the organic material. Glazes and oxide washes are applied on some forms and then they undergo a final firing to 1240°C (2264°F).

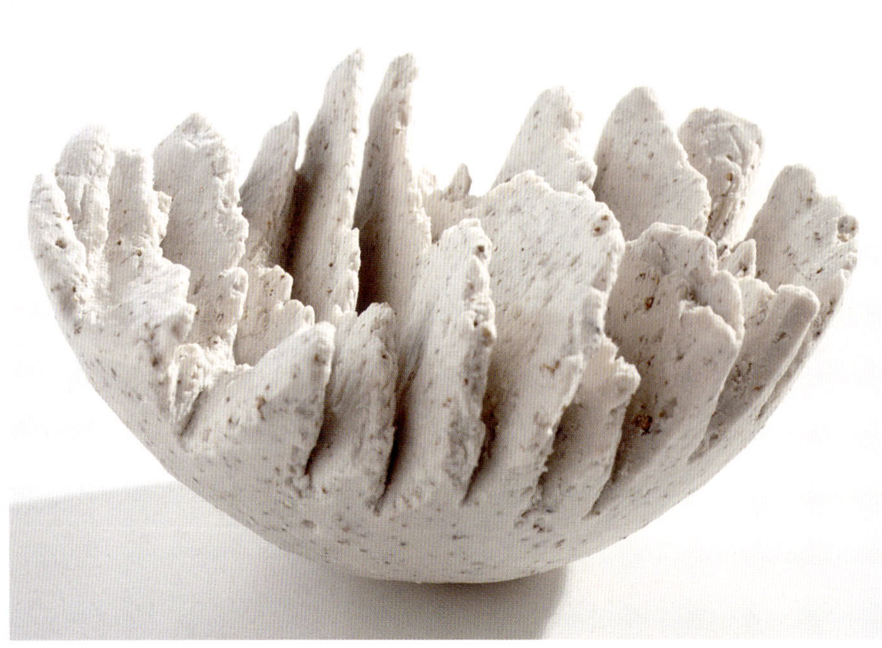

Dominique Bivar Segurado, *Calcium Bowl*, 2004. Porcelain clay, press-moulded and hand-cut, unglazed, 1240°C (2264°F), 7 x 12 x 10 cm (2¾ x 4¾ x 4 in). *Photo: Dougal Waters.*

Segurado's work features in private and public collections, and she is the author of a book on *Wall Pieces*, published by Bloomsbury Publishing (formerly A & C Black).

'The creative process is not in any way mysterious, magical or romantic; it's a matter of hard work and perseverance.' **Paul Philp** practices this philosophy and his large vessels and sculptures are the culmination of many years of research and testing. The forms are coiled, modelled and carved, and frequently left unglazed, to allow the colours of the raw clay to emerge. All work is fired to 1260°C (2300°F) in a gas kiln.

He blends a variety of clays and additions for any series of pieces he is starting: fireclay, buff clay, red clay, washed Bristol sea sand and 'strammin board' (an old form of insulation board made of wood wool and cement). Philp says that it took him years to discover how Bristol sea sand could be safely used. Bits of shell turn to quick lime in the biscuit firing, so the trick is to find the optimum size that will not cause the work to disintegrate, at least not to a destructive degree. In his work, the sea sand causes speckles but does not blow pieces out of the pots.

He tries not to stick to a safe working formula and believes that it is important to be prepared to fail, as fear of failure can inhibit creativity. This open-minded approach has led him to use strammin board in his work. It is broken up into manageable chunks and added to the clay mix or sometimes added as the form is modelled, then burns out in firing, causing erosions, marks or holes. Influences on Philps' work include Japanese ceramics, abstract expressionist painting and the Celtic practice of building walls using stones of different sizes.

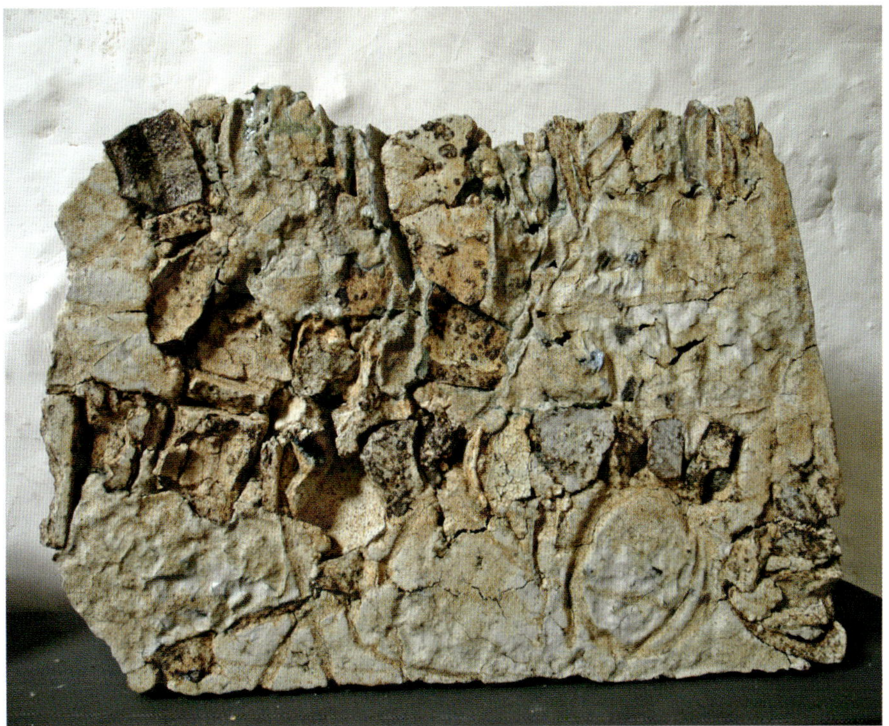

Paul Philp, *Untitled*, October 2008. Clay blends, sand and strammin board, 1260°C (2300°F), 50 x 43 cm (19¾ x 17 in). *Photo: Phil Boorman.*

Organics that leave shallow holes and patterns

Where small pieces of organic matter are added to clay, it is possible to create distinct patterns of holes. Seeds of all types, grasses and rice grains are just some of the organics that have been used successfully by artists. This can lend a delicacy to the work, as in the case of **Liz Emtage**'s lamps, or emulate erosion, as in some of my sculptural forms. Again, experimenting is the key to finding the best material for your work.

Chapter 5 has more information on Liz Emtage's lamps (pp. 81–83).

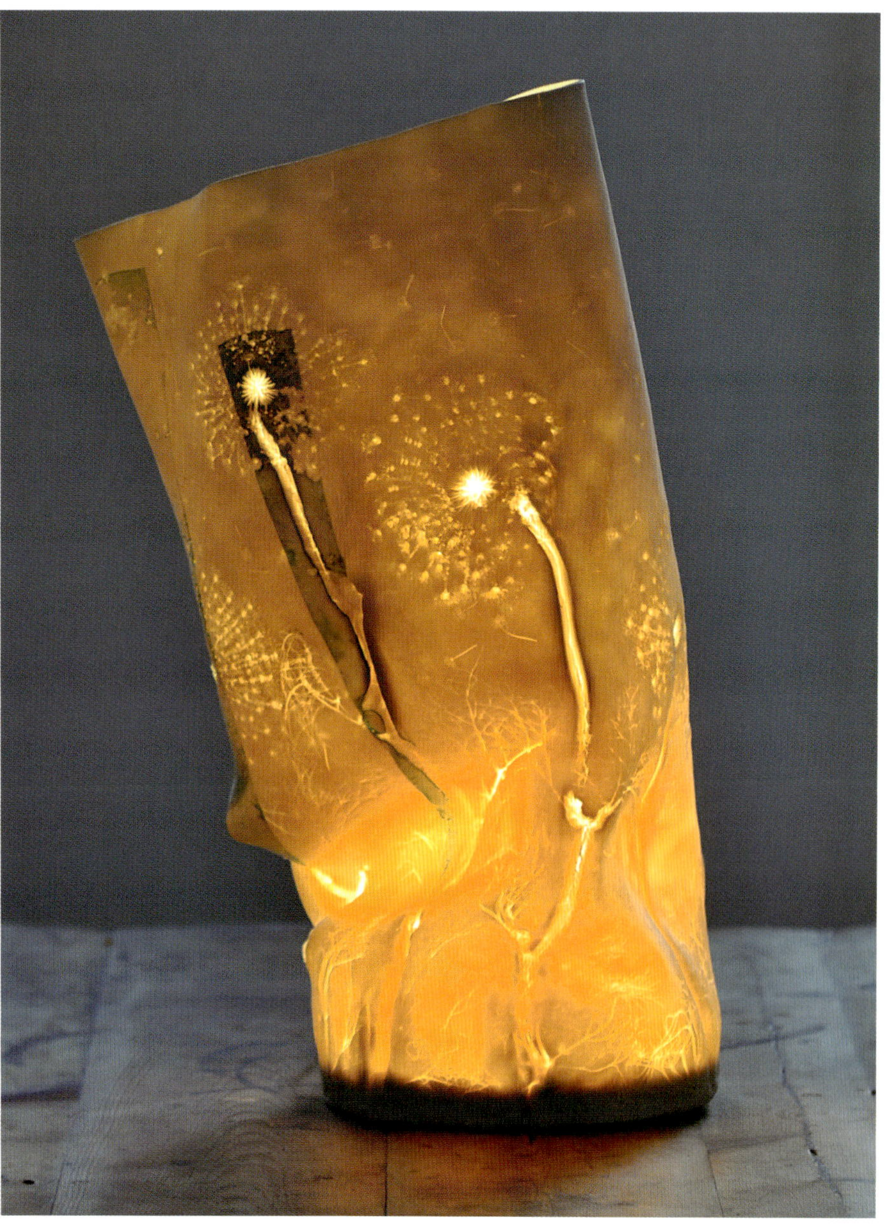

Liz Emtage, *Cowparsley-leaning*, 2011. Extra-large porcelain lamp inlaid with cow parsley pattern and glazed, 54 x 20 cm (21¼ x 7¾ in). *Photo: Sussie Ahlburg.*

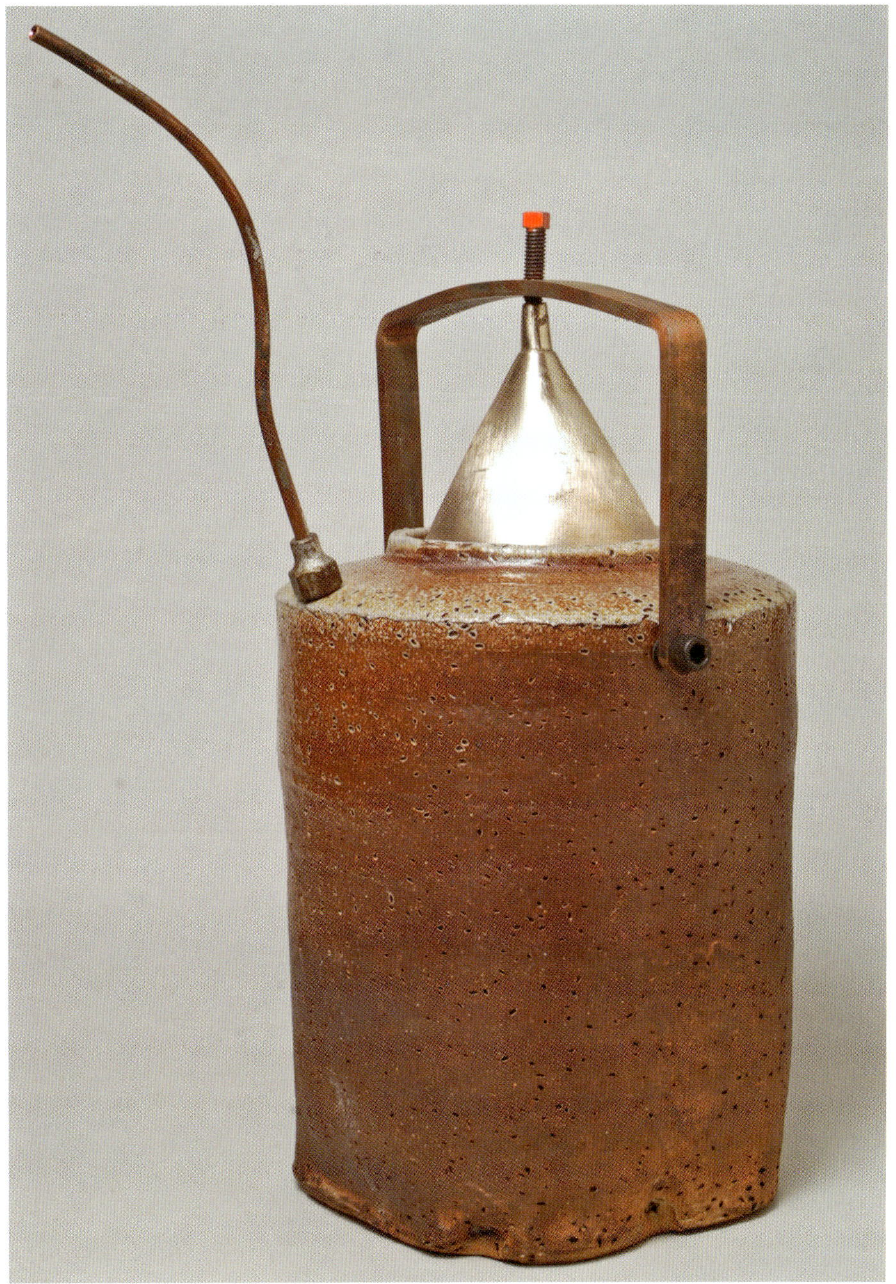

Richard Burkett, *Pressure Vessel: Regulated 1*, 2003. White stoneware clay with soya beans wedged into clay and thrown, with a very slow bisque firing, flashing slip, and soda-glaze firing to Orton Cone 10, 1315°C (2399°F). Found object lid, welded steel shelf, 30.5 x 20 cm (12 x 7¾ in). *Photo: by the artist.*

American ceramicist **Richard Burkett** is Professor of Art at San Diego State University, and exhibits his tea bowls and sculptures in galleries throughout the USA. His work hovers between pottery and sculpture. 'Ultimately,' he says, 'it's a reaction to living in a heavily corporatised, fast-paced world. The burnout clay and mixed media pieces, especially, address the apparent failure of industry to make the world a better, safer place.'

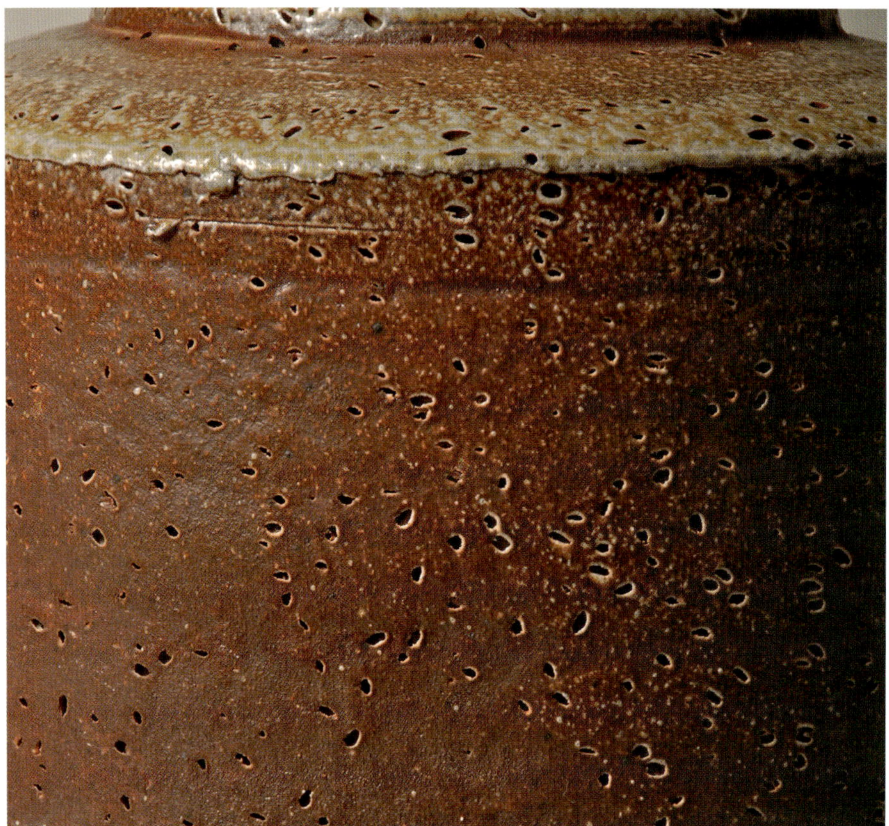

Richard Burkett, *Pressure Vessel: Regulated 1* (detail), 2003. *Photo: by the artist.*

Burkett wedges wholegrain barley into clay before throwing his forms, which are dried as quickly as possible to stop the grain swelling, sprouting or growing mould. Firing is carried out very slowly up until 550°C (1022°F). This includes holding the temperature for an hour at 220°C (428°F). This firing schedule aims to facilitate the release of moisture and carbon in the barley grain and to allow the grain to slowly char and decompose. He also stresses the importance in his practice of avoiding inhalation of the burn-out gases, with good ventilation of the room and the kiln. His *Pressure Vessel* (p. 51, and above) was then soda-fired to Cone 11 and the metal attachments fixed in position.

I was introduced to the notion of adding organics to clay by my tutor Robert Cooper whilst studying for a ceramics diploma at the City Lit Institute in Holborn, London. We were asked to bring in dried foods such as rice, lentils and oats. A local coffee outlet supplied used coffee grounds and someone collected wood shavings and sawdust from a joinery workshop. We created weird, wonderful and just plain awful forms in these early experiments, but they made an impression on me that remained. After several years of research and making, I have refined my use of organic material in clay to create sculptural forms with a strong narrative, connected to my family roots and home in Ireland.

My studio in Ireland is near the scenic fishing villages of West Cork, where the rocky coastline is punctuated by inlets and communities shelter from the Atlantic gales. I

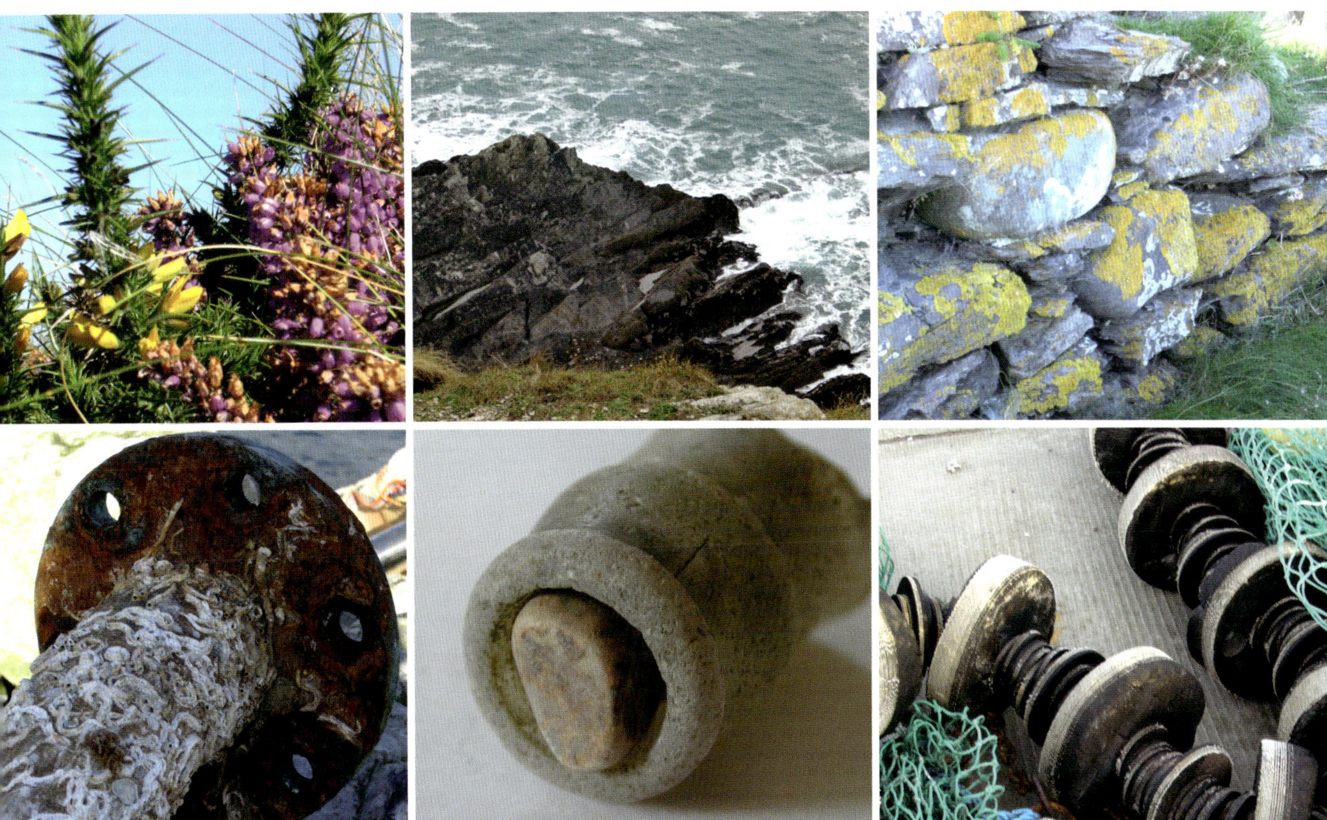

TOP ROW, LEFT TO RIGHT: Wild flowers on the headland; surging foam on the rocky promontory; lichen growing on rocks.

BOTTOM ROW, LEFT TO RIGHT: Barnacle encrusted pipe from a trawler; broken bottle with pebble stuck in its mouth; fishing floats made from recycled tyres. *Photos: Kathleen Standen.*

turned to incorporating additions in my clay, organic matter and colour in particular, to provide me with a colour pallete and range of textures that would emulate the forces of nature so evident in this part of the world. Grey and black twisted sedimentary rocks, deep yellow and bright white lichen, splashes of pink thrift and purple fuchsia, still water and surging foam, are a few snapshots of this special place, which provides the inspiration for my ceramic practice.

Research

Taking photographs, drawing with coloured pastels and beachcombing form part of my research when starting a new series of pieces. Sometimes a found object sets me off in a particular direction: part of a glass bottle with a pebble stuck in its neck; a barnacle-encrusted pipe from a fishing trawler; slices of tyres used as floats for nets; an eroded metal buoy; fragments of plastic containers washed up on the beach. Both inside and outside my studio, I keep 'collections' of my finds.

I often make a **maquette** to explore the possibilities for the form, and carry out colour tests to give me the best combinations of colours. I may research glazes at this stage too. Then the form is made and cast in plaster, and I am able to plan an individual piece, make the coloured clay and choose the organic additions.

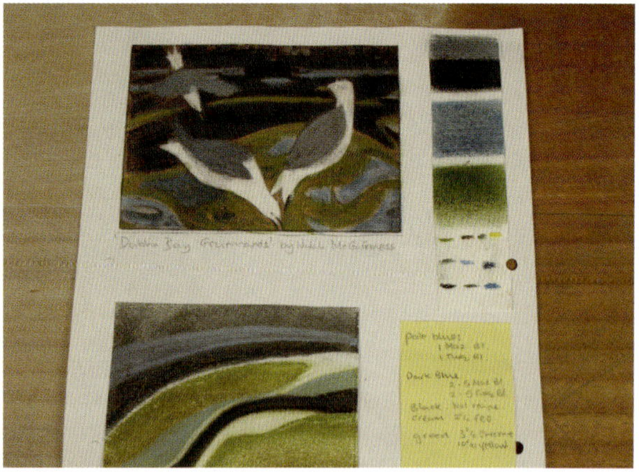

Sketches and colour studies.

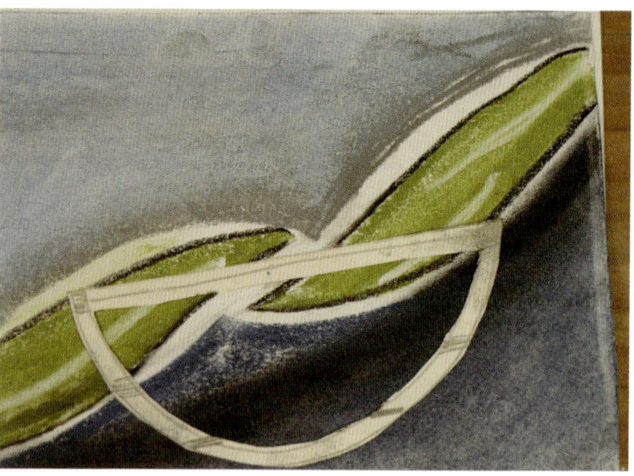

Exploring pattern and colour.

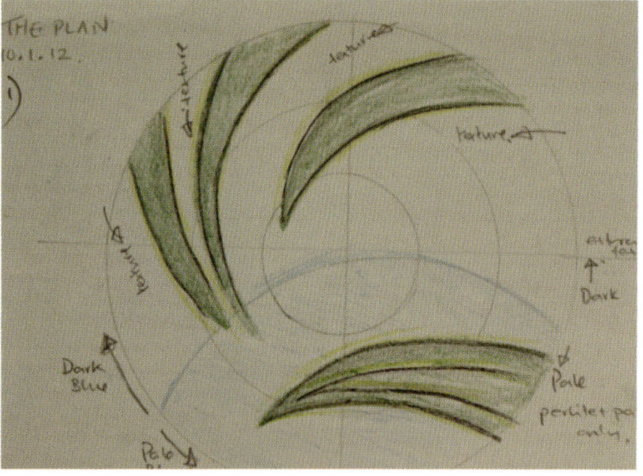

Drawing a plan.

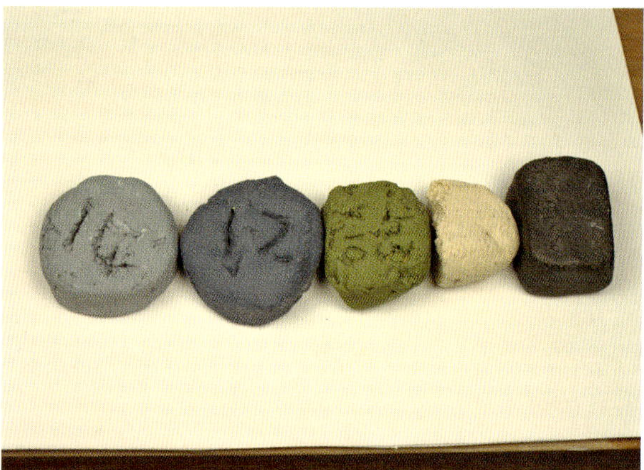

Choosing the coloured clay from a range of testers.
Photos: Kathleen Standen.

Plan

My usual procedure is to draw a plan showing the colour and organic inclusions, which I then use as a guide.

Filling the mould

While filling the mould, I work intuitively and some deviation from the plan occurs. Most of the moulds have internal curves and several forms are cut and rejoined, so this has to be factored in too. Wild bird seed, monkey-nut shells, olive and prune stones, pistachio-nut shells, cotton linter and perlite, and body stains and oxides are added to the clay in varying combinations. Sometimes I add the organic material to the clay as I am filling the mould, which gives specific areas of pattern and texture. Where a more uniform texture is required, the additions are stirred into the sloppy clay in a bucket, laid out on a plaster slab until just firm enough to handle, and then used to fill the mould.

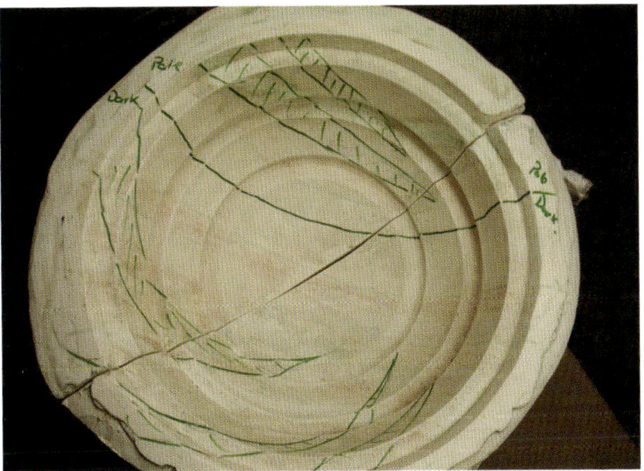

Markings are drawn on the mould to act as a guide.

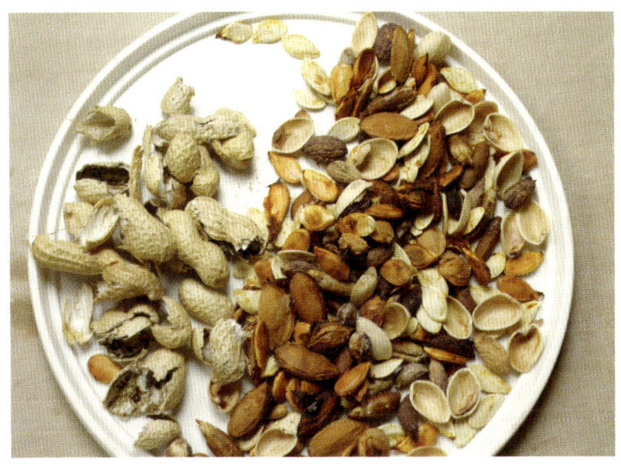

Any extra additions are selected.

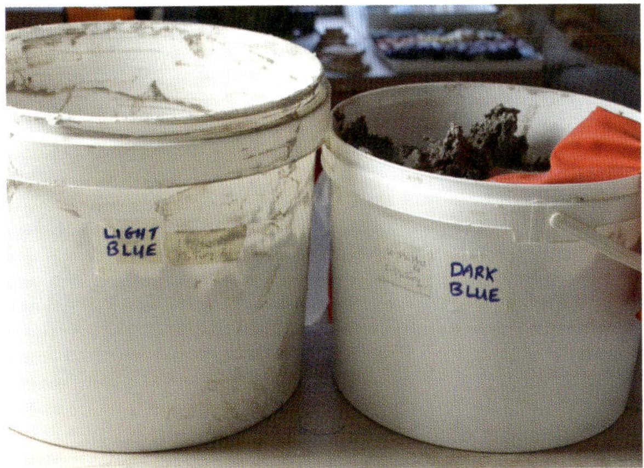

All the buckets of colour are labelled.

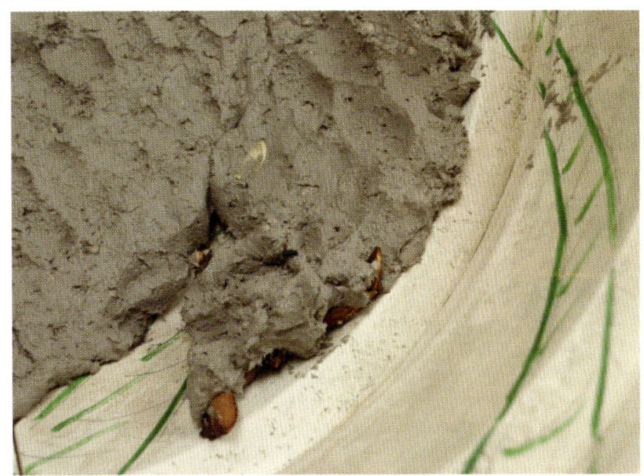

While filling the mould, extra seeds are added.

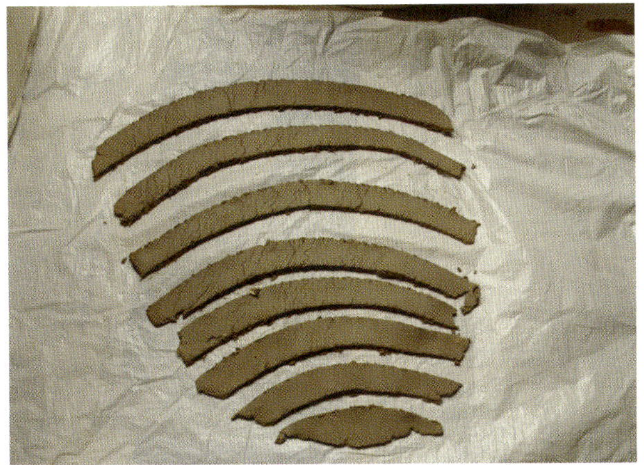

'Lines' of contrasting smooth colour are rolled and cut out.

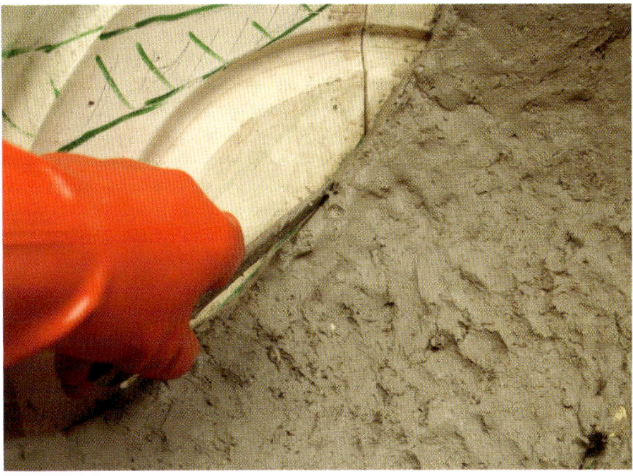

These are laid in the mould.
Photos: Kathleen Standen.

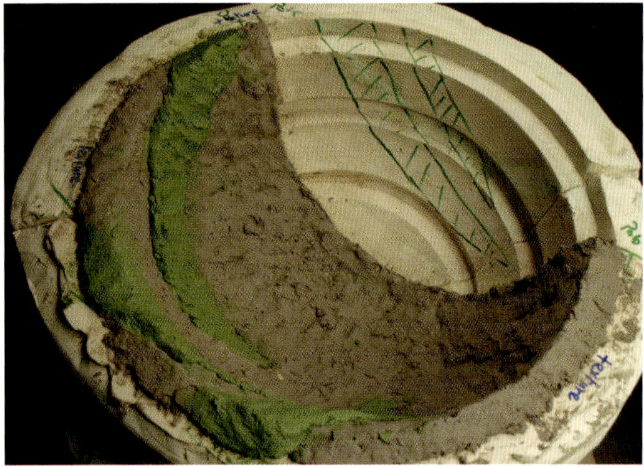

I continue to fill the mould.

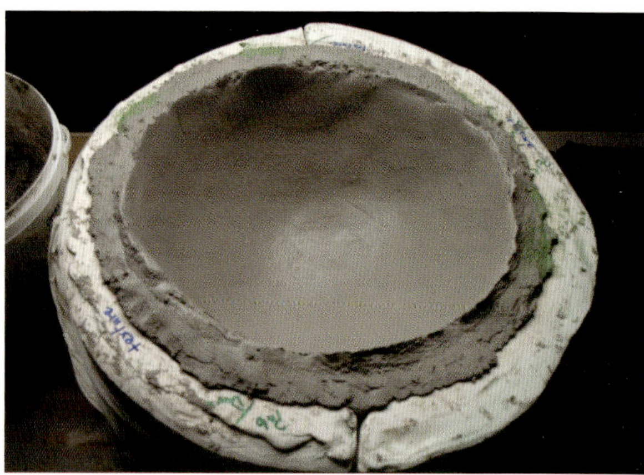

The interior surface is smoothed over. I check the thickness of the clay – it should be between 3 and 4 cm (1¼–1½ in) thick. It is then covered with plastic and left for 24 hours to firm up evenly before unmoulding.

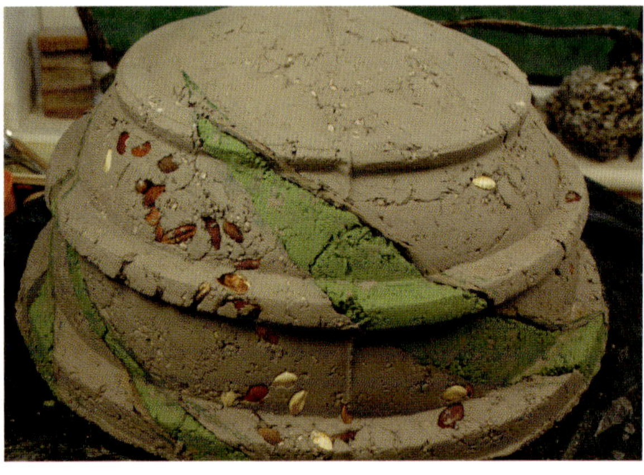

The form is unmoulded and the colour inlay and additions can be seen.

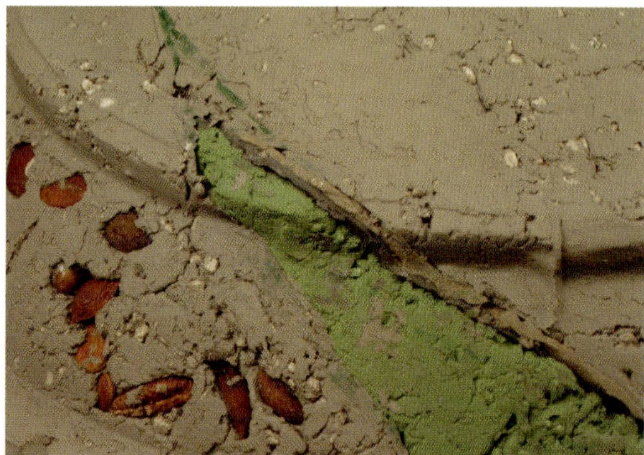

Close-up of the mould.
Photos: Kathleen Standen.

Note: All seeds are baked at a low temperature in the oven to prevent them from swelling and germinating. I put them in the slow oven of my Aga cooker, which is about 80°C (176°F).

Unmoulding, filling in holes, refining, cutting and rejoining

Once the moulded clay has firmed up, the form is carefully removed from the mould. With large moulds, this is a tricky process requiring a great deal of careful planning to ensure that the form is not placed on an edge, which could be damaged or distorted. Lots of soft padding, such as sponges and towels, and two people are needed to ensure the safe unmoulding of the form.

The series of images opposite and on the following pages shows the next stages in the making of *Dockpool*. Holes are filled, then the surface is scraped back to reveal

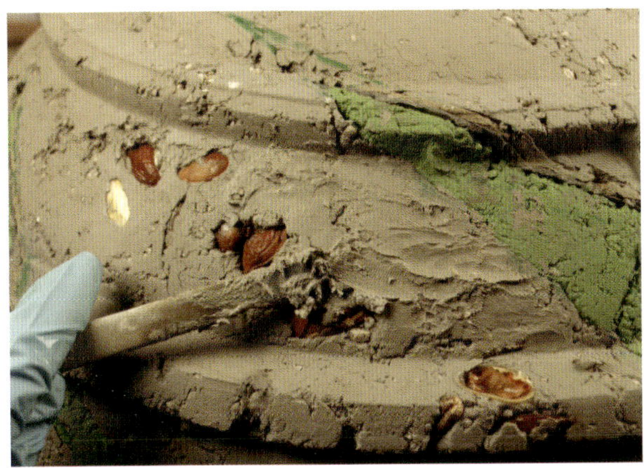

Filling in the holes with soft clay.

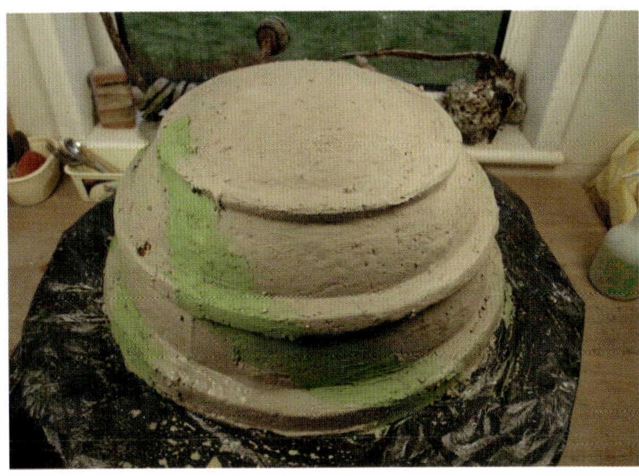

When all the holes are filled in, it will be wrapped up in plastic for a few days.

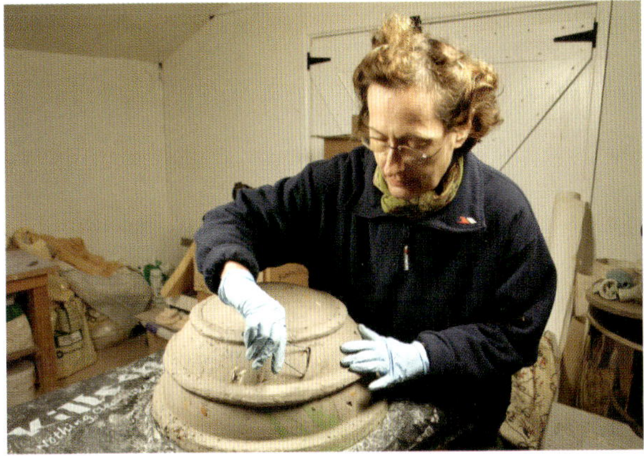

Using a metal tool to scrape and refine the surface to reveal pattern and texture.

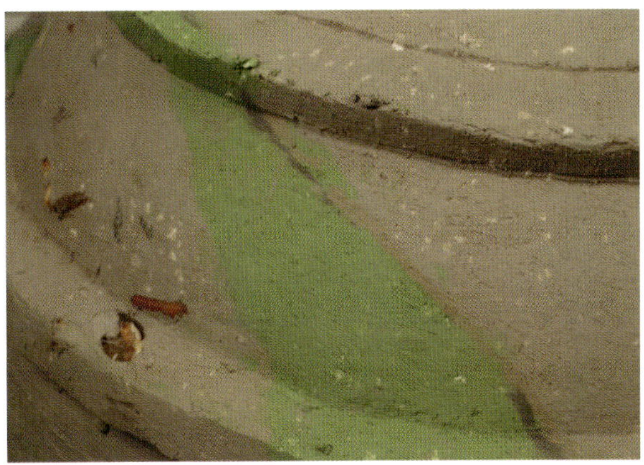

Close-up of pattern and texture.

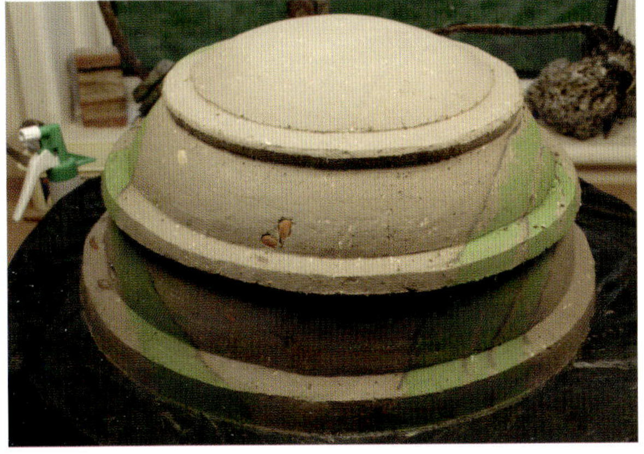

The refining continues.

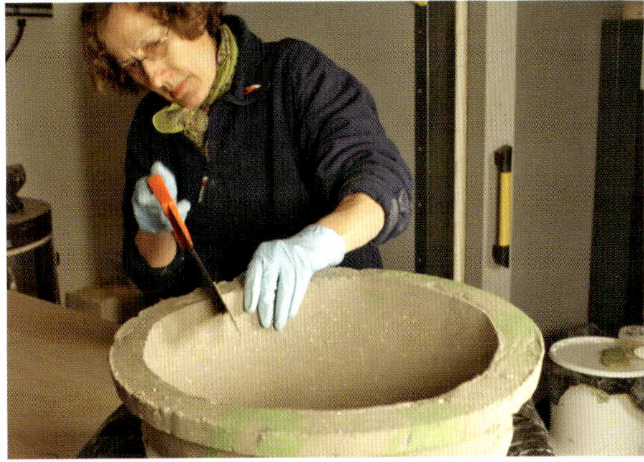

Marking and then cutting through the form. *Photos: Kathleen Standen.*

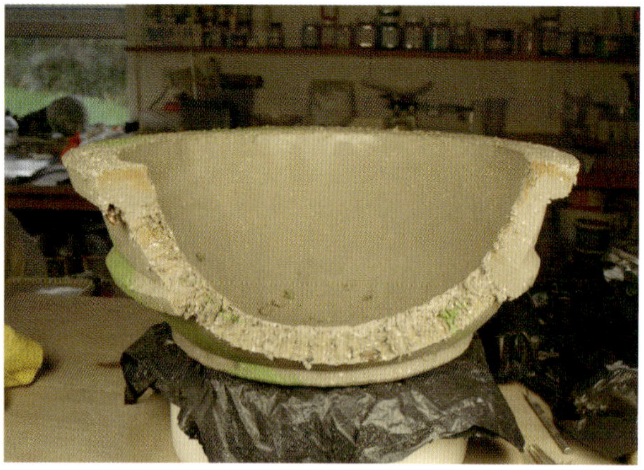

The cut piece is removed.

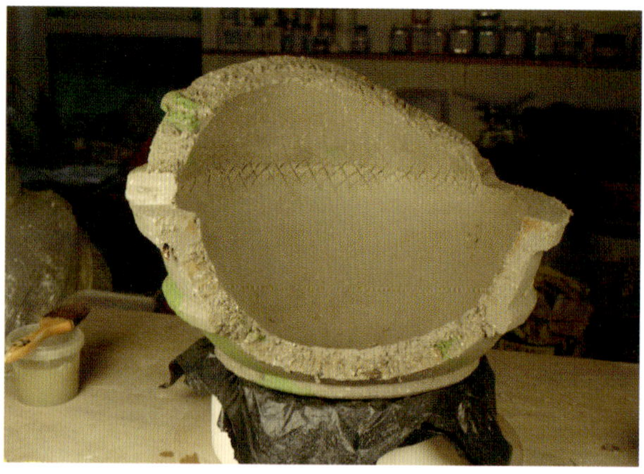

Another piece has been joined onto the form.

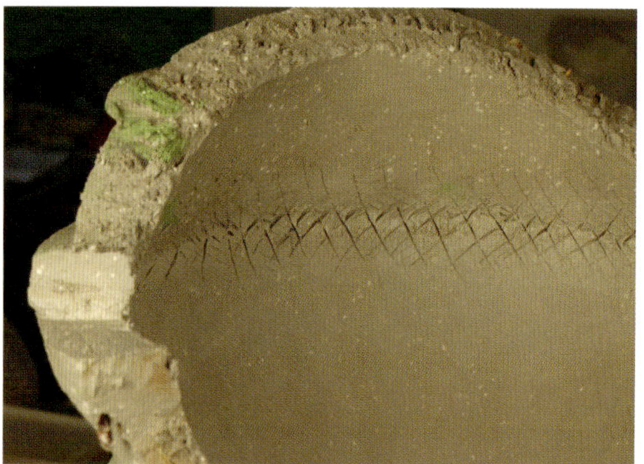

The form is scored and soft clay added to re-establish the internal curve.

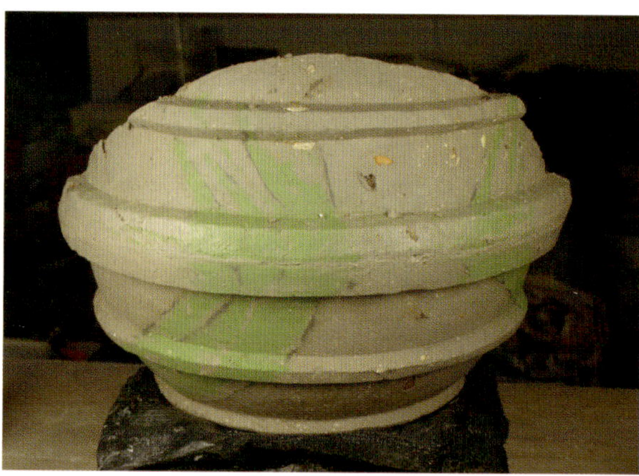

The outside of the form.

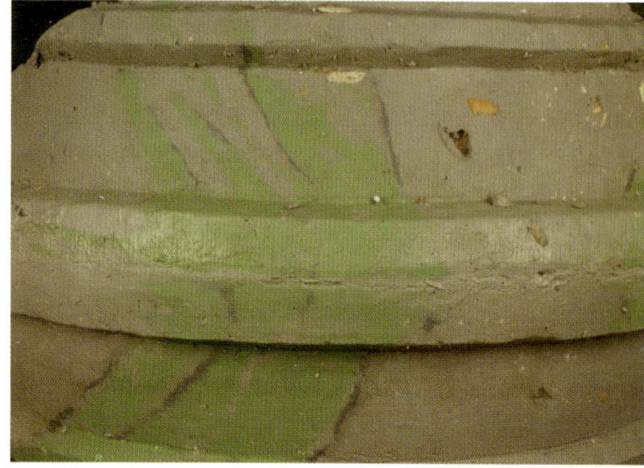

Close-up of the joined sections, showing that the patterns have been matched.

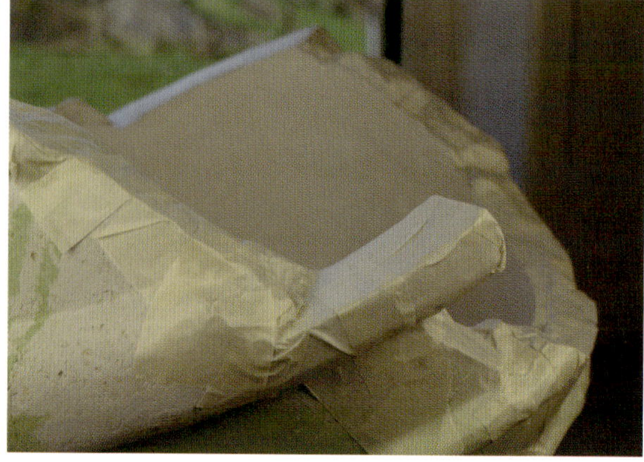

The edges of the form are covered with masking tape before the interior is glazed. *Photos: Kathleen Standen.*

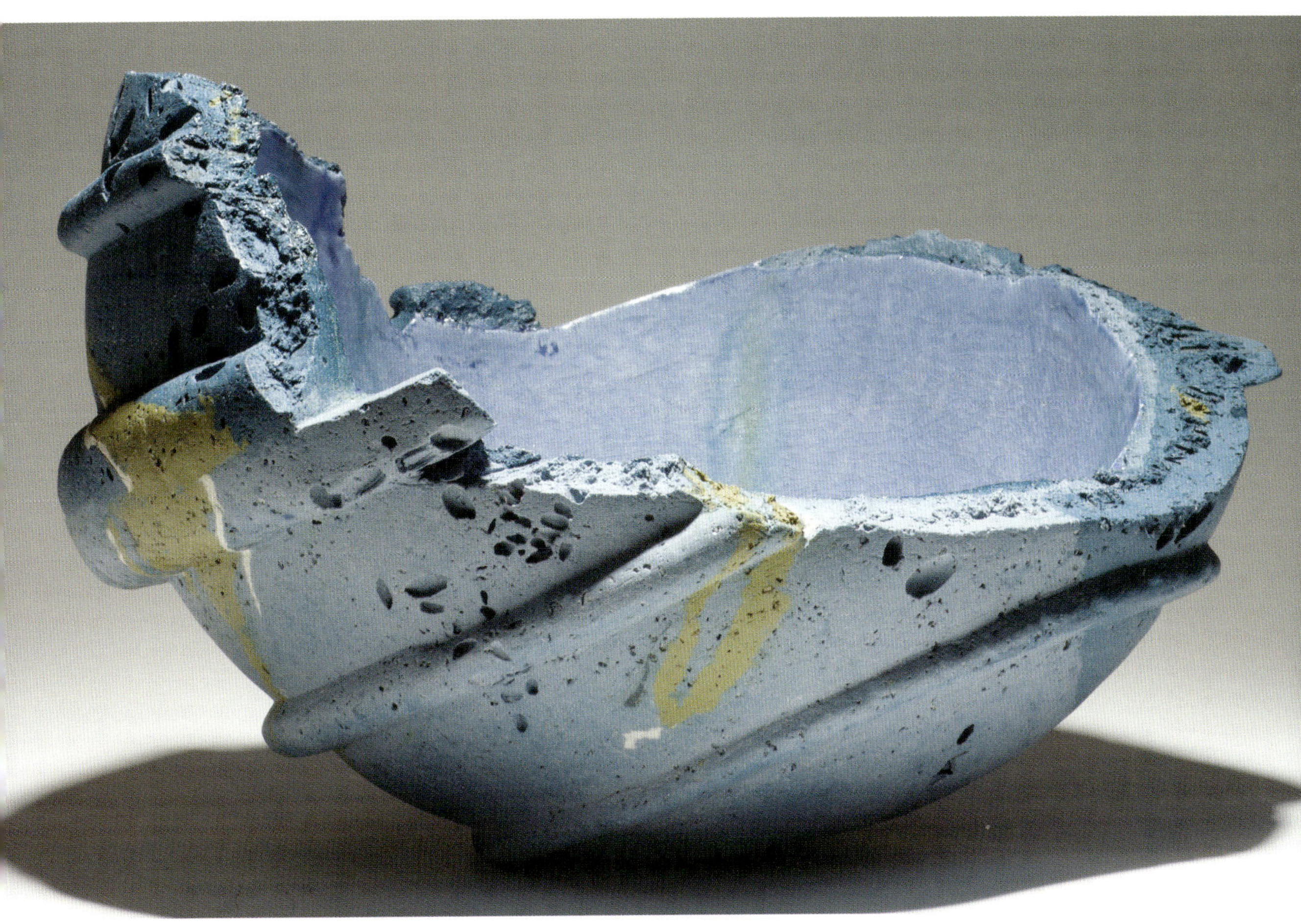

Kathleen Standen, *Dockpool*, 2012. Coloured, glazed porcelain clay with organic additions, 32 x 38 x 40 cm (12½ x 15 x 15¾ in). *Photo: Roland Paschhoff.*

the pattern of colours. Two forms were made in this way. I cut and broke off a section from each form and then attached it to the other one. The internal curve must then be re-established and the outside repaired and refined. Sometimes the cutting and breaking continues, although on a reduced scale. In this way I turn a whole form into something that resembles a fragment. When I am satisfied with the piece it is allowed to dry slowly and then it is slowly biscuit-fired in a well-ventilated kiln.

Before glazing the interior, all the holes are cleaned with a wooden tool, sandpaper and the vacuum cleaner. Finally, the outside edges are covered with masking paper to prevent glaze from splashing onto the coloured clay. The glaze firing is to 1220°C (2228°F) with a 20-minute soak.

Surface refinements are carried out at the leatherhard, biscuit and final fired stages. A variety of tools are used: metal kidneys on greenware; wet and dry sandpaper, rounded, long wooden tools and vacuum cleaner on biscuitware, and an electric stone polisher on some pieces after the higher firing. This last procedure renders the surface silky smooth, with a weathered look, as it reveals variations in surface colour. Beeswax is sometimes rubbed in, too.

Growing plants in clay

Whilst on a residency at the Fule International Ceramic Museum in Shaanxi Province, China, I experimented with growing plants in clay.

Soya beans were a staple part of our diet, so I had the idea of planting these seeds in porcelain clay, together with a few grape seeds saved from fruit snacks. The white porcelain was rolled and cut into the shape of a tea rose, many of which grew in the gardens nearby. These were then attached with slip to a terracotta, double-walled, thick tile. This latter form is one of many shapes that were extruded in huge numbers in the Brick and Tile Factory next to the museum.

Some of the soya beans were soaked for 24 hours to encourage them to swell. Soaked and unsoaked beans were then 'planted' in the porcelain flowers by pushing them below the surface. Five tiles were made in this way and covered with plastic to keep the clay damp and encourage germination. After a few days, I removed one cover each day for the next five days, thus varying the growing conditions for each tile. The support staff in the factory set up a drying tent over my table, comprising plastic sheeting and a very high-wattage light bulb. The soya beans flourished for a while and were a source of great amusement to staff and visitors.

Eventually they were biscuit-fired to 1000°C (1832°F), all debris was cleaned away, and copper carbonate was painted into the cracks and crevices before the final firing to 1270°C (2318°F).

I was delighted with the results: deep cracks had formed where the porcelain pulled away from the terracotta and more delicate cracks and marks, picked out in subtle shades of green, charted the growing pains of the soya beans.

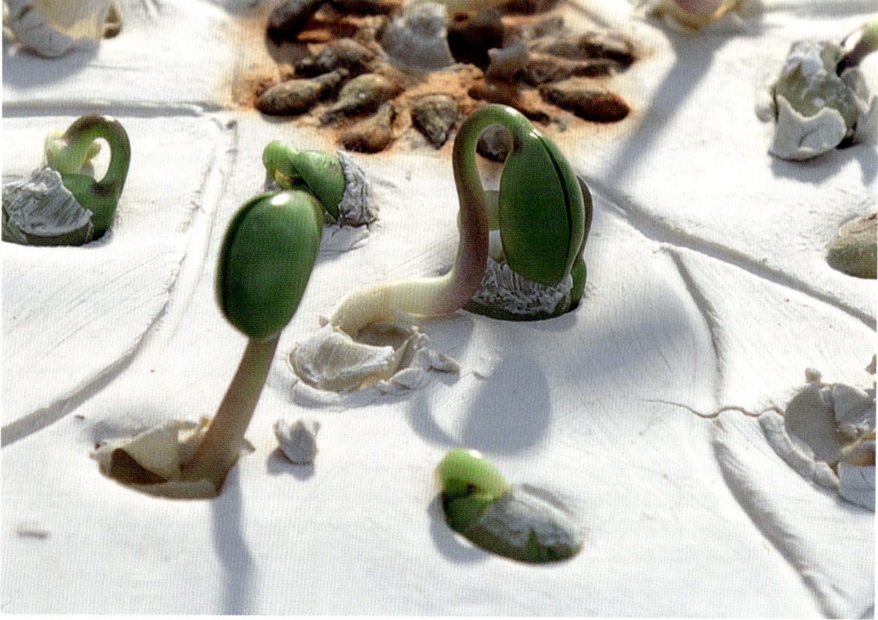

Sprouting soya beans, Fule International Ceramic Museum, Irish residency, September 2011. *Photo: Andrew Standen-Raz.*

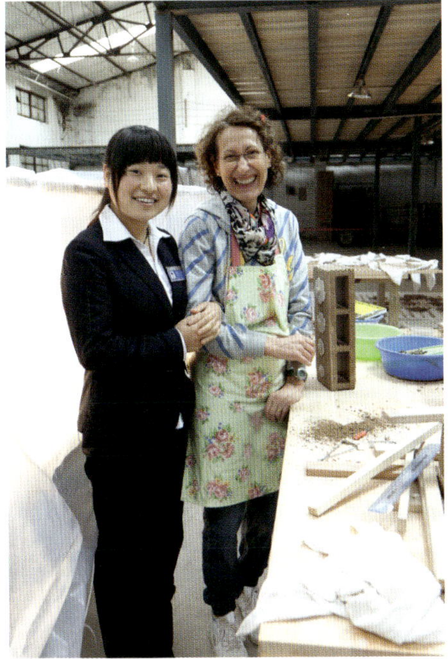

Kathleen Standen with Melody (Interpreter), Fule International Ceramic Museum, Irish residency, September 2011. *Photo: Andrew Standen-Raz.*

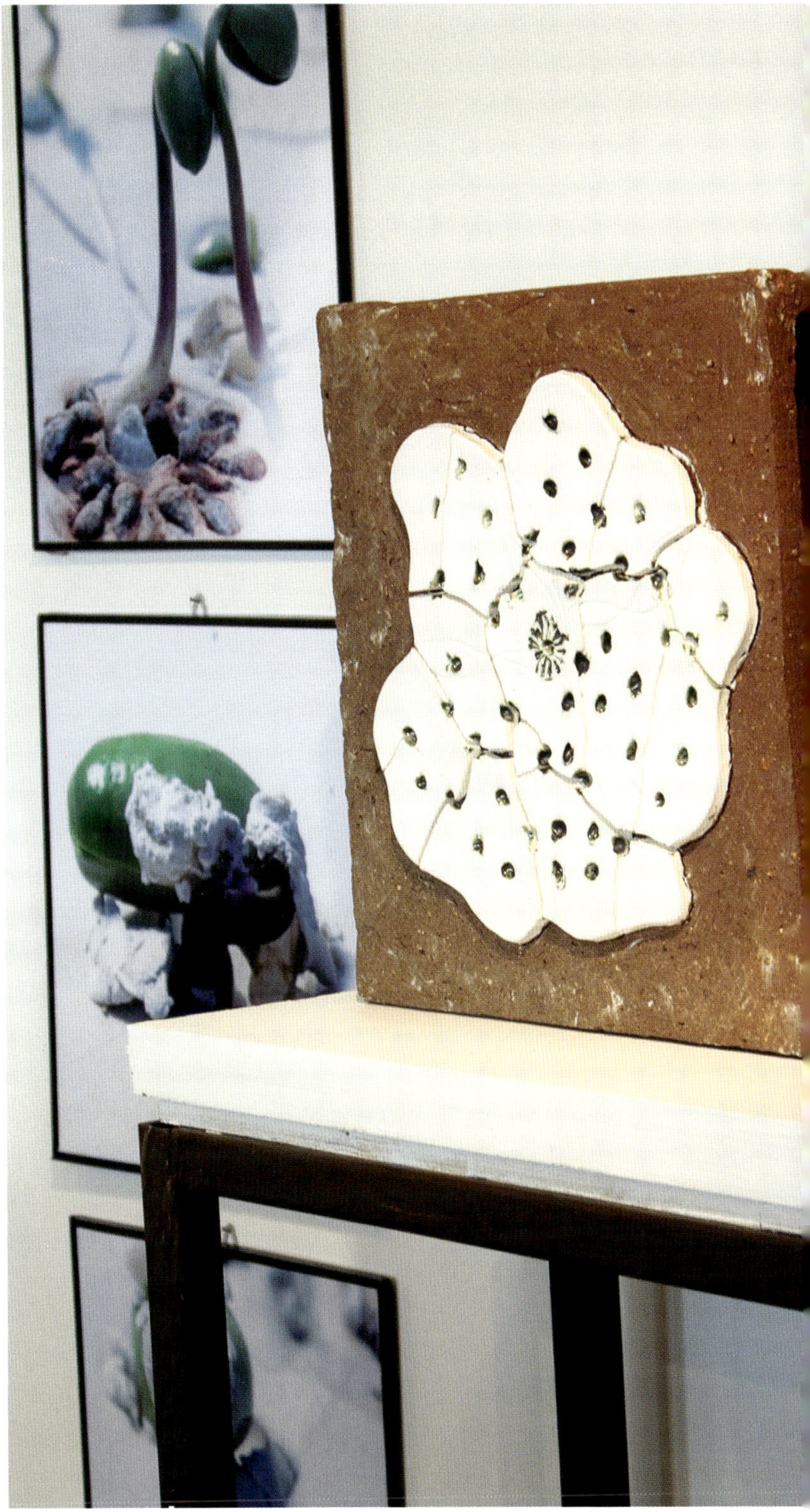

Kathleen Standen, porcelain flower with soya bean marks, 2011. Terracotta tile, porcelain flower, soya beans and grape seeds, 1270°C (2318°F), 30 x 10 cm (11¾ x 4 in). Fule International Ceramic Museum, Irish residency, Sept 2011. *Photo: Andrew Standen-Raz.*

Deirdre Hawthorne describes her 'one-off pots' as 'a little story in their own right'. Her imagery and voice are rooted in the Irish landscape where she grew up and has now returned to live. 'Specific places,' she says 'hold a charge for me – seashores, gardens, houses, city streets. I draw, photograph and write, sifting through individual memories and feelings, and this process leads me to making a series of small pots.'

Her simple, cylindrical forms with paper-thin walls may be marked with textures, imprinted with objects or pierced with tacks and staples. She often incorporates plants or their imagery into the clay, using screenprinted flowers on the surface, photographic cyanotypes developed directly on the fired porcelain, rolling plants into the clay or encasing plants in slips, which form part of the walls.

Her *Behind the greenhouse* pot (opposite) was made by casting earthenware clay and mung beans in a cardboard mould. The beans were allowed to grow by keeping the clay damp, followed by a drying period, then placed inside a sealed saggar containing combustible material. Pine cones, seaweed and banana skins are just some of the combustibles used, which catch fire in the kiln, burning up the oxygen to create a smoky reduction atmosphere. The work is fired to 1090°C (1994°F). Hawthorne says that 'many pots are lost in the firing but the pieces that survive are idiosyncratic and unrepeatable, fragile, dark, yet inherently resilient'.

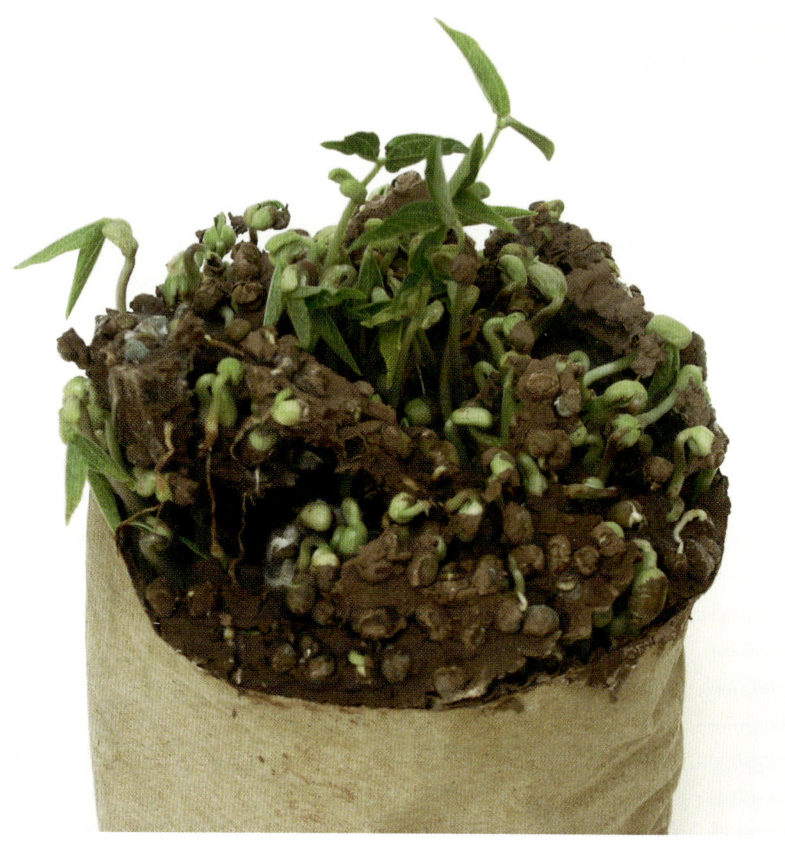

Deirdre Hawthorne, mung bean pot, work-in-progress (detail), 2005. Earthenware and mung beans cast in a cardboard mould. Beans are allowed to grow then fired inside a sealed saggar (with combustible material) to 1090°C (1994°F). This one disintegrated during firing, but was made by the same process as *Behind the greenhouse*, opposite. Height: approx. 14 cm (5½ in). *Photo: Leon Coole.*

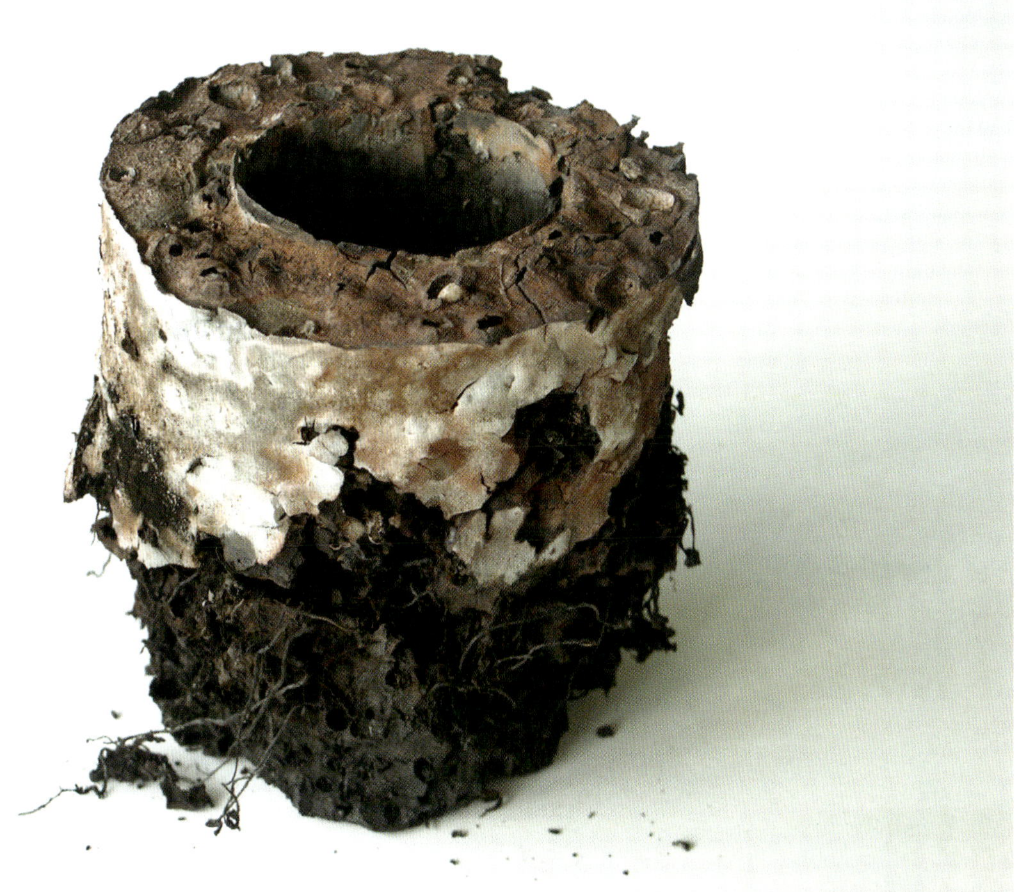

Deirdre Hawthorne, *Behind the greenhouse*, 2005. Earthenware and mung beans cast in a cardboard mould. Beans are allowed to grow then fired inside sealed saggar (with combustible material) to 1090°C (1994°F), about 14 cm (5½ in) high. *Photo: Leon Coole.*

4 Impressions, imprints and dipping

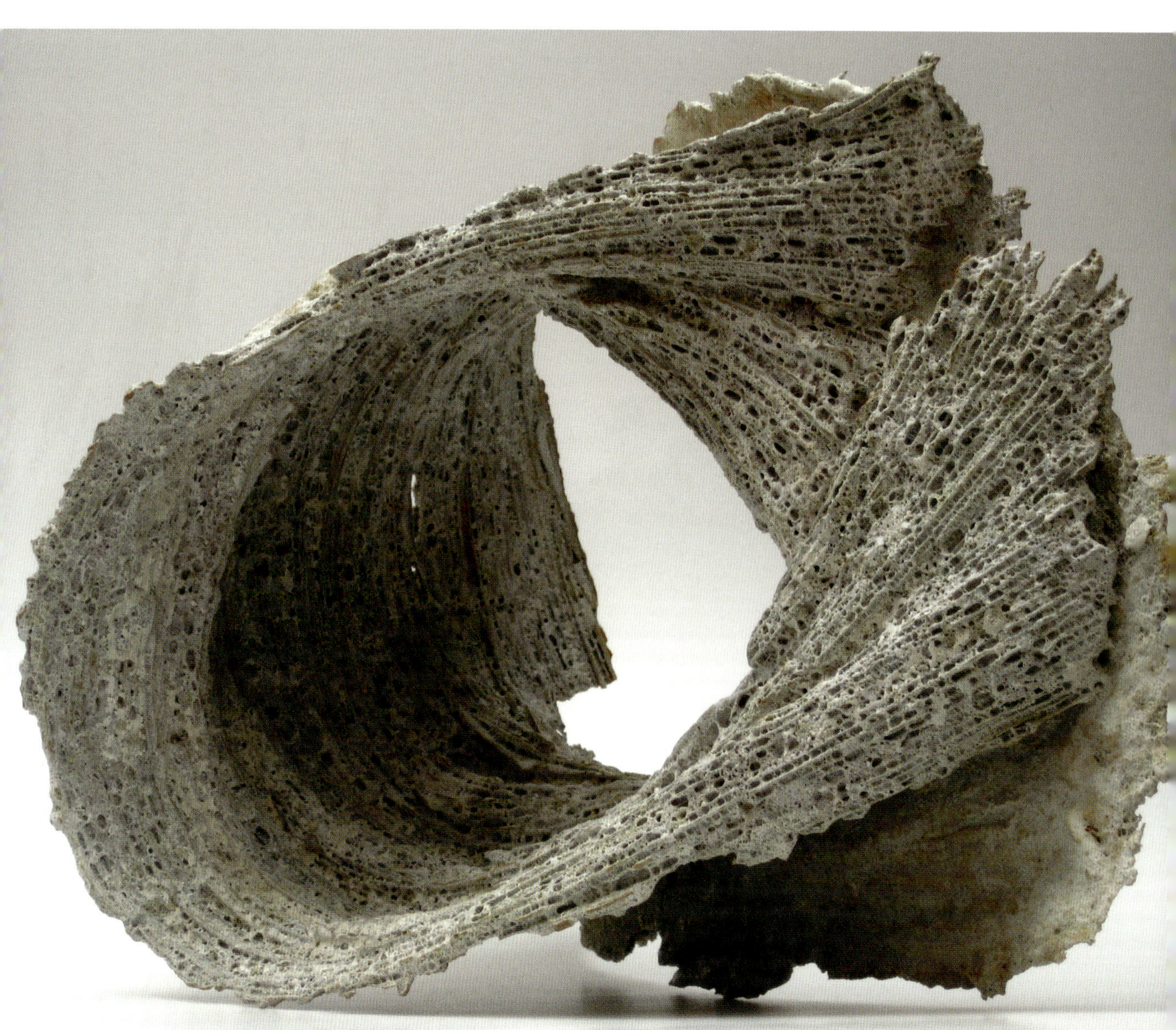

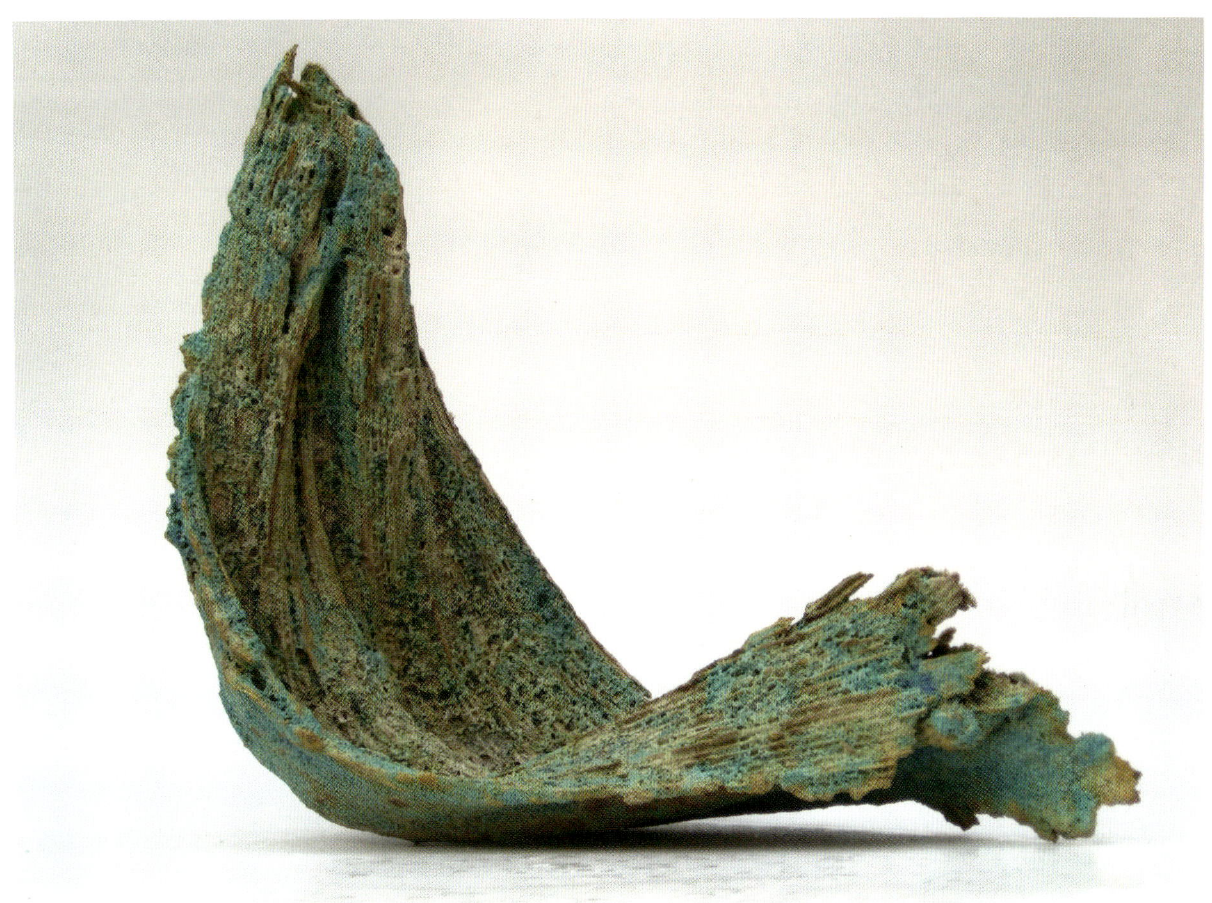

She uses sections of bamboo window blinds, which she cuts up, ties with thread and wire into curved wave-like forms, and hangs from the ceiling to create a free-flowing form. Soft stoneware clay, with additions such as molochite, paper pulp, acrylic fibres, **bentonite** and sand, is then spread onto one side of the form and allowed to dry. This procedure is repeated several times until the required thickness has been achieved – a slow process that takes several weeks. A biscuit firing to 800°C (1472°F) takes place in an outdoor gas kiln, because lots of smoke is produced from the burning bamboo. Wood ash is brushed off before a second biscuit firing to 1140°C (2084°F) in an electric kiln.

A range of glazes are applied to the curved forms, with repeat firings on many occasions, until Gregersen is satisfied with the depth of surface achieved. Glaze firings go up to 1280°C (2336°F).

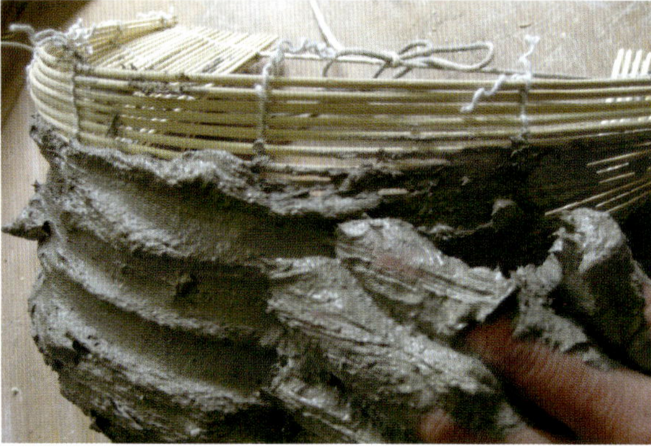

ABOVE: Applying the prepared paperclay in layers on the bamboo blind. Each layer is left to dry before applying the next one.

RIGHT: Hanging the bamboo blind from the ceiling enables the structure to become a free-flowing form.

BELOW: The dried piece is ready to fire.
Photos: Mette Maya Gregersen.

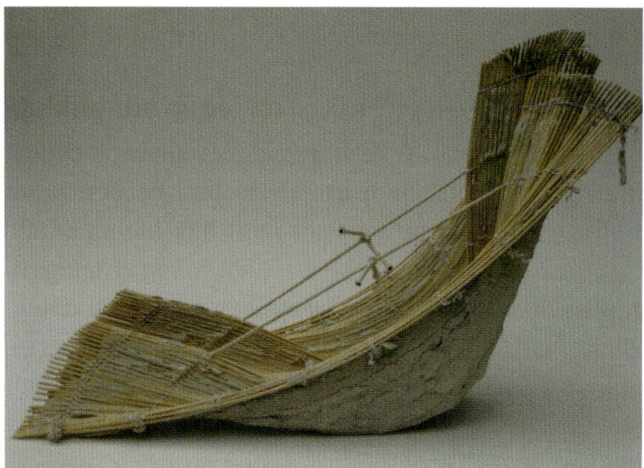

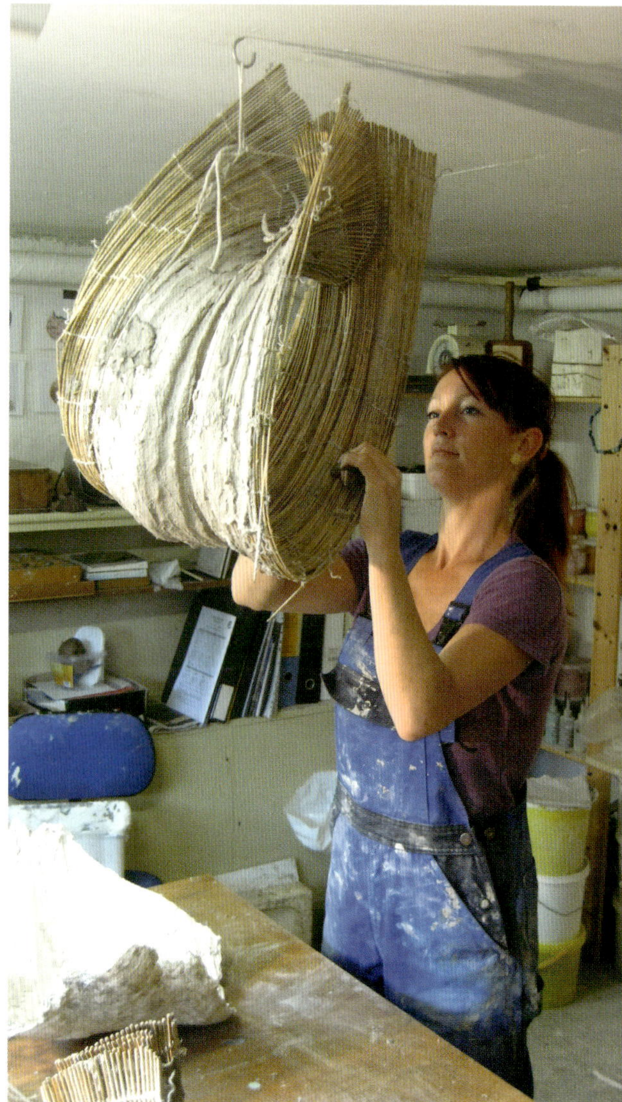

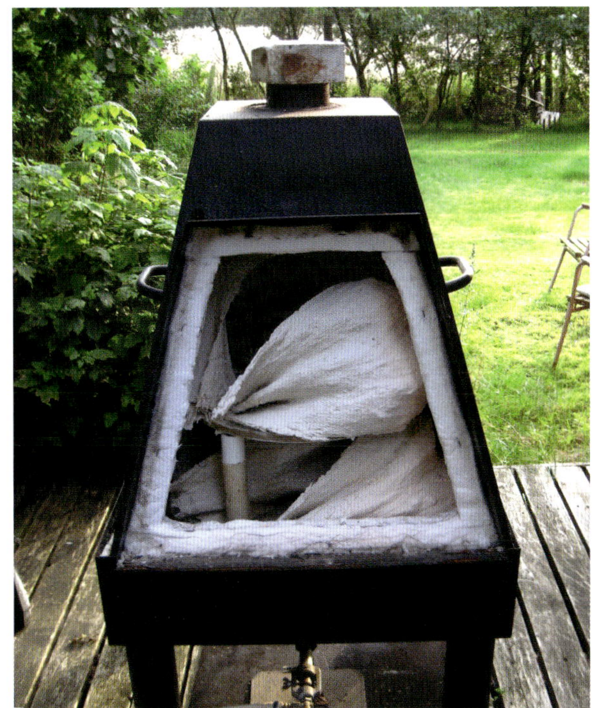

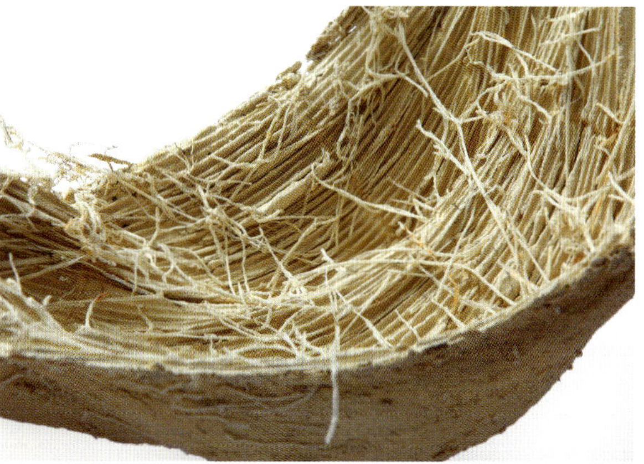

LEFT: The pieces are fired in a gas kiln outside, as there is a lot of smoke from the wood. Two biscuit firings: first to 800°C (1472°F) in a gas kiln then to 1140°C (2084°F) in an electric kiln
ABOVE: After the first firing, the wood ash is brushed off and fired again in an electric kiln.

BELOW: Often the pieces are glazed several times, and fired as many times, in order to obtain depth in the surface.
Photos: Mette Maya Gregersen.

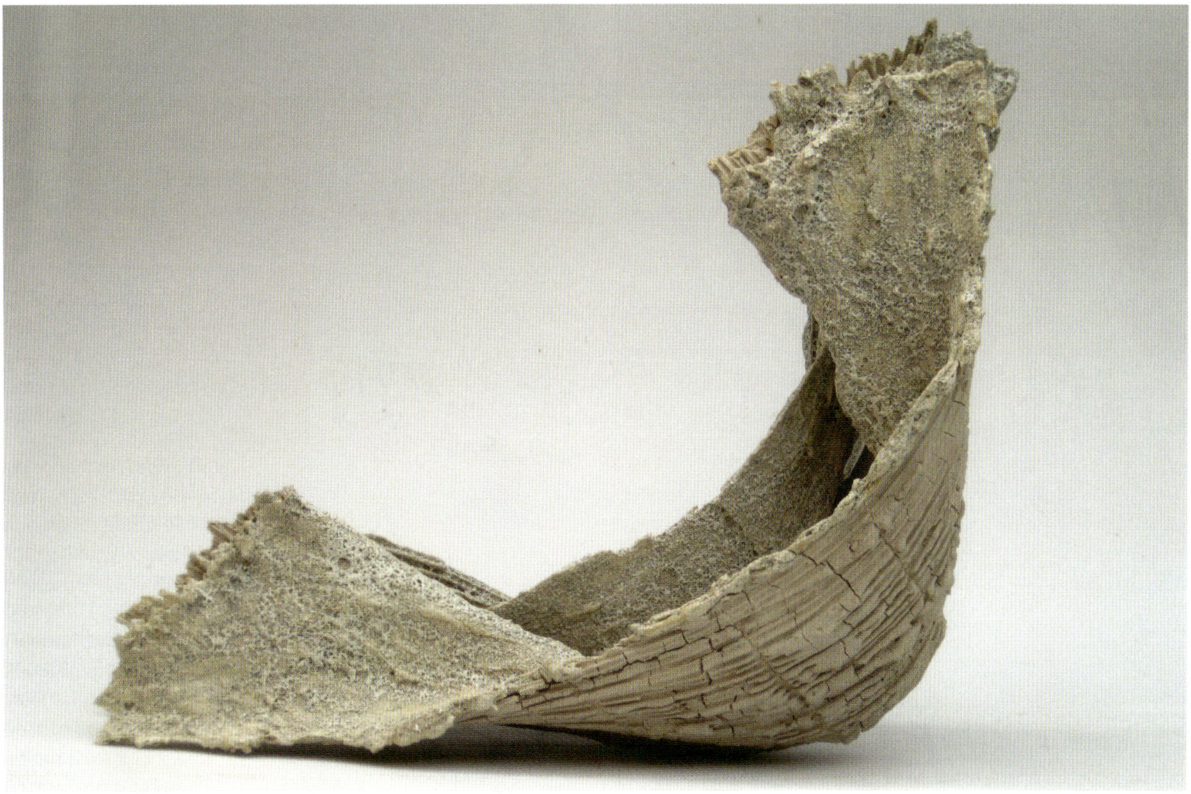

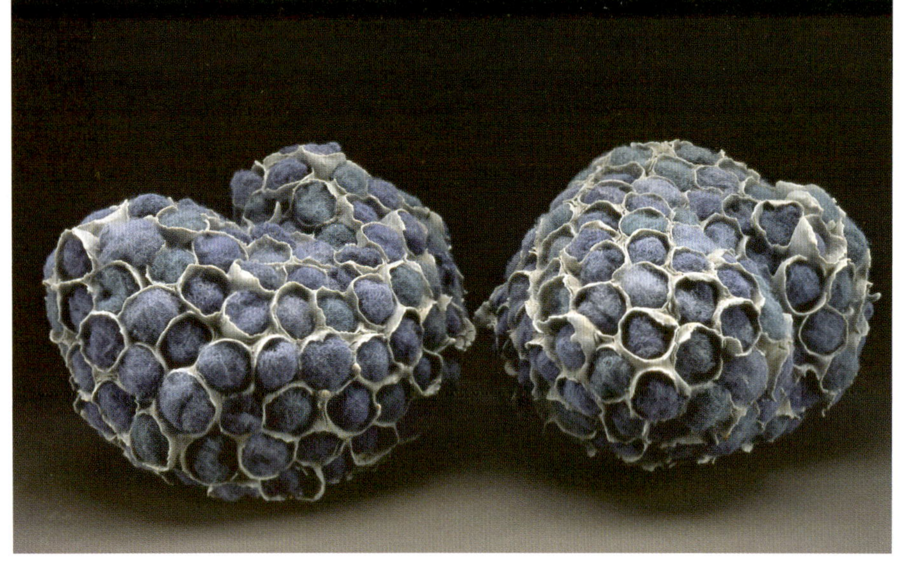

Katie Queen, *Objected Blue*, March 2004. Press-moulded and coil-built porcelain, polyester fill, Cone 10 oxidation, 16.5 x 45.5 x 25.5 cm (6½ x 18 x 10 in). *Photo: by the artist.*

Honeycomb forms using cotton fibre

The objects made by **Katie Queen** are inventions of her own imagination, but they resonate with details from the world around us. A seedpod, or the delicate connection between a berry and its stem, are examples of what Queen calls 'the minute perfection of nature'.

Porcelain is her chosen material, coiled, slabbed, press-moulded using custom-made moulds, extruded or thrown on the wheel. The method depends on the design of the piece. She uses organic material, in the form of cotton fibre, on some of her work.

While the form is leatherhard, balls of cotton fibre, partly dipped in **deflocculated slip** are attached. These burn away in the bisque firing (1022°C/1872°F), leaving a hollow cavity that Queen likens to a honeycomb or barnacle. Sometimes she fills this cavity with dyed polyester fibre, as seen in *Objected Blue*. In the piece titled *Crux*, recycled glass pieces were placed in a shallow depression. The pieces melted, fractured and formed a pool on the surface of the porcelain. Firing was to 1288°C (2350°F).

Queen divides her time between teaching and making ceramics in Los Angeles, California.

BELOW LEFT: Porcelain casting slip is poured into the mould and allowed to sit until the thickness is right. The remaining liquid slip is poured back into the container.

BELOW RIGHT: Once the castings have become leatherhard, they are easily removed from the mould. *Photos: by the artist.*

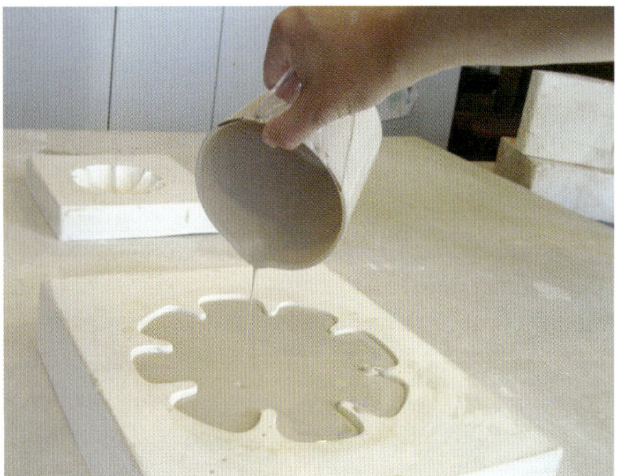

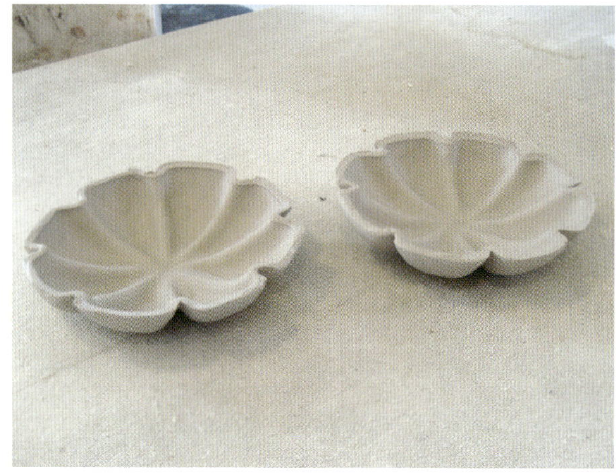

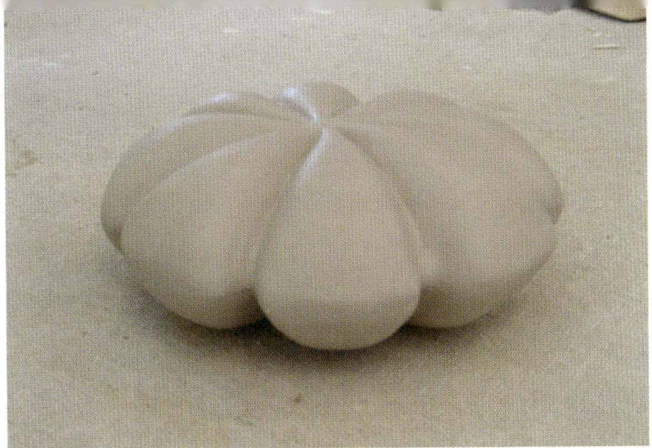

Cast forms have been cleaned, scored and joined together to create the desired form.

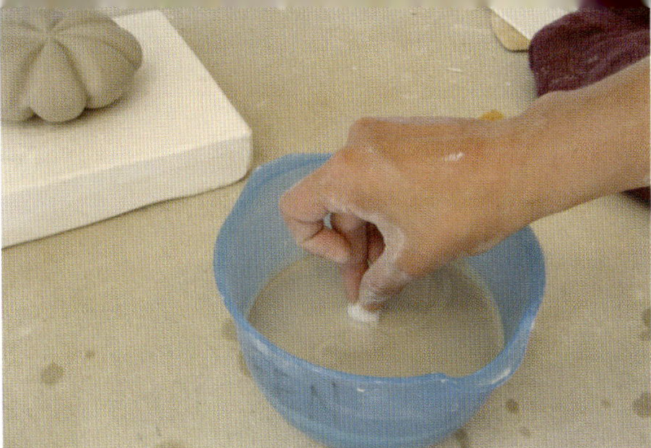

Cotton fibre is dipped into casting slip, only half to three-quarters of the way up, to allow a cavity to form.

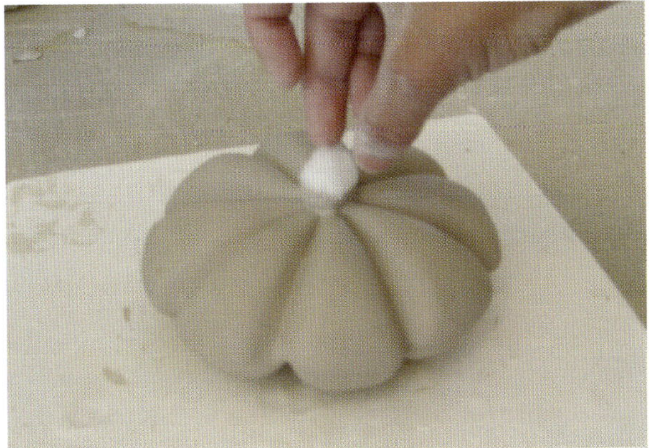

Dipped cotton is attached to the cast form.

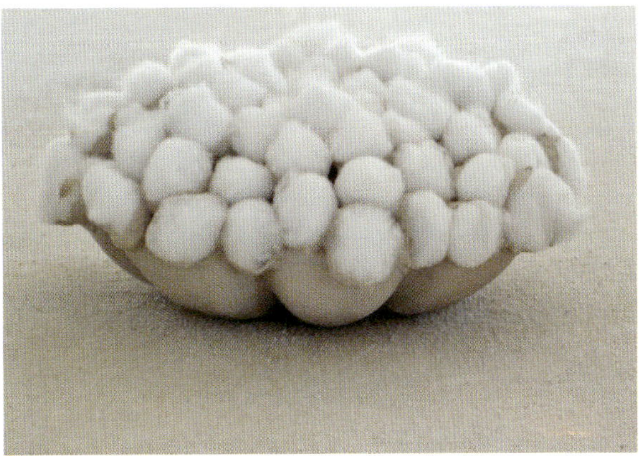

Complete form with cotton fibres attached, ready to be bisque-fired upside down. *Photos: by the artist.*

BELOW: Katie Queen, *Crux*, 2009. Completed form after glaze firing. Press-moulded and coil-built, porcelain, recycled glass, Cone 10 oxidation firing, 12.7 x 35.5 cm (5 x 14 in). *Photo: Ian Arenas.*

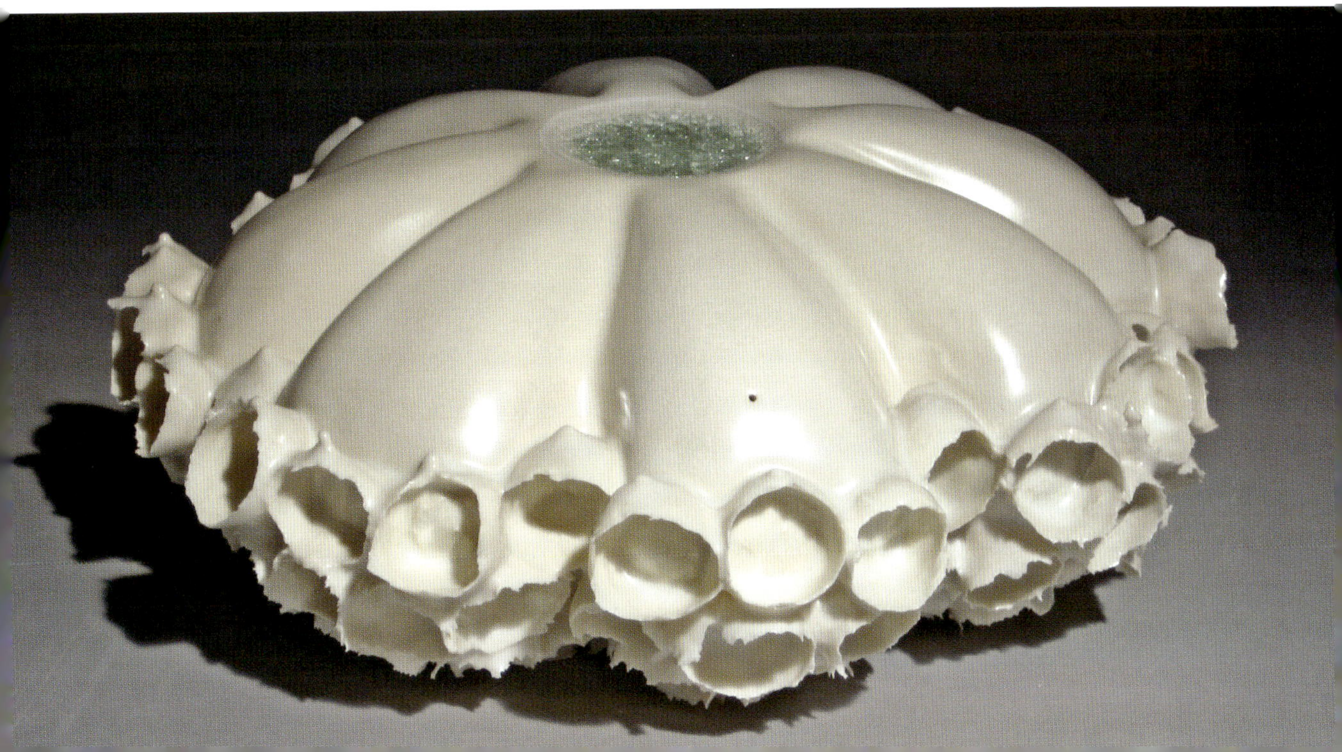

Knitted tableware

Helen Gilmour's work explores the connection between ceramics and traditional crafts such as knitting and crochet. She deconstructs functional pottery by soaking cotton yarn in porcelain slip to produce knitted ceramic vessels, which are totally non-functional. She began experimenting with these materials while studying at the Glasgow School of Art and has continued to develop this work, improving her techniques and seeking new possibilities. Her ceramics appear delicate but are easily strong enough to be handled and transported.

Process

The first step is to knit the pieces – teacups, saucers and teapots – using 100% pure cotton knitting yarn. They are then thoroughly soaked in porcelain slip and wrung out several times before being stretched over a former and left to dry. Inflated balloons work well as formers for teapots. More slip is applied while the form is still on the balloon: spraying, dipping and painting are the different methods used. Through experience, she knows when the right amount of slip has been applied in order to

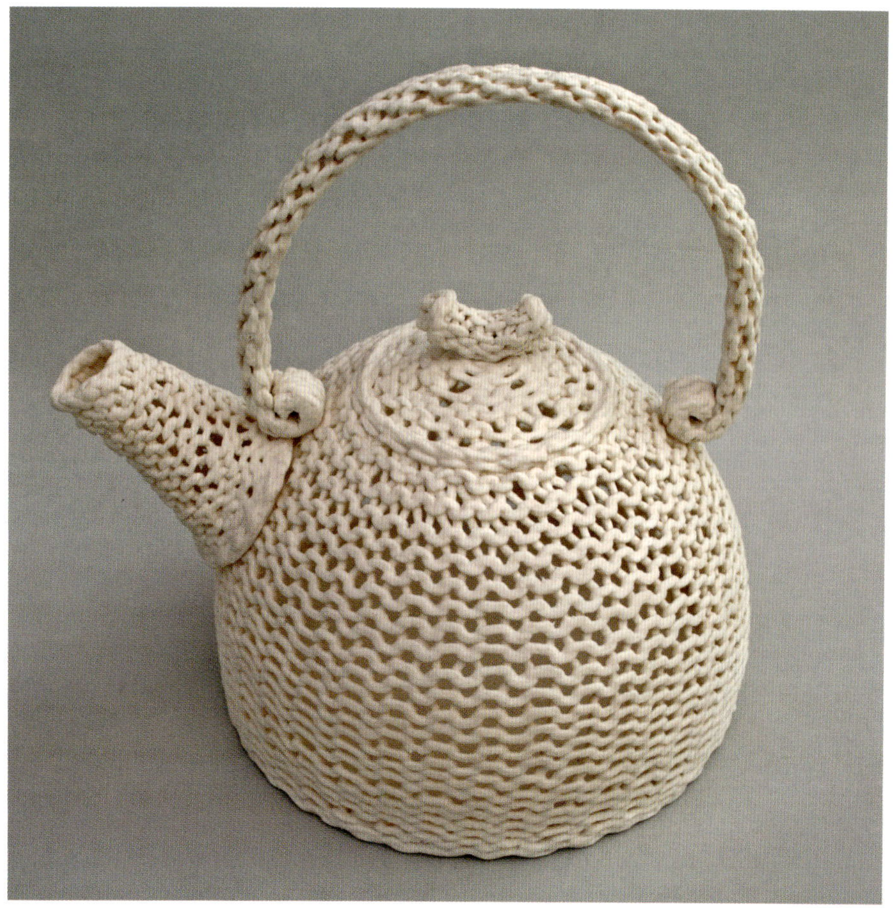

Helen Gilmour, *Teapot*, 2011. Knitting soaked in porcelain slip, 20 x 20 cm (7¾ x 7¾ in). *Photo: by the artist.*

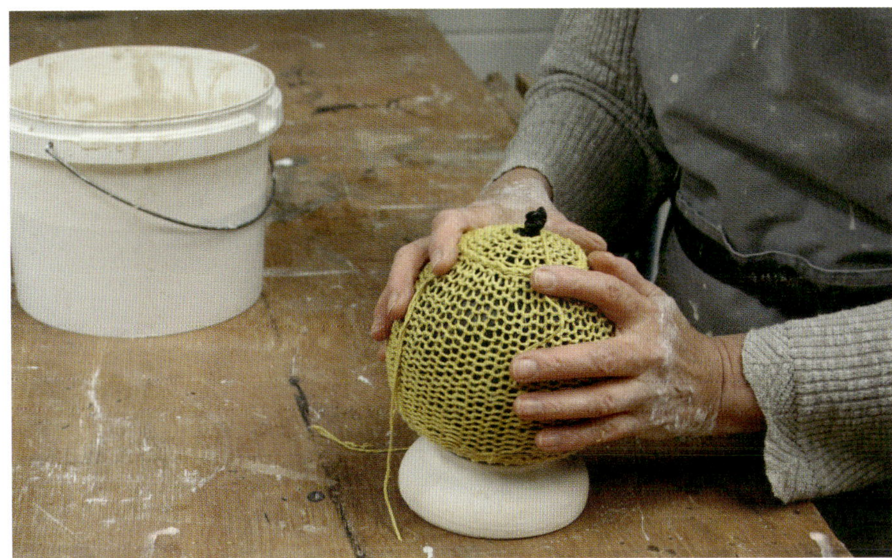

Stretching soaked knitting over balloon former
Photo: by the artist.

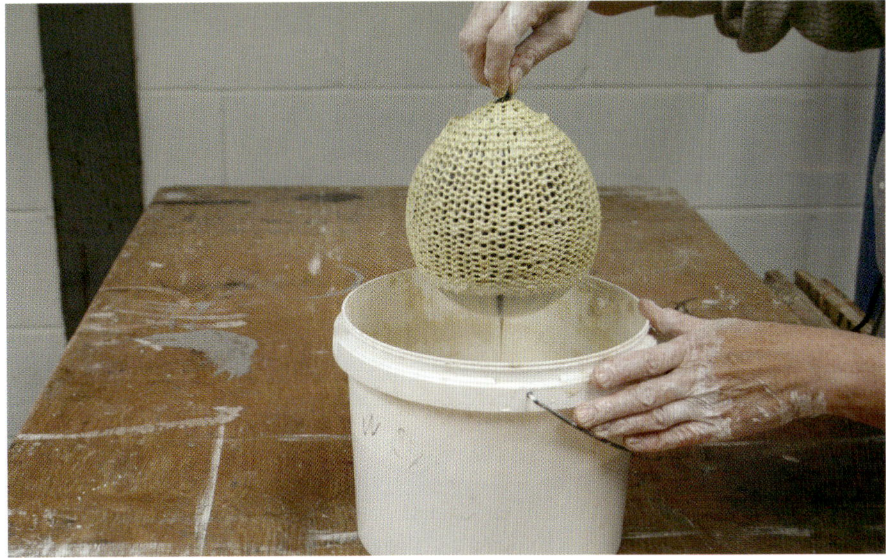

Applying more slip while still on balloon.
Photo: by the artist.

produce a finished piece that will be strong enough to handle but still clearly reveal every stitch of the knitting. This process can take several days.

Gilmour describes in detail the next stage, which is the removal of the balloon. She says, 'I wait until the piece is properly dry and stiff before removing the balloon. If it hasn't already started to deflate it is best to remove it by letting the air out slowly. Sticking some tape on the balloon and making a small hole through it prevents it bursting.

'The work is extremely fragile at this stage and great care must be taken while handling it, avoiding any damaging bumps or dents that might affect the strength of the pot.'

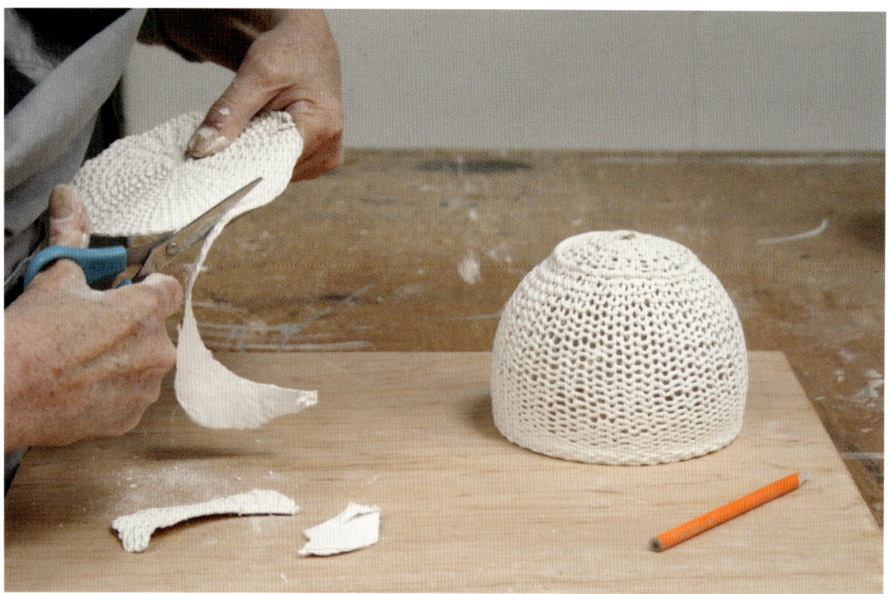

Cutting out the base made from Flax paperclay.
Photo: by the artist.

As the teapot was knitted without a base, the next stage is to form the base and attach it to the teapot.

Flaxed paperclay porcelain from Scarva Suppliers is rolled out thinly onto a **plaster batt** to form the base. The clay picks up the knitting texture on the cast plaster and is then cut to size. The base is joined with slip to the teapot body when they are both bone dry. Gilmour says that, in her experience, the shrinkage of both the porcelain slip used on the teapot body and the paperclay in the base is the same, so cracks are avoided.

The work is fired to 1280°C (2336°F), with provision for good ventilation, while the cotton burns out. Slumping can occur at these temperatures, which can enhance a piece, but where it is not desired she takes care to try and avoid it. For this reason, when making teapots, she adds the spout and handle after they have been fired. Smaller pieces such as cups and jugs are often fired upside-down with their handles attached, allowing the slumping to compliment the form.

Figurative work with fabric and lace additions

'Conversation pieces and miniature worlds' is how **Penny Green** describes the work she loves to make. But on closer inspection, these seemingly tranquil scenarios reveal underlying tensions, paradoxical landscapes and uneasy characters.

Inspiration is derived from objects and paintings from the past and this can inform a whole body of work. Her *Thomas Dundas* piece is part of a series titled *Obelisk Treasury of Ancient Coins*, commissioned by a private coin collector. This is based on the story of Lord Dundas, who was an eminent collector; his travels in Italy in the 18th century are well documented.

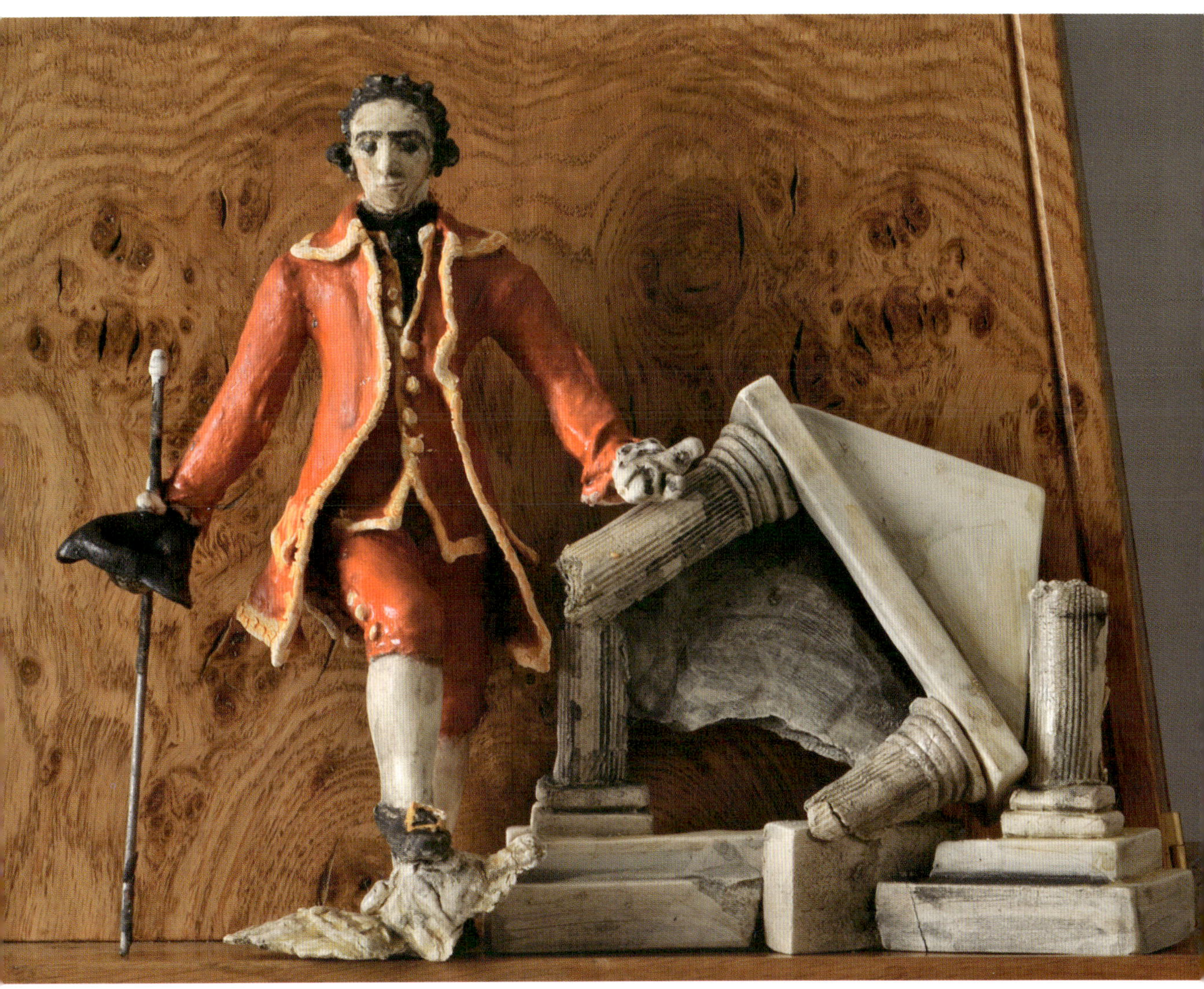

Penny Green, *Thomas Dundas posing in Rome for his swagger portrait by Pompeo Batoni*, 2012. Slip-cast and hand-built; clothes on figure made by dipping cloth – a soft, open weave works best – in casting slip and forming around the figure. Further coatings of slip are added when clothes harden. Glazed and fired to 1060°C (1940°F), 20 x 28 cm (7¾ x 11 in). *Photo: Sussie Ahlburg.*

Green uses a variety of making techniques: slip-casting, press-moulding, silkscreen printing, transfer printing and slab-building. In addition, she carries out glaze testing and research to create a range of textured glazes, by overloading the glaze with specific materials. The clothes are cut from an open-weave cloth, which is then dipped in casting slip before draping around the figure. Once the clothes have hardened, further coatings of slip are applied. The fabric burns out in the biscuit firing, leaving clay with the texture and shape of the original material. Glaze is fired to 1060°C (1940°F).

Green's former, successful career in costume and fashion design continues to exert a strong influence on her ceramics, together with old books and catalogues, to which she has good access, as her husband is an antiquarian book dealer. Her ceramics are held in numerous private and public collections.

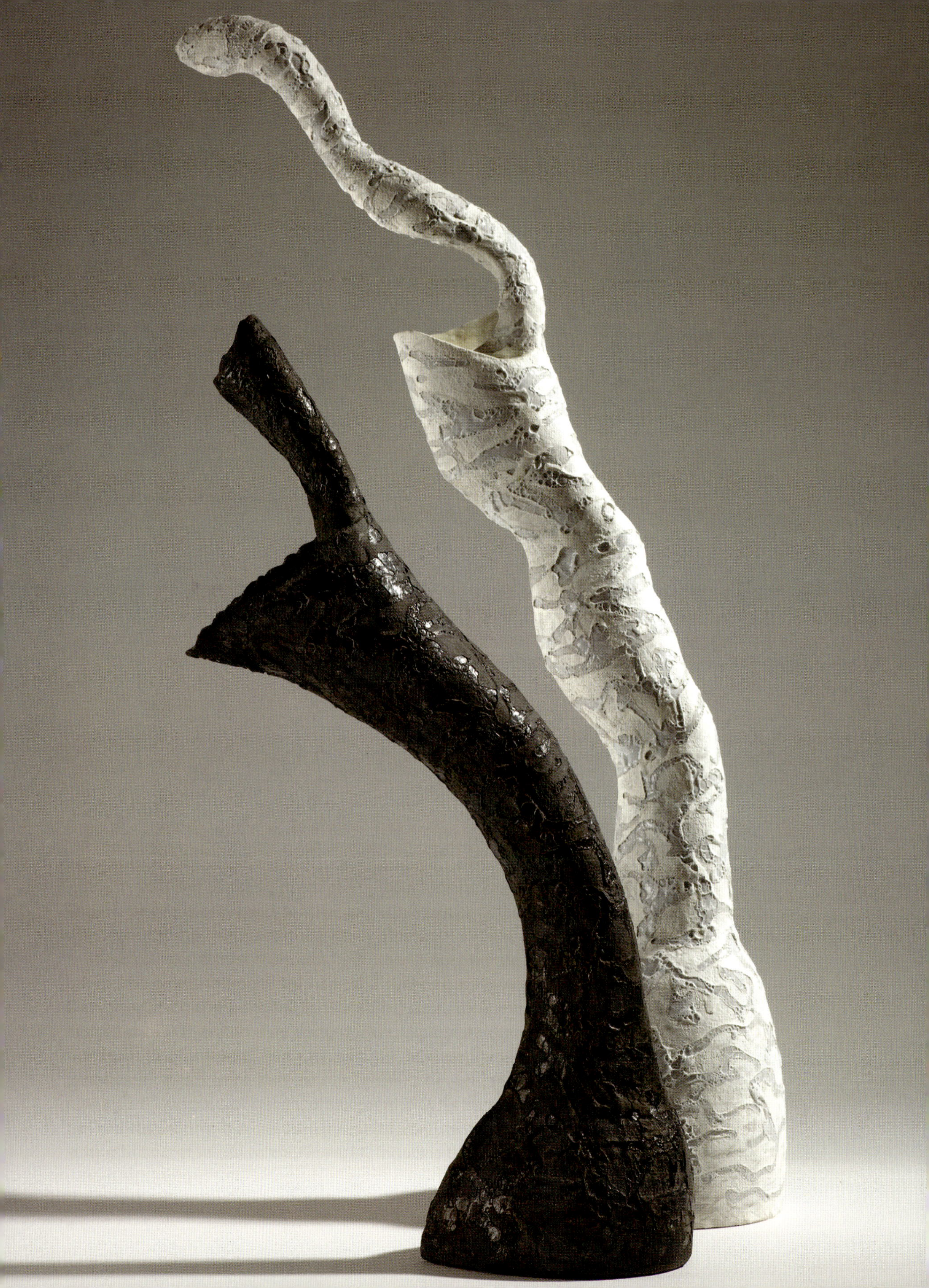

5

Fibres

The additions covered in this chapter display one particular characteristic that is unique to them: they leave almost no visible residue after firing. However, they do convey strength to the clay, which is especially useful for greenware. This characteristic of fibre additions has been used in the construction of buildings for thousands of years.

Adobe and cob houses

Who could imagine that straw, sand and clay, mixed together and left unfired, would make a material strong enough to build a two-storey house, complete with roof? The old town of Ghale Nouv in Sistan, Eastern Iran, is testament to the success of this building technique.

How does it work?

Mostafa Arefhaghi is a college lecturer and independent researcher in the field of adobe architecture in Iran. His photo (top left, next page) shows the mixing together of sand, straw and clay in the proportions by weight of half sand, one-third clay and one-sixth straw.

This mixture is then packed into wooden frames to make uniform bricks, which are laid out in the sun to dry. Compare the two images of bricks: one shows bricks

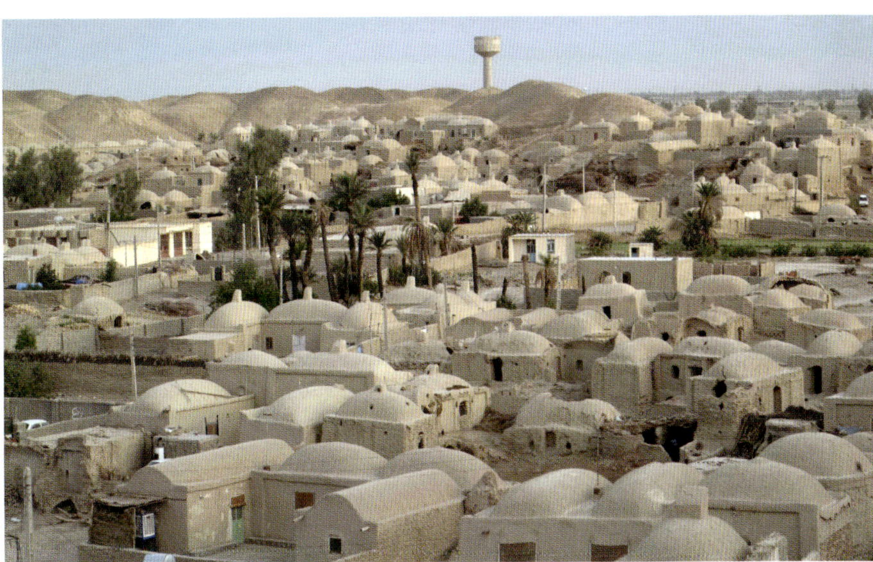

LEFT: Jim Turner, *Black and White Bottles*, 2009. Thrown and extruded altered forms, fibre slip on top of glaze with fibre, once-fired to 1300°C (2372°F), height: 65 cm (25½ in) and 55 cm (21½ in). *Photo: Roland Paschhoff.*

RIGHT: Village of adobe houses, in Eastern Iran. *Photo: Mostafa Arefhaghi.*

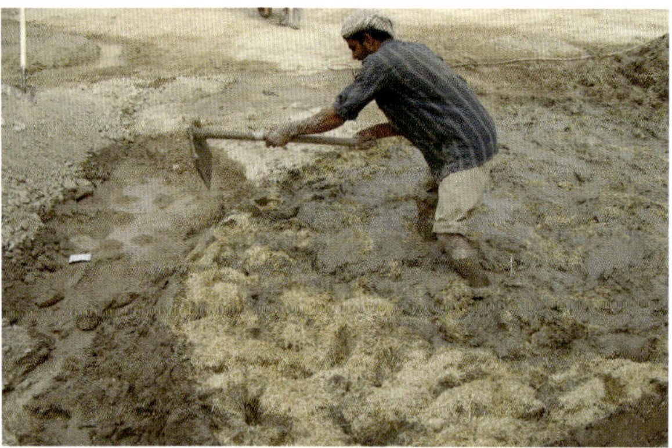

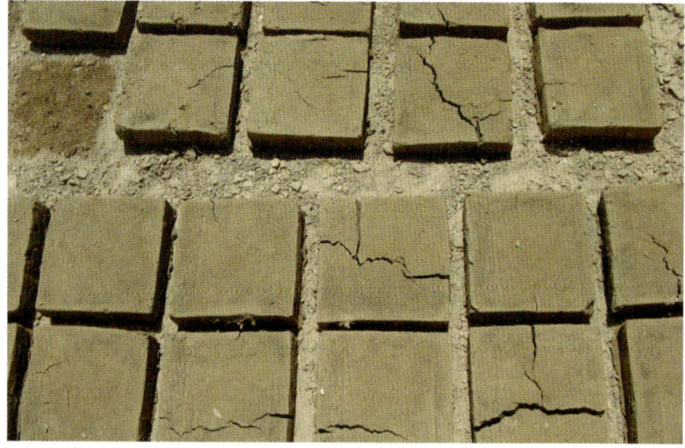

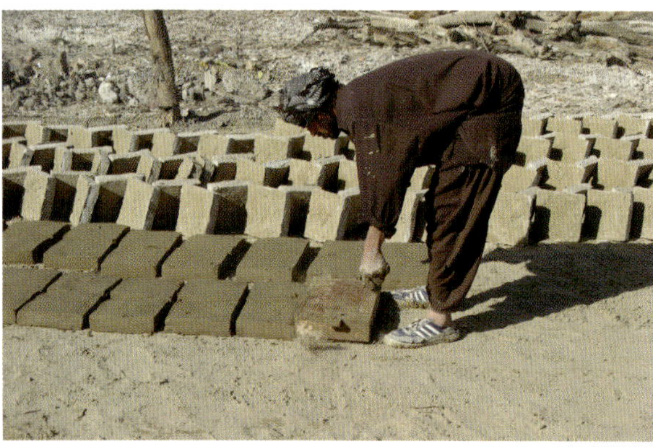

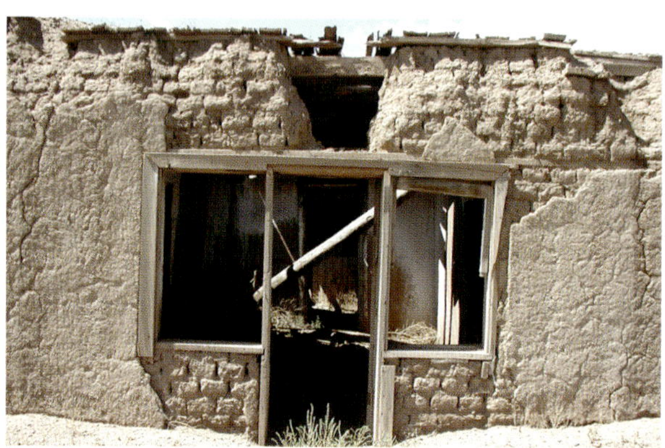

TOP ROW, LEFT TO RIGHT: Mixing sand and straw with clay; clay bricks without straw crack and disintegrate.

BOTTOM ROW, LEFT TO RIGHT: Laying out the adobe bricks to dry in the sun; and an old house made of adobe bricks.
Photos: Mostafa Arefhaghi.

made with the correct mixture of clay, sand and straw, whereas the other shows bricks without the addition of straw. The straw fibres help to bind the clay and sand together, and most importantly, allow the clay to dry evenly, reducing the chances of weakening cracks appearing.

The unfired bricks are then laid out in a single layer to form the first course and using adobe mortar (same mixture, but without the straw), the next layer of bricks is set out on top until the desired height is reached. Adobe dwellings have been found in Africa, South America and Asia, as well as Europe and in all sorts of climates, including rainy and windy regions.

Clay houses are better known in the UK as 'cob houses'. There are many similarities with adobe buildings – certainly the materials used are very similar – but the method of construction differs. The walls are built directly with the clay mixture, starting off with a wide base and tapering in as the wall rises. Each layer of clay mixture is allowed to dry before the next is built upon it.

Cob can be shaped and moulded during building, allowing bas-relief, shelves, alcoves and even furniture to be built right into the walls. Cob, being earth, is totally fireproof, so even a fireplace can be built into the design. The images of cob houses on the opposite page are from The Hollies, a centre for practical sustainability in West Cork, Ireland.

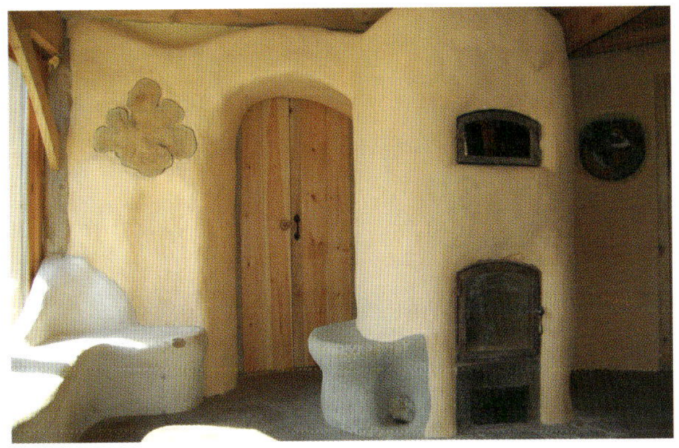

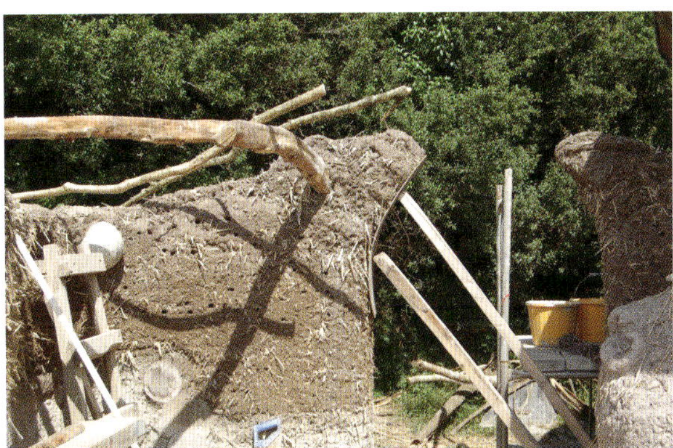

ABOVE, LEFT TO RIGHT: Interior view of a cottage at the Hollies showing the fireplace and built-in seats; and wall under construction.

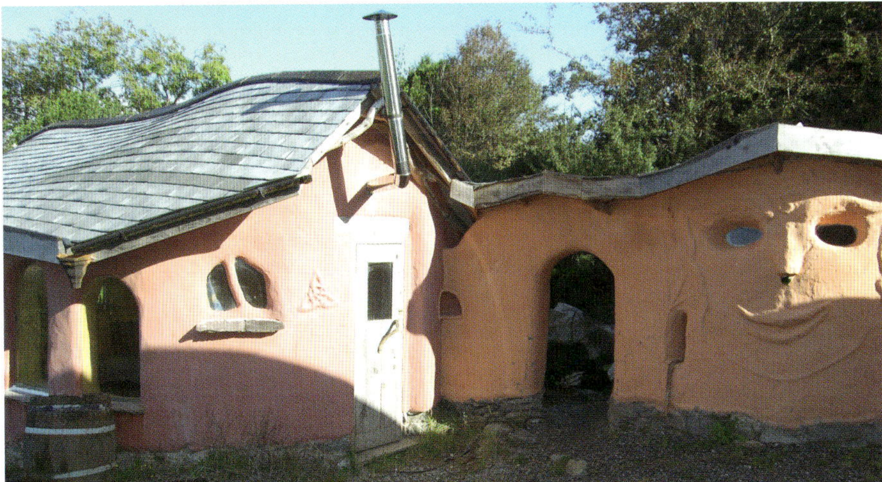

RIGHT: Cob cottage in West Cork, Ireland. *Photos: Jonathan Reidmuller.*

Paperclay

The strengthening property of organic fibre mixed with clay is exploited by ceramicists today when they use paperclay for hand-building and throwing forms.

Barbro Åberg uses paperclay to construct her large-scale intricate structures, such as *Fossil Fantasy II.* The presence of paper and perlite in the clay she uses conveys strength to the form and promotes even drying.

Useful properties of paperclay

- Increased dry strength of the body, so there is a decreased risk of damage when handling greenware pieces.
- The cellulose fibres in the body 'opens up the clay' allowing you to work with thicker walls with a reduced risk of cracks and fractures.
- When working on sculptural forms, you can add multi-layers of clay at several stages: you can add wet to wet, wet to dry, and wet to bisque. Repeat wetting and forced drying can be carried out with less risk of cracking.
- Fired work will be lighter, a quality that is useful for large-scale pieces.

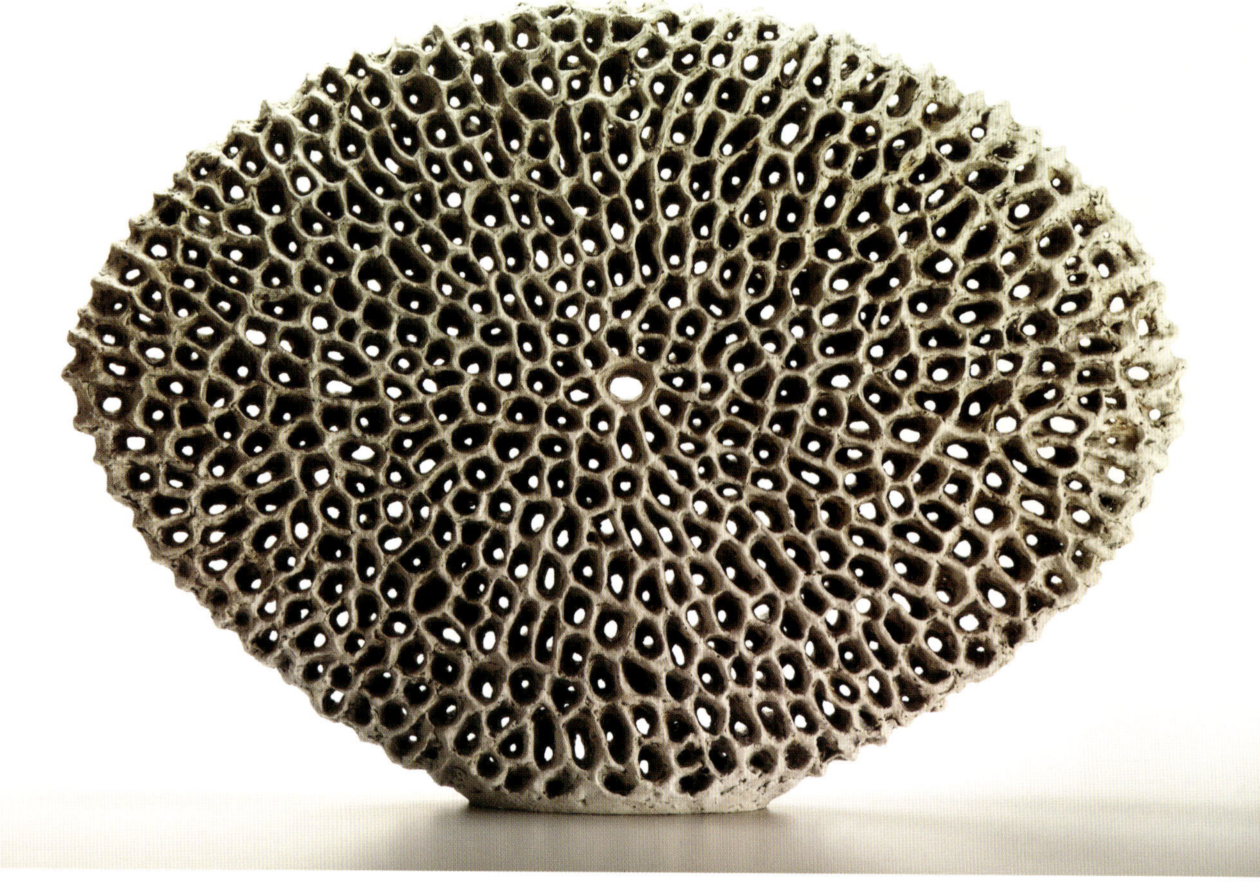

Barbro Åberg, *Fossil Fantasy II*, 2011. Clay with perlite and paper fibres, 69 x 48 x 8 cm (27 x 19 x 3 in). *Photo: Lars Henrik Mardah.*

In essence, when fibres are added to clay, the appearance of the clay is unchanged but its handling properties are different.

Making paperclay

The most commonly used fibre is **cellulose**, made from paper pulp. Ceramicists generally have a favourite paper they use, such as newspaper, egg cartons or toilet paper. The proportion of clay slip to paper pulp varies, but a typical sample would be 4:1. The clay slip and paper pulp are mixed thoroughly together, with the best results achieved using a blender or electric mixer. The blended mixture is then laid out on plaster batts to dry a little so it can be wedged into balls of clay. The proportions can vary from 5% to 25%; carrying out your own investigations is the best way to find out what suits your work.

Jim Turner makes paperclay from wheel trimmings, which are frequently a mixture of white earthenware and reduction bodies. These are blended to a thick slip with cellulose fibre, which is usually shredded newspaper, broken down to individual fibres with boiling water. Persistent blending with an electric mixer breaks down the paper, but he advises that it takes more boiling water than one expects and can make for a very sloppy paperclay mix.

Making your own paperclay is economical and versatile, as any clay body can be used. There are some issues to be aware of:

LEFT TO RIGHT: A ruler in the bucket measures the depth of slip.

Adding the cellulose fibre.

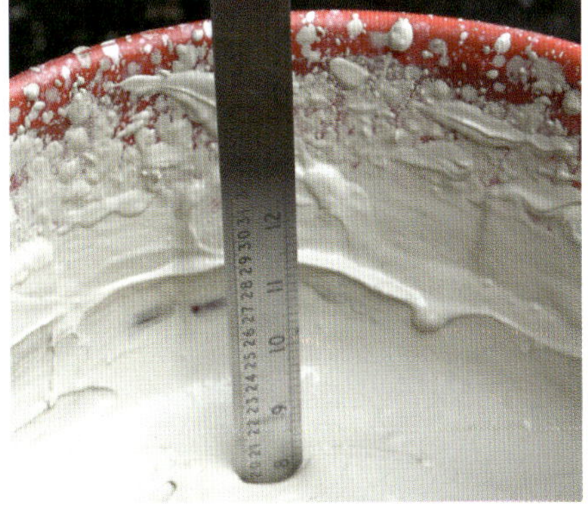

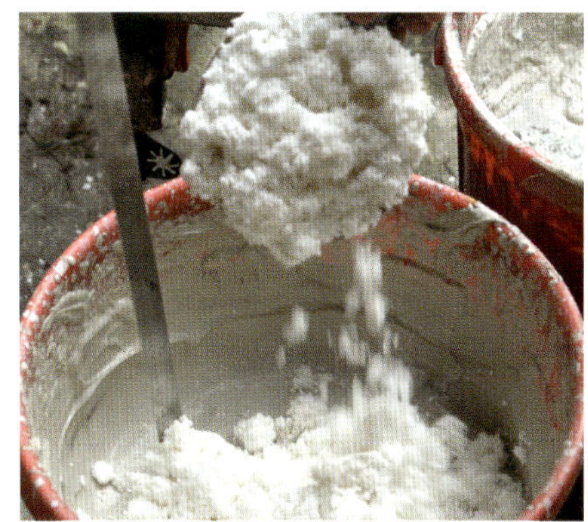

LEFT TO RIGHT: Blending the mixture.

Pouring the paperclay slip onto plaster to firm up.

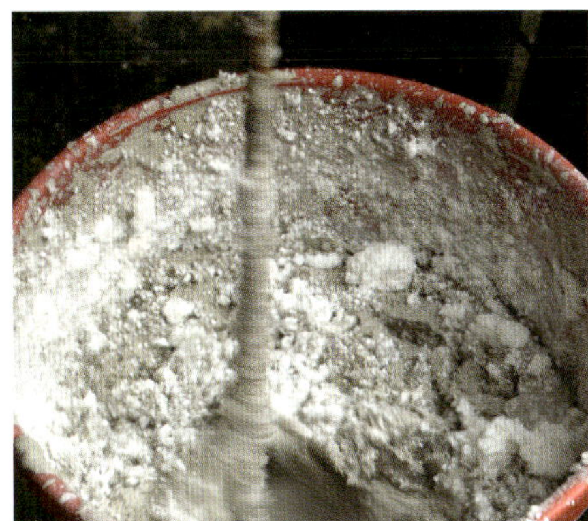

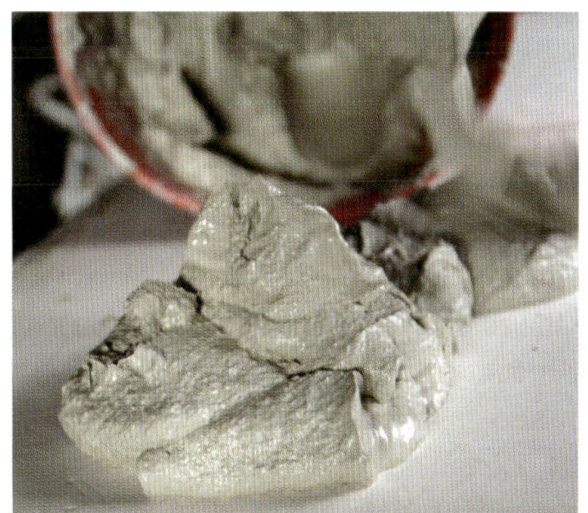

- The shelf life of homemade paperclay is about two weeks, so it needs to be used up quickly; if kept for longer, the organic cellulose starts to break down and decay, with all the health issues explained in Chapter 3 (p. 46).
- When paperclay decays, the tubular structure of the cellulose fibres breaks down and the paperclay loses the properties associated with it; toilet paper is more prone to rapid decay because of a corn-starch coating on the cellulose fibres.
- The usability of paperclay can be extended by adding a small amount of Milton sterilising liquid or disinfectant (but not bleach) to the wet mixture before drying.
- Alternatively, rolling out unused paperclay into thin sheets and allowing them to dry completely preserves the tubular structure of the fibres. They can be stored, and later softened up by laying them out on a damp cloth.

Cotton fibre and clay

An excellent alternative to paper pulp is the addition of cotton fibres. This can be purchased in sheets as cotton linter. Preparation of the materials is the same as for paper but cotton fibres don't break down as easily as paper, so it can be stored in its wet form for longer.

If you don't want all this hassle, then the pottery suppliers listed at the back of the book will sell you a ready-made paperclay with an unlimited shelf life (as long as it is wrapped up well).

Most suppliers also sell air-hardening clay, which is a blend of modelling clay and nylon fibres and, as the name suggests, dries hard and strong without the need to be fired in a kiln. It is worth checking out the websites of several pottery suppliers to check the product description and compare prices.

Glass fibre sheets and tape are also used by artists to strengthen the clay to which it is bonded. Its application will be discussed in greater detail during the descriptions of **Tamsyn Trevorrow** and **Paul Payne**'s ceramics (pp. 87–91).

Fired and unfired paperclay

Rebecca Hutchinson is Professor of Artisanry/Ceramics at the University of Massachusetts. Her large-scale sculptural work straddles textiles and ceramics, constructed of handmade paper brushed with porcelain paperclay slip, or woven with paperclay-coated sisal thread.

Her complex and delicate structures resemble massed floral forms, spiders' webs or bird nests and are usually site-specific: outdoor sculptures invariably deconstruct

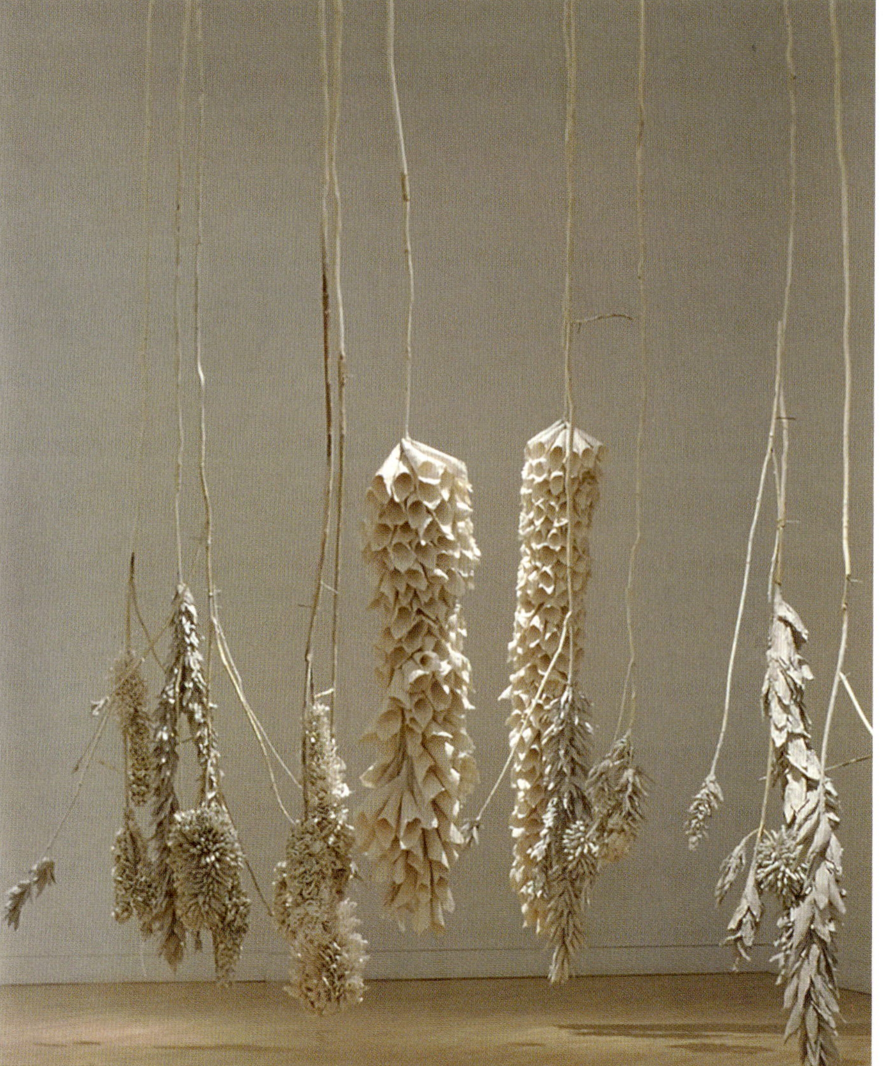

Rebecca Hutchinson, Holter Museum Installation, 2009. Porcelain paperclay, fibre and organic materials, 55 x 40.5 x 35.5 cm (22 x 16 x 14 in). *Photo: Holter Museum of Art, Montana, USA.*

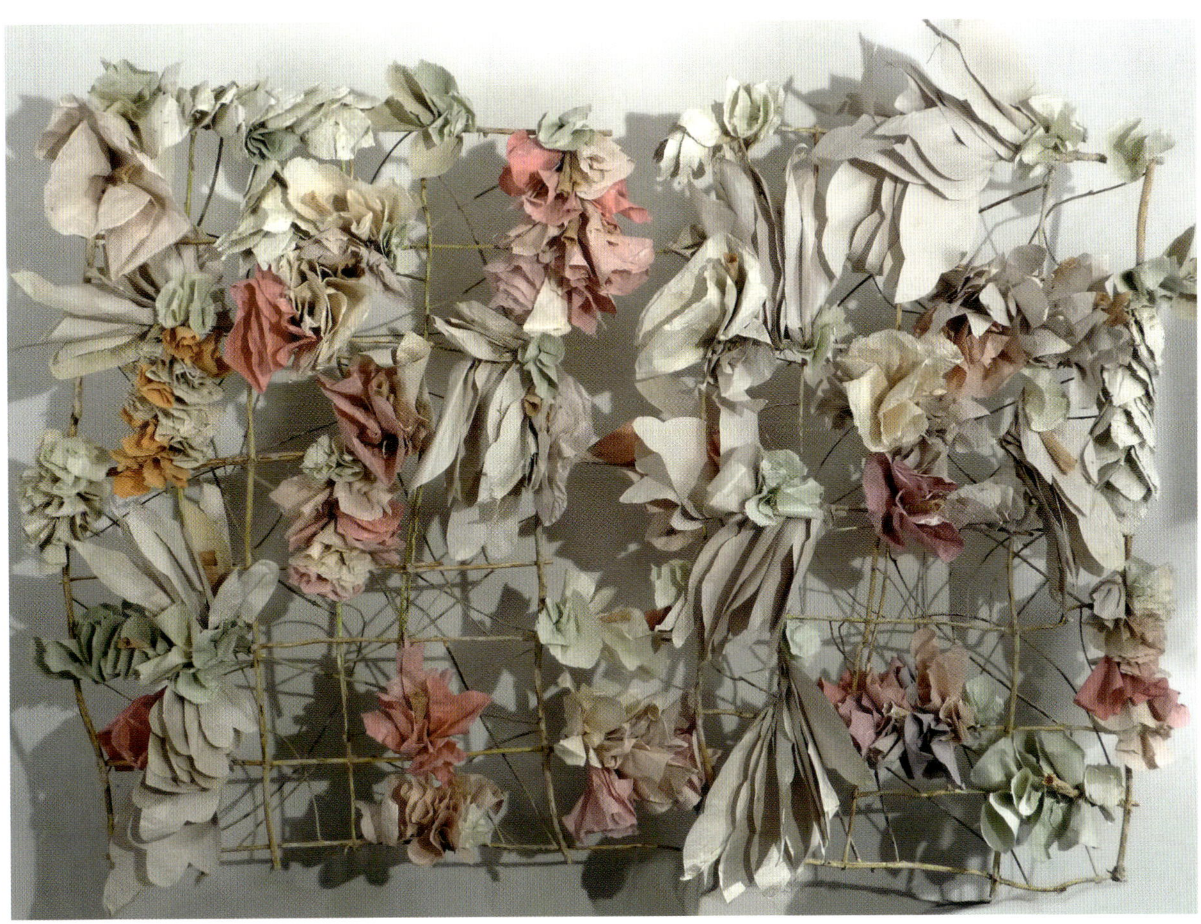

Rebecca Hutchinson, Islip Museum Installation, 2011. Porcelain paperclay, fibre and organic materials, 30.5 x 20.5 x 45 cm (12 x 8 x 18 in). *Photo: Islip Museum.*

over time with the effects of weather, and gallery works only exist in the spaces for which they are created. The recognition that all life is ephemeral is important to Hutchinson.

Her forms contain 20 to 30 per cent cellulose fibre (cotton, abaca, sisal or flax) and a range of techniques are employed, from dipping, brushing, hand modelling, slip trailing, cutting and constructing to achieve the fragile works. Fired and unfired elements are assembled together. She uses an adhesive to increase the strength of unfired pieces, methyl cellulose, which is found in Elmer's glue and wallpaper paste, and wears a respirator during this application. Firing is to 1148°C (2098°F).

Translucency and paperclay

Bespoke, translucent, porcelain lighting, inspired by the beauty of the natural world, is the genre of ceramics in which **Liz Emtage** specialises. Illuminated, her lamps emit an ethereal glow, converting the surface decoration into textures of light. When turned off, the lamps become sculptural pieces, rich with subtle surface pattern.

They are all made using porcelain paperclay, into which she lays a variety of grasses and seeds, which leave a delicate impression in the clay surface. Some organics are removed before firing but others are left to burn off in the kiln. Sometimes she mixes stains into the clay body or paints or screenprints onto the surface of the lamps; more recently she has been experimenting with final glaze firings to 1260°C (2300°F). Firing is always at night, when the studio is empty and the extractor hood on the kiln removes the smoke from the organics. Emtage's work also appears in Chapter 3 (p. 50) and Chapter 7 (p. 118).

Paper fibres, perlite and clay

Barbro Åberg's large-scale sculptures are not easily categorised. As a Swede living in Denmark, combined with a five-year stint in the US, she has developed her own distinctive style. She exhibits her ceramics in galleries and events throughout Europe and the US.

She was introduced to additions early on: to perlite by US artist Bob Shay and paperclay by Rosette Gault. Testing of several different mixtures followed, until she found the correct formulae to suit her way of working. 'During the years, I have developed several specific clay bodies – one for large, solid work, one for small pieces and one for open structures,' Åberg says. 'They give me a range of possibilities for working freely with my sculptures.'

Most of her ceramics are modelled by hand, a slow process that allows Åberg to change the form as she constructs it. Larger pieces can take 6–7 weeks to finish. 'I allow myself to reflect, alter and change, follow the impulses that emerge, and give room for a dialogue with each sculpture.'

The work is fired to 1135–1140°C (2075–2084°F) in an electric kiln, often more than twice, or until the right surface is achieved. **Terra sigillata** is sometimes applied to the surface.

Irish-based artist **Jim Turner** constructs large forms from lightweight slabs, composed of paperclay laminated with a perlite and clay mixture. He has fired solid blocks of this to 1300°C (2372°F) and raw raku-fired to 1100°C (2012°F) in six hours from fairly wet, with a 50% perlite mix, and seen no ill effects!

The perlite mixture consists of waste-clay trimmings, cellulose fibre, grogs and perlite, all of which is blended together. This is sandwiched between two layers of porcelain paperclay. For large pieces, he recommends adding molochite to the paperclay slip, because it will give extra strength to the forms and help reduce shrinkage and cracking.

Jim Turner's porcelain paperclay mix (%)	
Grolleg China clay	70
Petalite	25
White bentonite	5
White cellulose fibres	25-30% by volume (see p. 79).

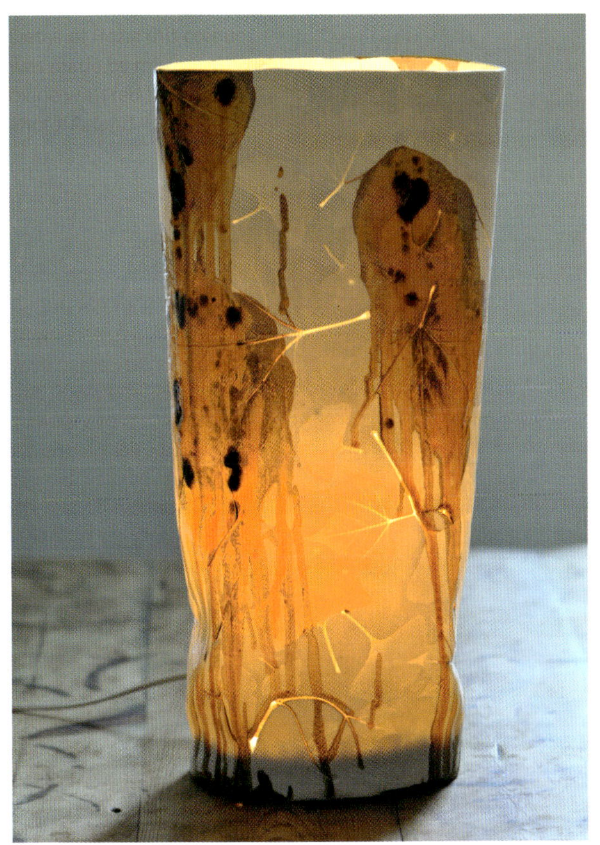

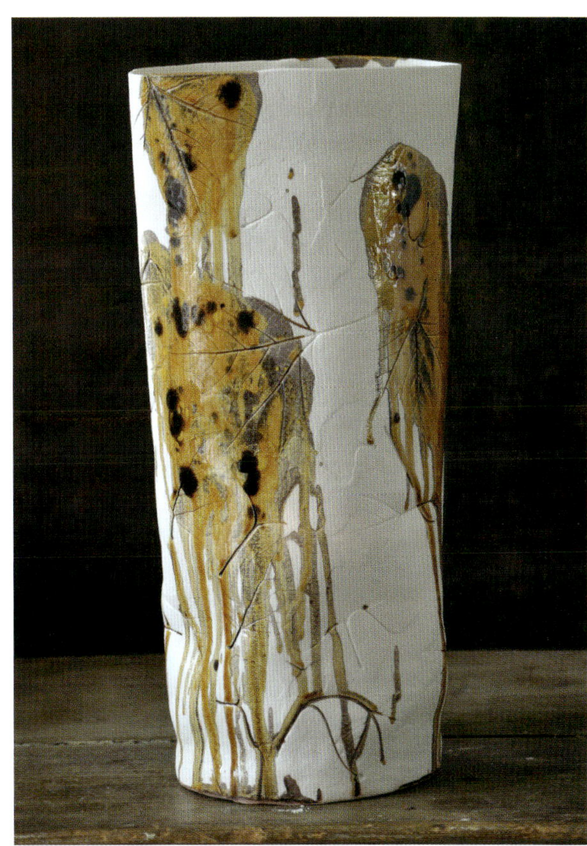

ABOVE, LEFT TO RIGHT: Liz Emtage, *Autumnal Lamp*, 2011. Large porcelain lamp, glazed, light on, 48 x 16 cm (19 x 6¼ in). *Photo: Sussie Ahlburg.*

Liz Emtage, *Autumnal Lamp*, 2011. Large porcelain lamp, glazed, light off, 48 x 16 cm (19 x 6¼ in). *Photo: Sussie Ahlburg.*

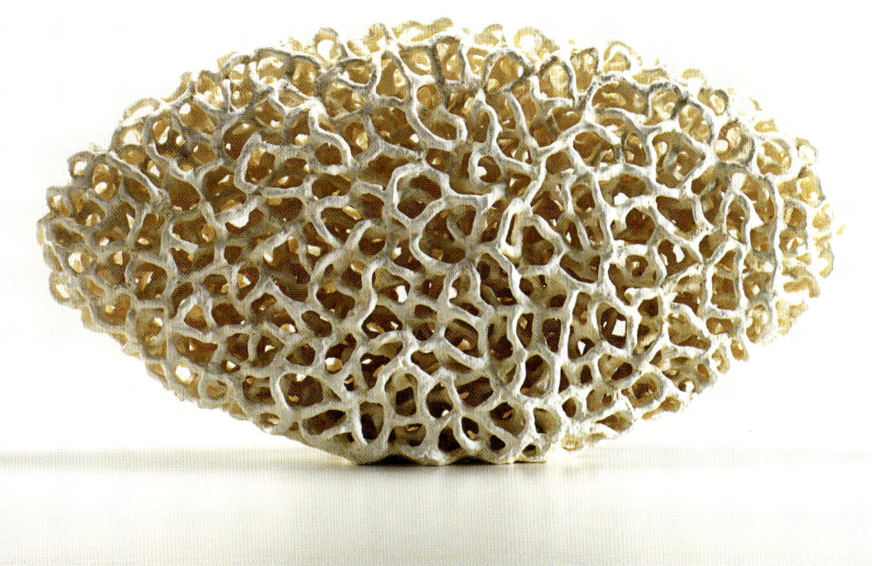

RIGHT: Barbro Åberg, *Time Yarn*, 2008. Clay with perlite and paper fibres, 68 x 35 x 12 cm (26¾ x 17¾ x 4¾ in). *Photo: Lars Henrik Mardah.*

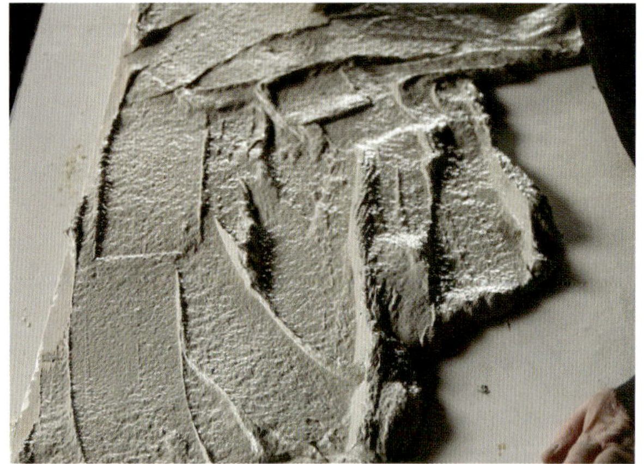

A layer of porcelain paperclay slip is laid out on the plaster.

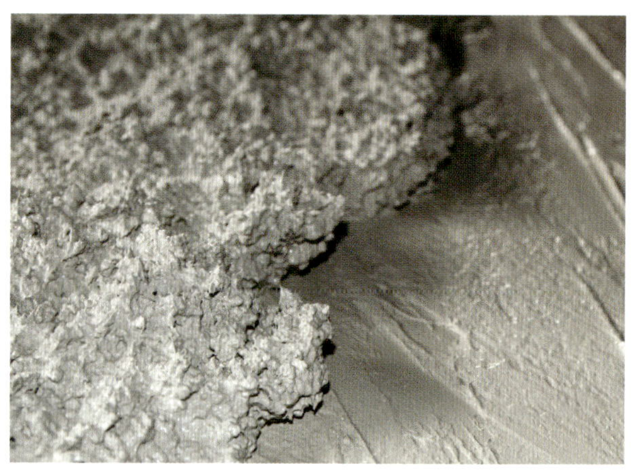

Perlite and paperclay mixture is spread on top.

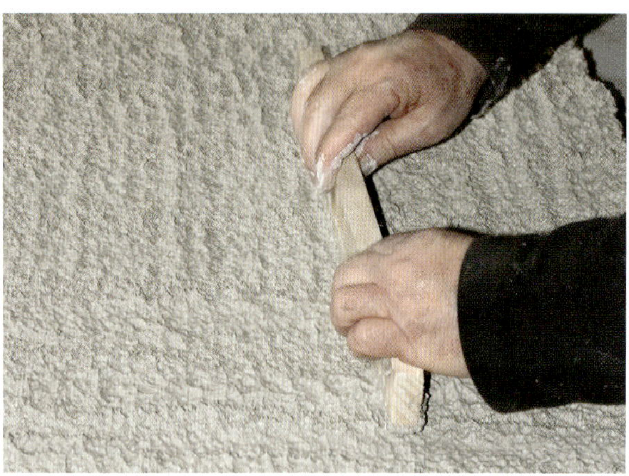

A batten is used to tamper down the perlite mixture.

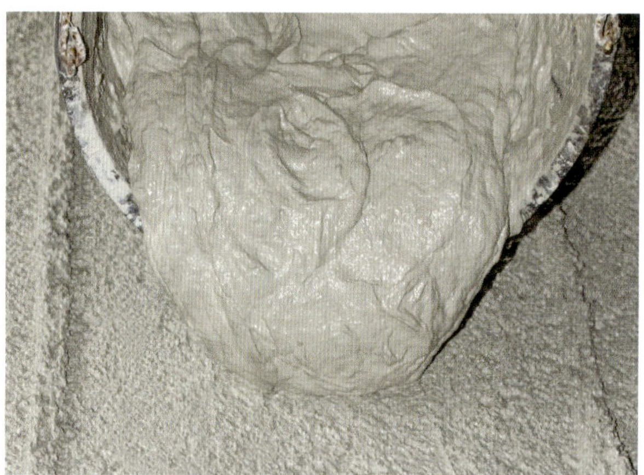

A final layer of porcelain paperclay slip is poured on top.

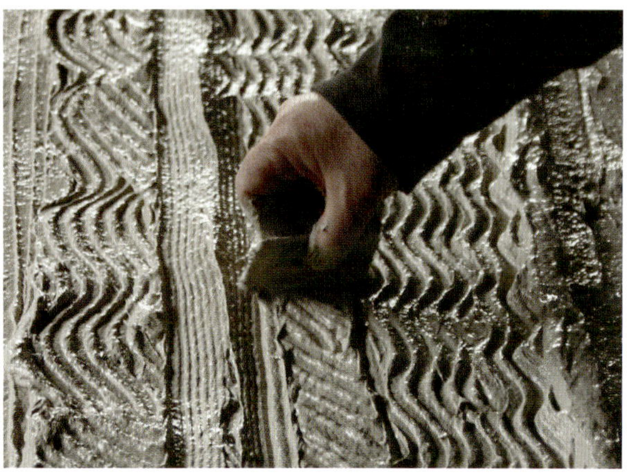

Patterns are made on the surface.

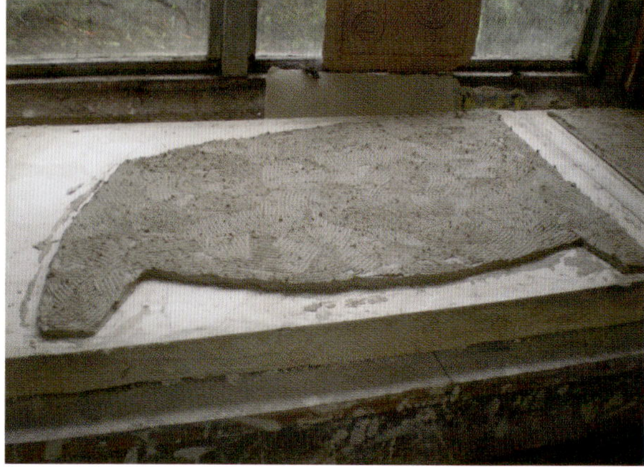

Firm slabs are cut into shapes. *Photos: Jim Turner.*

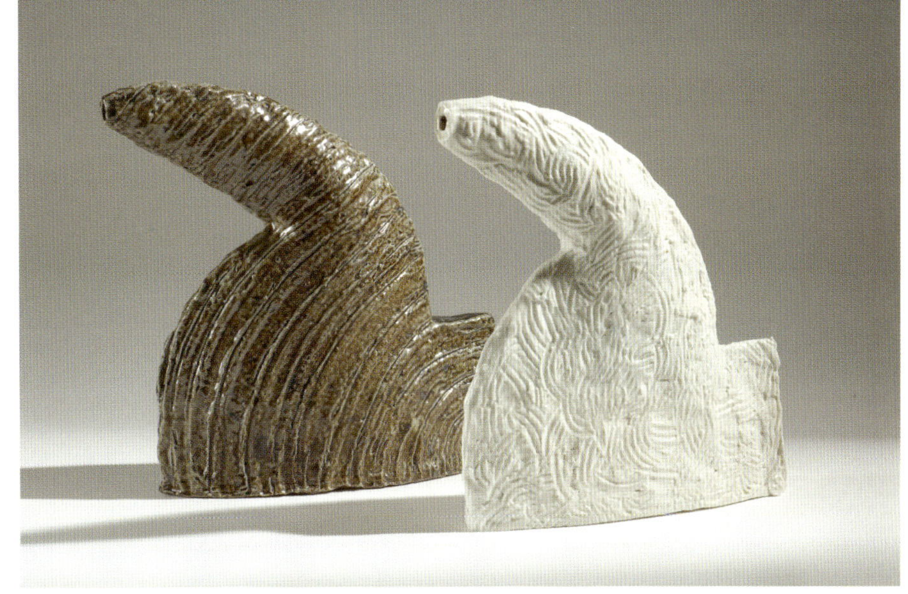

Jim Turner, *Liminal Forms*, 2009. Slabbed paperclay, wood-fired and salt-glazed to 1320°C (2408°F), height: 40 cm (15¾ in). *Photo: Roland Paschhoff.*

Drying is carried out on plaster batts. Jim says that wet sheets are interesting to manipulate as they dry on the plaster, and extra additions such as sawdust, pine needles, ceramic pellets and peat briquette crumbs can be added as the work dries. Manipulating the paperclay while it is extremely wet gives immediacy to the surfaces created.

Turner has used an interesting technique in his *Black and White Bottles* (below). Cellulose fibre was added to the glaze to help it adhere to unfired work. Then porcelain paperclay slip was painted on top and the work was once-fired to 1300°C (2372°F). This procedure results in a volcanic surface, one of the distinguishing features of his ceramics.

Turner has inspired generations of students with his knowledge and ideas, and exhibits his work widely.

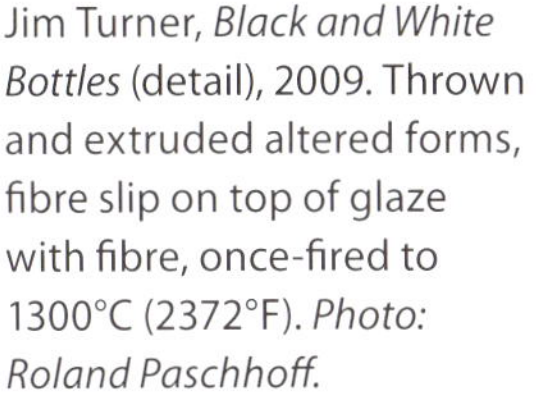

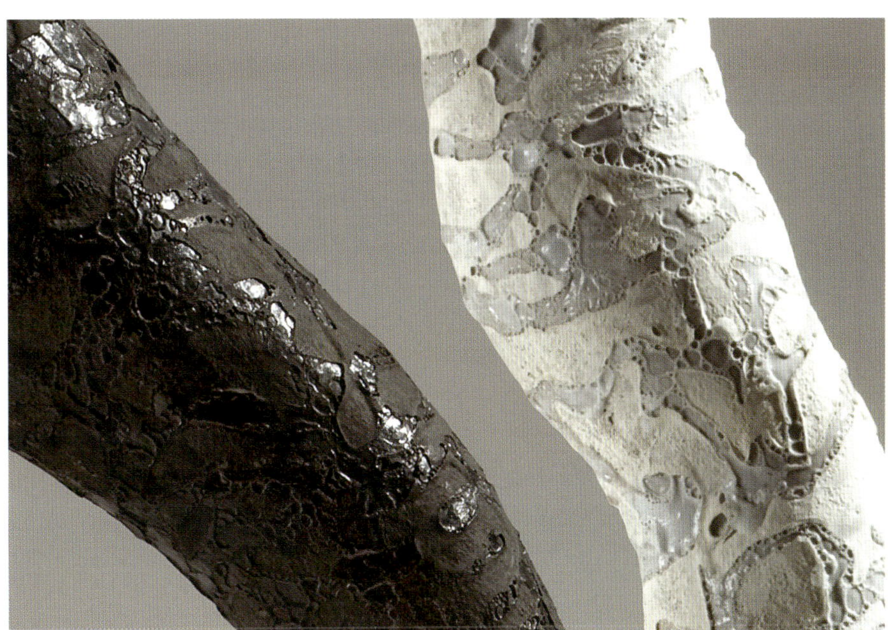

Jim Turner, *Black and White Bottles* (detail), 2009. Thrown and extruded altered forms, fibre slip on top of glaze with fibre, once-fired to 1300°C (2372°F). *Photo: Roland Paschhoff.*

Scottish ceramicist **Jenny Pope** is an avid beachcomber and her frequent coastal wanderings have nurtured a fascination for eroded rock and the effects of weathering on materials.

She also collects fragments of bone. 'I find they are an amazing mixture of original functional orthopaedic structures overlaid with weathered eroded surfaces,' she explains. Her choice of additions to clay, which include paper, perlite, nichrome wire and plant materials such as seaweed, helps her to create interesting surfaces pitted with cracks and holes, reminiscent of the landscapes she visits.

Recent pieces are hand-built using a mix of porcelain and paper, in the ratio of 75% clay to 25% paper pulp, and also perlite. Sometimes larger lumps of paper pulp are left in, leaving holes after firing. The work is bisque-fired to 1000°C (1832°F) then sanded with wet and dry paper to achieve crisp edges and fired again to 1250°C (2282°F).

The range of Pope's work is considerable: jewellery reminiscent of weathered beach pebbles; installations of bone-like fragments set out in glass cabinets or shelves which draw parallels with museum collections; large sculptures for indoor and outdoor display.

Research into the development of an environmentally friendly version of concrete, used in outdoor sculptures, is also ongoing at her studio in Edinburgh.

Jenny Pope, *Open Form*, 2010. Stoneware clay and porcelain, perlite, paper, hand-built and fired to 1250°C (2282°F), 35 x 45 cm (13¾ x 17¾ in). *Photo: Shannon Tofts.*

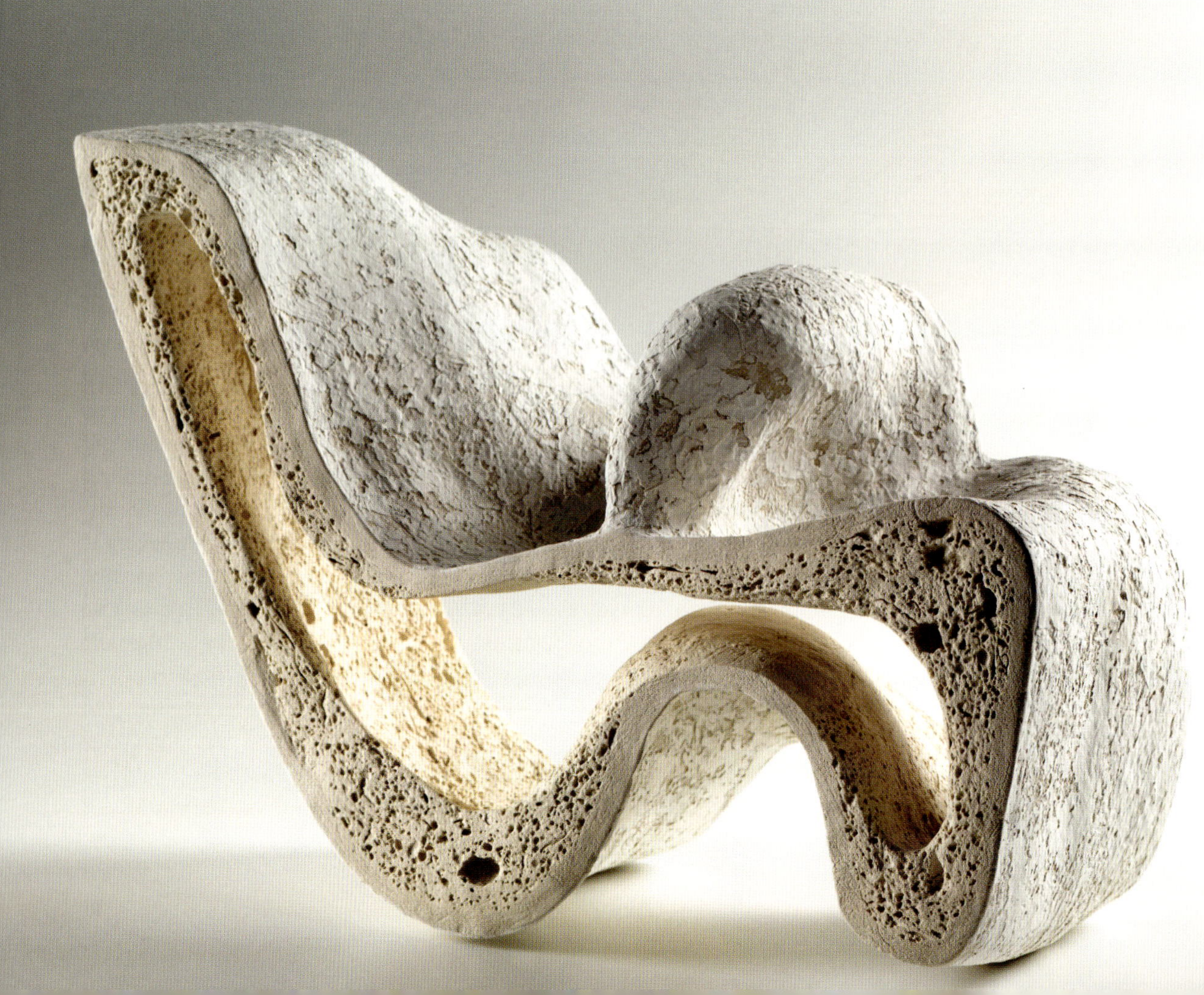

Jenny Pope, bead necklace, 2010. *Photo: Julia Douglas.*

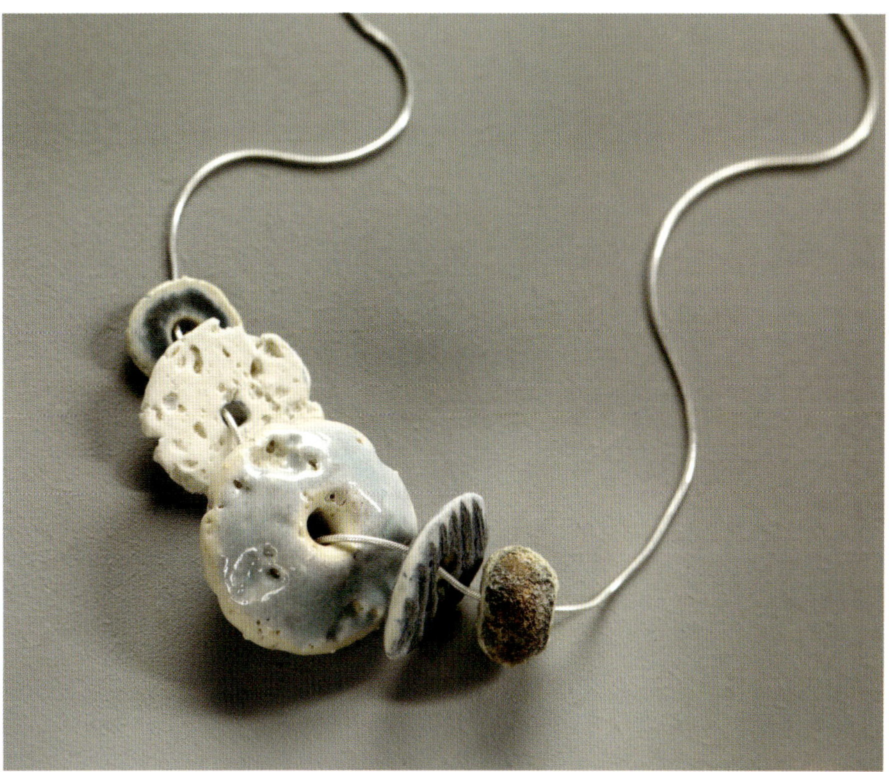

Paperclay and glass fibre tape

The experience of growing up beside the sea in St Ives, Cornwall, is clearly evident in the ceramics of **Tamsyn Trevorrow**. In a similar way to Jenny Pope, she has noticed the effects of weathering on the rock strata of this rugged part of the country. Debris from shipwrecks and the corroding effects of water and wind have also caught her imagination.

Trevorrow photographs both the details of her finds and the panorama of the ever-changing landscape that is sculpted by the elements, and captures the essence of this in her ceramics by use of colour, form and texture.

Trevorrow uses a variety of additions to create her textured, weathered surfaces, which she likens to coral or barnacles. Paper and grog are mixed into stoneware clay. This is coiled and slabbed, and the emerging forms cut, reshaped and sculpted to create work that must be explored from all angles.

At the leatherhard stage, sand, wire and scrim are used to build up layers of texture. The scrim tape, a form of glass fibre, can be purchased from builders' merchants. Trevorrow says it is safe to handle because it has a plastic coating that covers the glass fibres. It is cut into lengths, dipped in slip and then attached to the surface. This may be repeated several times, with sand and wire sandwiched between layers of tape.

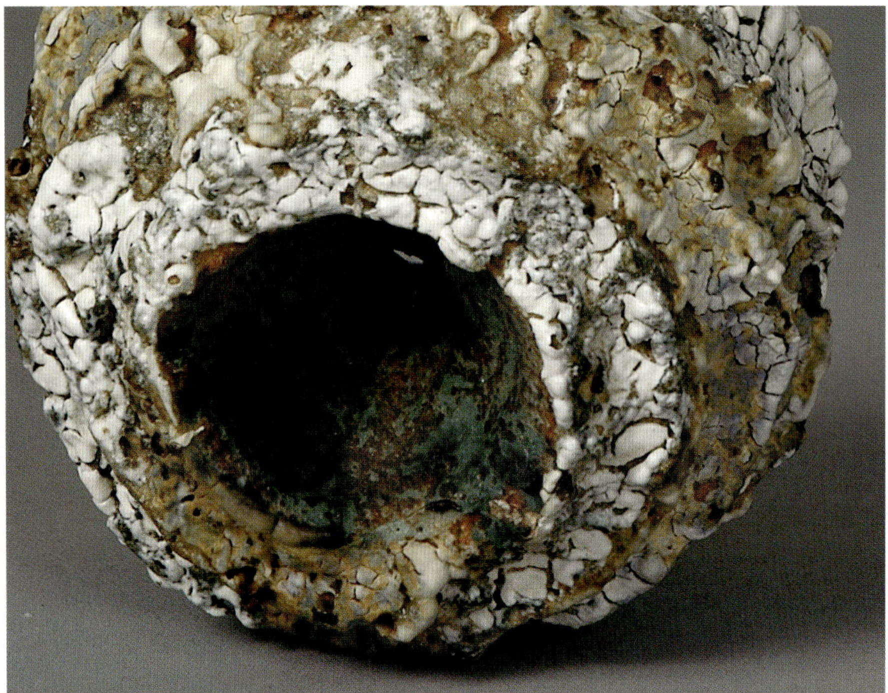

Tamsyn Trevorrow, *Small net weight*, 1998. Slab- and coil-built, paperclay, scrim, sand, wire, 20 x 20 cm (7¾ x 7¾ in). *Photo: by the artist.*

After a bisque firing, the forms are glazed and refired to 1260°C (2300°F). Multiple glazing and firing is sometimes carried out until the correct depth of texture and colour is achieved. The resulting surfaces are frequently unstable, with a propensity to shedding small pieces, a situation she likens to the uncertain outcome of the forces of change in the environment.

Porcelain and glass fibre sheets

Daniel Rhodes was one of the first people to write about the properties that glass fibre tissue can offer to ceramics. He discovered that it had all the useful properties of organic fibres, but in firings up to or above 1190°C (2174°F), the fibre would melt and remain as glassy threads. These threads increase the strength of the fired form, the reverse result to when organic fibres are burnt out. Rhodes went on to suggest its application in large complex sculptures to reduce cracking, and to reinforce joints and corners.

Paul Payne combines porcelain with glass fibre surfacing tissue, which he buys in a roll and cuts to size. Like scrim, this tissue is sealed with a plastic coating, so it is safe to handle, according to the supplier, Glasplies.

Porcelain casting slip is combined with fibreglass surfacing tissue to create a strong structure that retains its translucency. The slip-coated tissue can be used as a single-ply sheet (about 1 mm thick) or a number of laminates. The sheets are joined together with water-like pastry and any cracks that appear whilst drying out are smoothed over and sealed with water. Colouring oxides can be painted between layers to create a coloured, translucent surface. (For more on colouring oxides see Chapter 7, pp. 111–21.)

The ceramic pieces are biscuit-fired to 1000°C (1832°F), then glazed and fired to 1260°C (2300°F). The glass fibre bestows strength and flexibility to the thin sheets of porcelain so that they can be manipulated without risk of cracking. When glazed and fired to 1260°C (2300°F), the glass fibre melts to become part of the translucent clay body without leaving a visible residue.

Payne's work *Hedgerow vessels* was inspired by patterns of light between a lattice of plant stems and leaves. His making method is shown in the photos below.

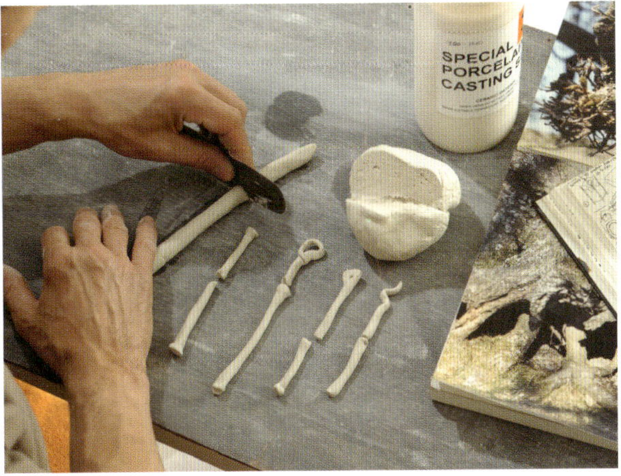

Porcelain clay is rolled out and cut to form 'uprights' that will support the structure of the vessel.

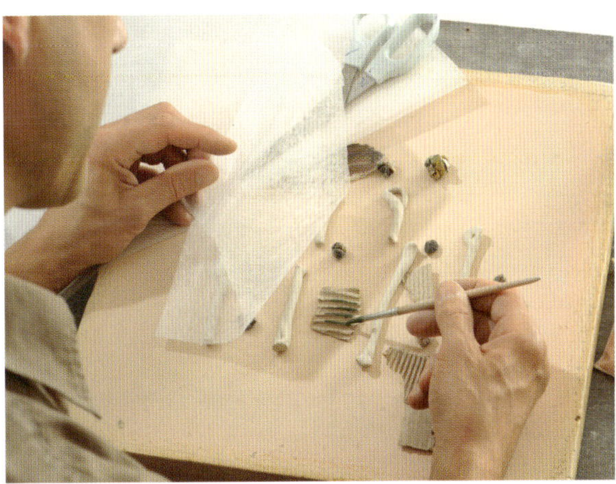

Glass fibre surfacing tissue covers the porcelain uprights. Colour and texture is added with paper and card shapes, painted with oxides.

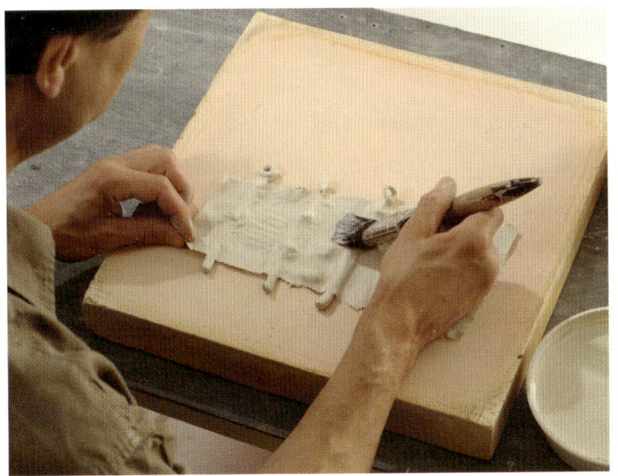

Casting slip is brushed onto the glass fibre.

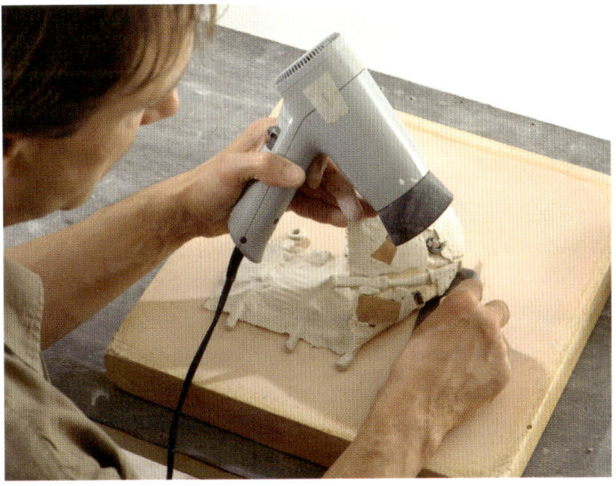

When the collage of materials is dry enough, it can be peeled off the plaster in a single layer. A metal kidney helps, and a hairdryer speeds up the drying process. *Photos: Florence Morris Photography.*

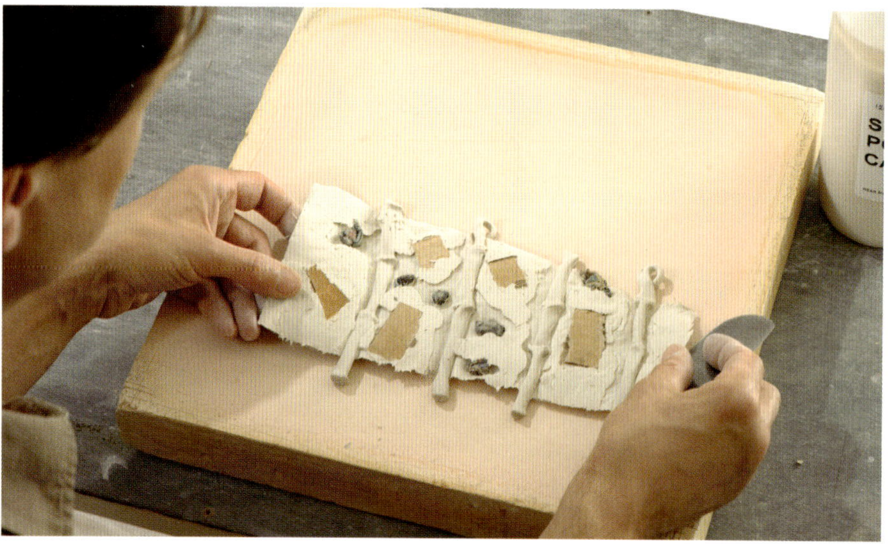

The completed panel, turned over.

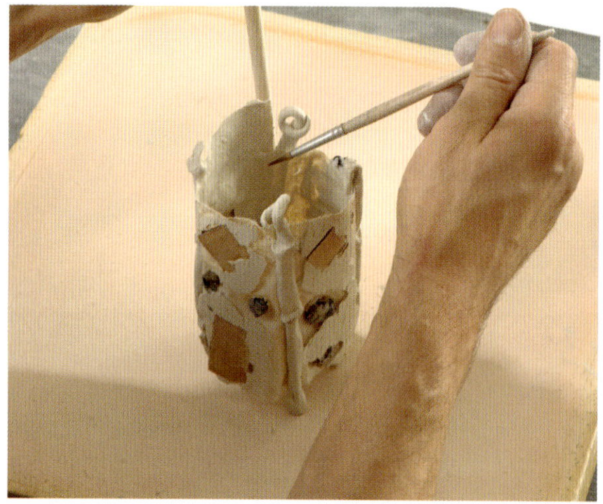

The vessel is assembled by bringing the two ends of the length together and sealing the join by brushing with water.

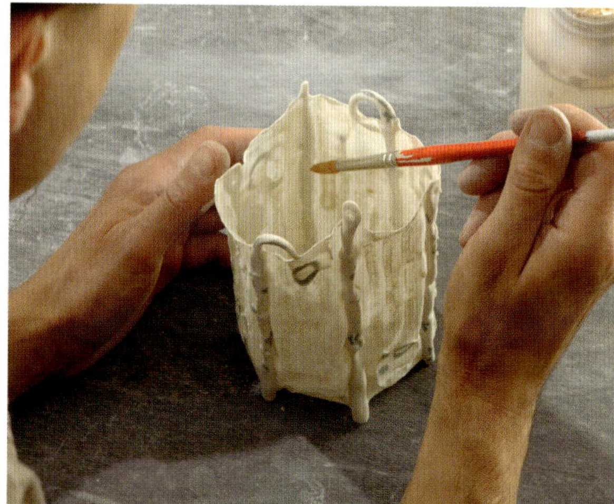

After the first biscuit firing to 1000°C (1832°F), glaze is applied. The vessel is re-fired to 1260°C (2300°F), making it translucent and waterproof. *Photos: Florence Morris Photography.*

His present focus is on lighting; he designs and makes bespoke atmospheric lighting and lithophanes. Embossed surface 'mark-making' is achieved by using lino-cut designs or carved wax blocks ranging from repeat patterns to figurative lithophanes. The design is planned and carved on a lino block, so that when a sheet of clay is pressed against this, the pattern that emerges is embossed. Firing and glazing is carried out as previously described.

Paul Payne works from his home near Bath, Somerset, on commercial and private commissions.

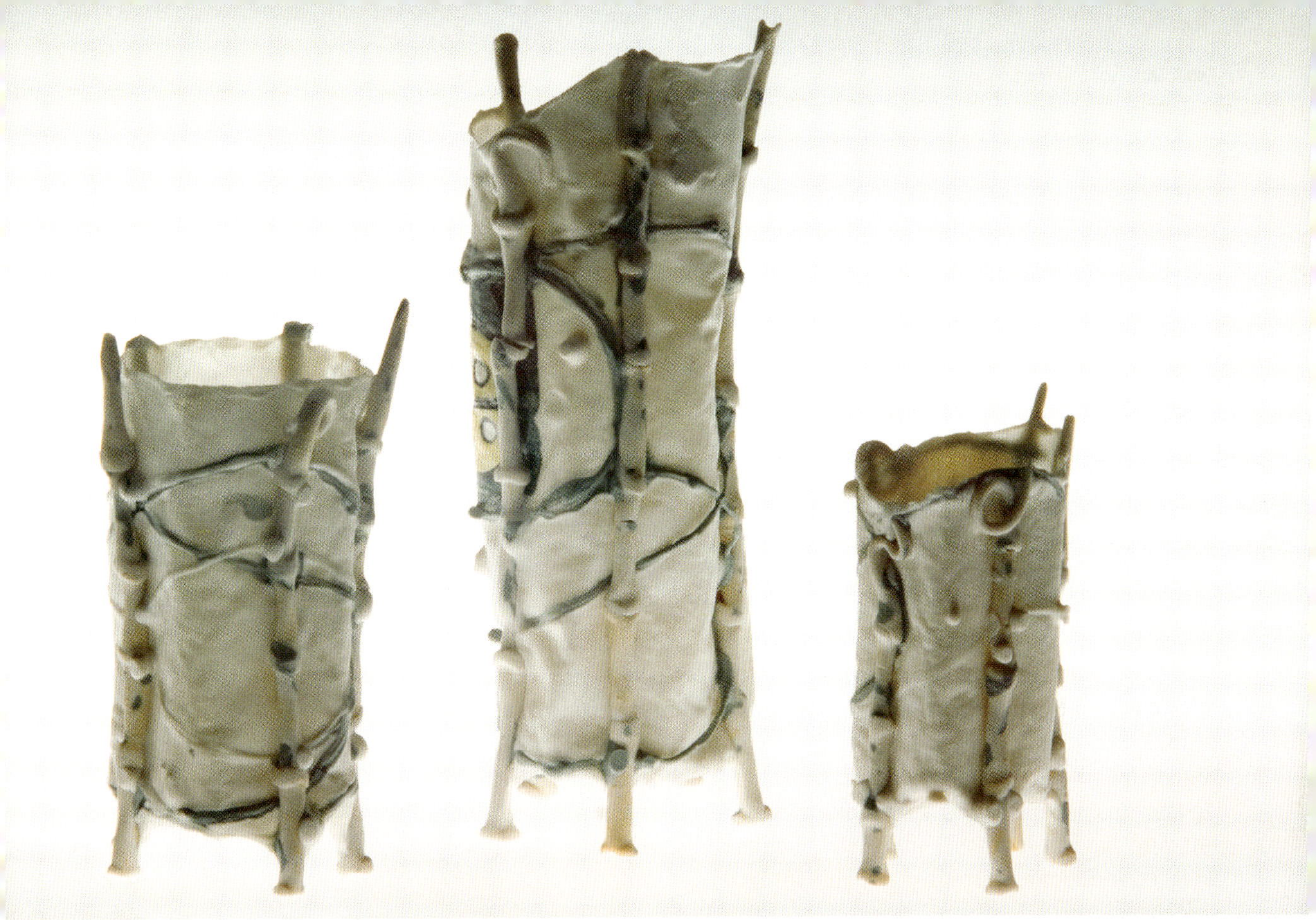

ABOVE: Paul Payne, *Hedgerow vessels*, 1990. Porcelain casting slip, porcelain clay, fibreglass tissue, oxides, two firings to 1000°C (1832°F) and 1260°C (2300°F) respectively, 16 x 10 cm (6¼ x 4 in). *Photo: Alan Bye.*

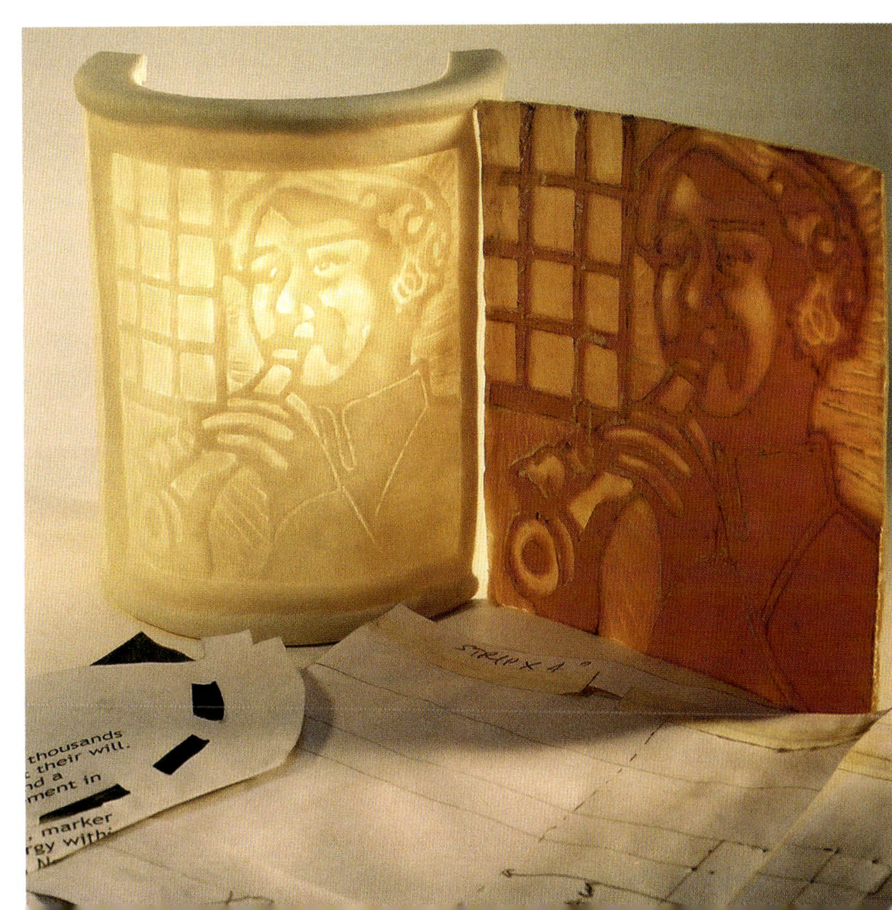

RIGHT: Paul Payne, *Lithophane Night Light*, 2009. Drawings, lithopane patterns, completed light, 10 x 9 cm (4 x 3½ in). *Photo: by the artist.*

Clay, sand and cement

This next item does not really fit the fibres genre, as fibres are not added to the clay. Instead, cement and sand are mixed in. But as these materials also do not leave a residue, I have included this unusual work here.

Writing about his own work, **Jonathan Roberts** explains how 'soft expressive clay cylinders compacted within their container jostle with an intense exuberance, within a restrained form'.

Roberts uses a mixture consisting of clay, sand and cement in order to eliminate the firing process, yet still capture the momentum of throwing clay directly on the wheel. This method was developed by Roberts in response to what he sees as the absurdity of creating objects laboriously by hand, and also to question the hierarchical relationship that exists between an object and the way in which it is presented. **Caution:** cement is highly caustic! Dust mask and gloves must be worn before any measuring, mixing, throwing or handling takes place. Clay, sand and cement are mixed as dry powders and then enough water is added to give a consistency suitable for throwing. The mix is spiral wedged in the conventional way prior to being thrown. A container, usually a piece of furniture, is positioned alongside the wheel. Component thrown cylinders are created and immediately stacked upright within the container. The piece is allowed to dry and excess cement mix is cleaned away. The work is not fired.

Jonathan Roberts, *Here Gentlemen come try your skill, IV*, 2011. Thrown concrete mixture, furniture, 62 x 36 x 45 cm (24½ x 14¼ x 17¾ in). *Photographed by Sally Roberts.*

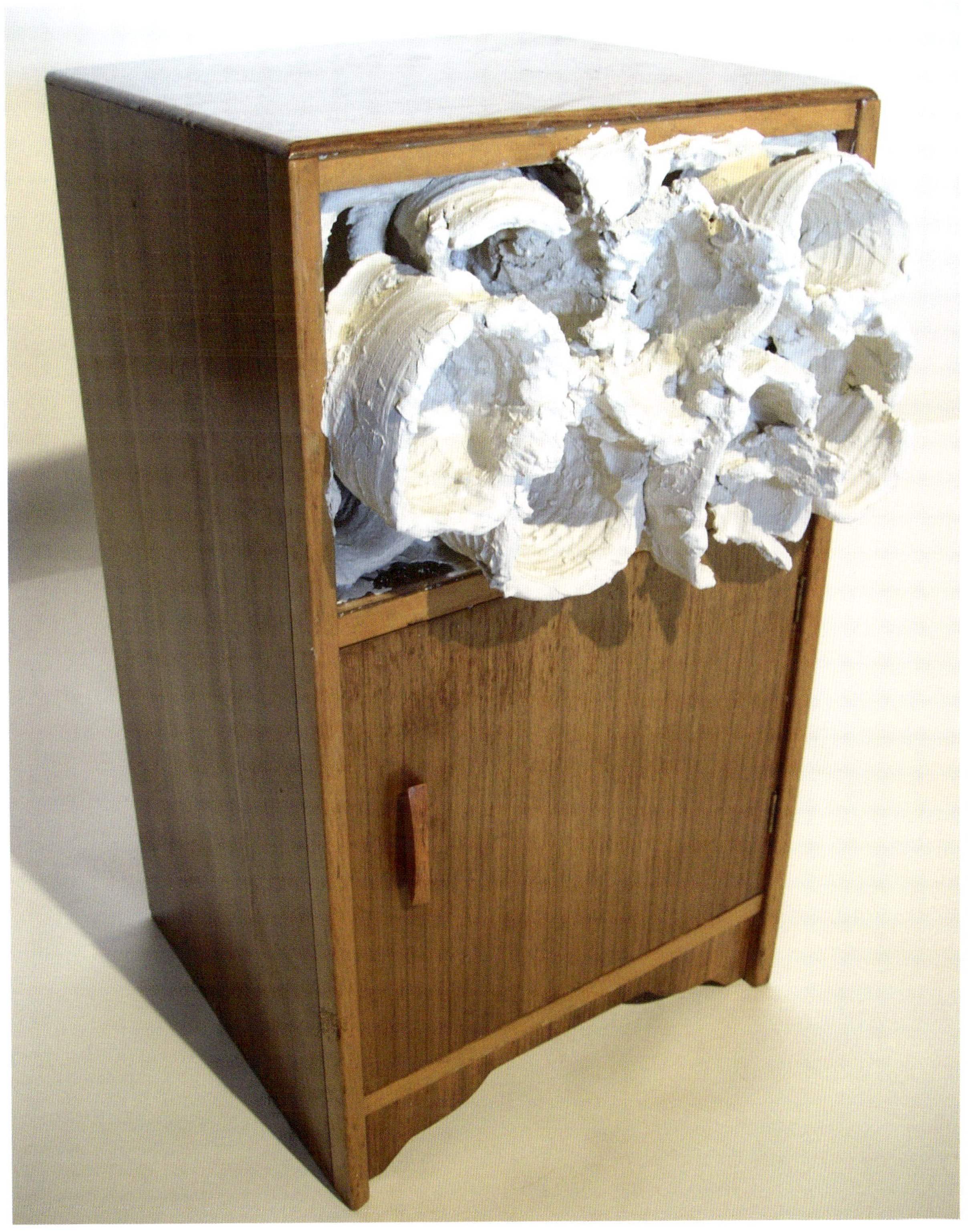

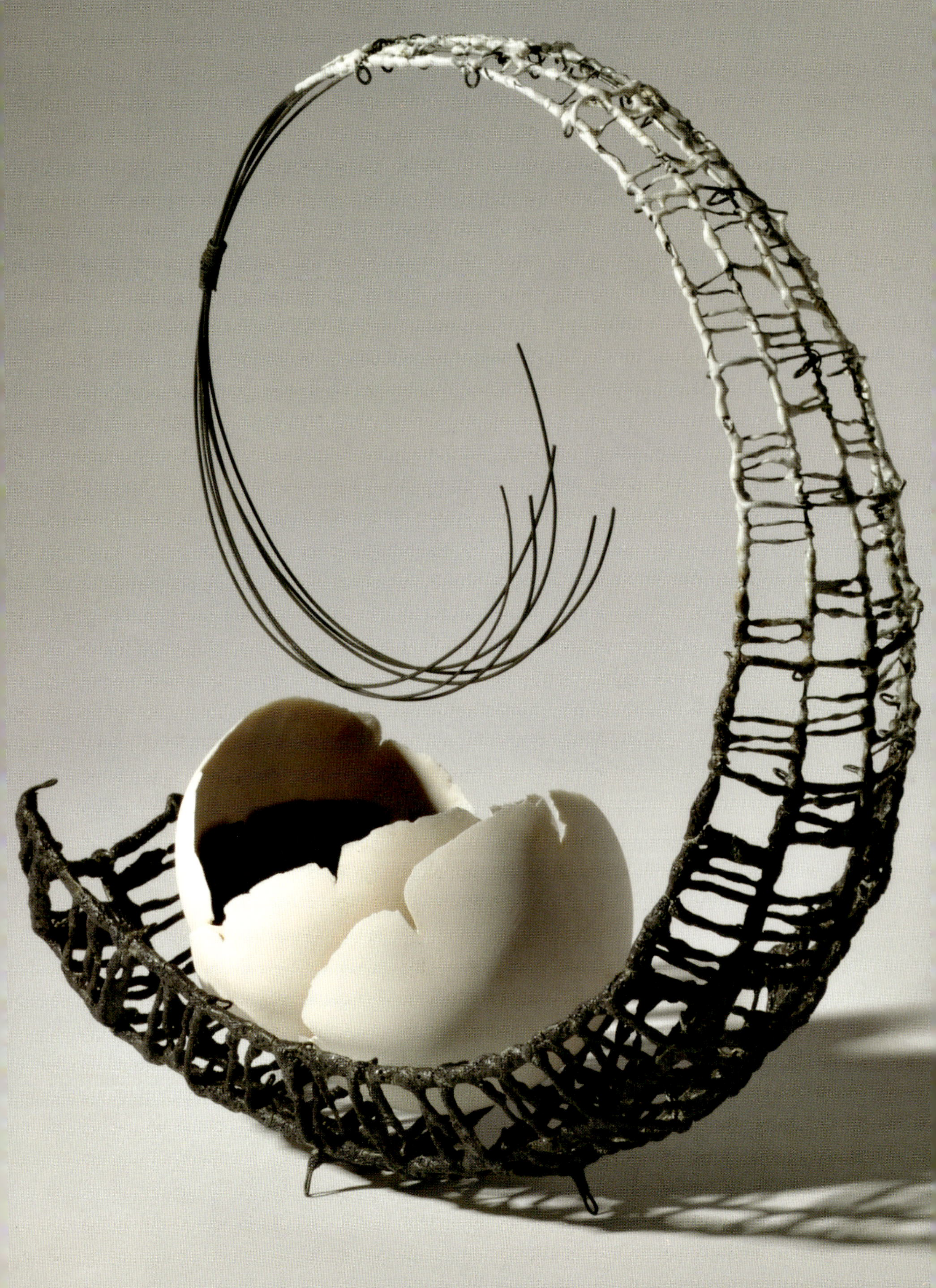

6

Metal

Nichrome wire, steel rods, mesh and wire, nails and tacks, recycled metal from kilns, clocks and buildings: all of these metals have been added to clay bodies by the artists featured in this chapter.

Sometimes, the metal is chosen for support, sometimes for interest, and frequently a combination of both. But a good match between the clay and the metal must be found, because metals melt and lose their strength at different temperatures. Nichrome wire is used by many artists because it retains its strength at stoneware temperatures. This is important for Susan O'Byrne, who uses the wire to support sheets of printed paperclay draped into animal forms.

Recycled kiln elements are also able to withstand heating to high temperatures, a feature explored in an intriguing way by American artist Todd Leech, with his application of foaming glazes directly onto the coils.

On the other hand, steel in all its many forms (mesh, wire, rods and nails) starts to disintegrate at temperatures above 1200°C (2192°F). This does not present a problem for Deborah Sigel, as she uses steel wire to support low-firing Egyptian paste.

Metal is also used to add interest to a form, as in the vessels of Deirdre Hawthorne and Emma Rodgers. And then, of course, there is the extraordinary installation work of Andy Glass, who buries wire inside his clay structures and then 'switches on' the electricity, with exciting results.

Clay with metal additions should be fired in a well-ventilated area and precautions should be taken to avoid inhaling fumes.

Support: nichrome wire

LEFT: Lesley Risby, *Protection series I*, 2009. Made from porcelain and nichrome wire by hand-building and press-moulding. The wire form is glazed and once-fired to 1220°C (2228°F) with a 30-minute soak. The cups are unglazed, stained porcelain, bisque-fired to Cone 04 and sanded before firing to Cone 7, 30 x 30 cm (11¾ x 11¾ in). *Photo: Sussie Ahlberg.*

It might have been a deer or a calf, but when I think back to the first time I saw one of **Susan O'Byrne**'s life-size sculptures, I was both in awe and a little confused. How could these creatures be made of clay and fired in a kiln? The answer, of course, is in the unique way she builds a metal skeleton, which she covers with a skin of clay and imagery.

Her sculptures depict everyday animals of the English countryside. Calf, hare, deer and badger, together with the garden birds of the hedgerow, orchard and lawn, are all included in her repertoire. Her intention is not to make representations of actual, living creatures, but rather to use the animal forms as vehicles for the expression of human emotions. She references the wonder of childhood, when we are introduced to storytelling, legend and folklore, all of which use animals to simplify the complexities of adult life.

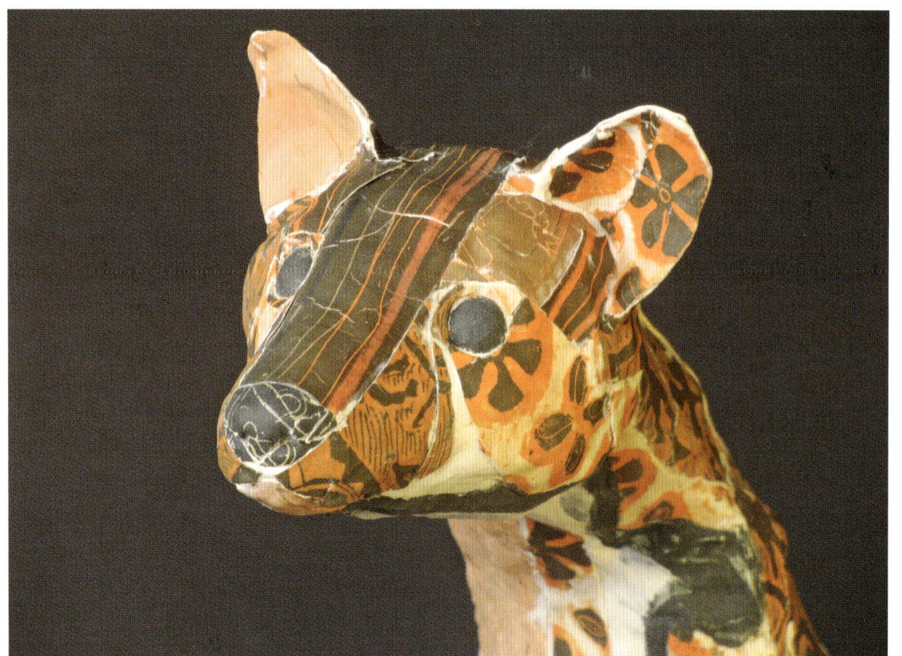

Susan O'Byrne, *Pine Marten* (detail), 2011. Hand-built, nichrome wire and porcelain paperclay. Reduction-fired to 1260°C (2300°F), 55 x 25 x 20 cm (21¾ x 9¾ x 7¾ in). *Photo: by the artist.*

Susan O'Byrne, *Calf*, 2011. Hand-built, nichrome wire and porcelain paperclay. Reduction-fired to 1260°C (2300°F), 80 x 105 x 50 cm (30½ x 41¼ x 19¾ in). *Photo: by the artist.*

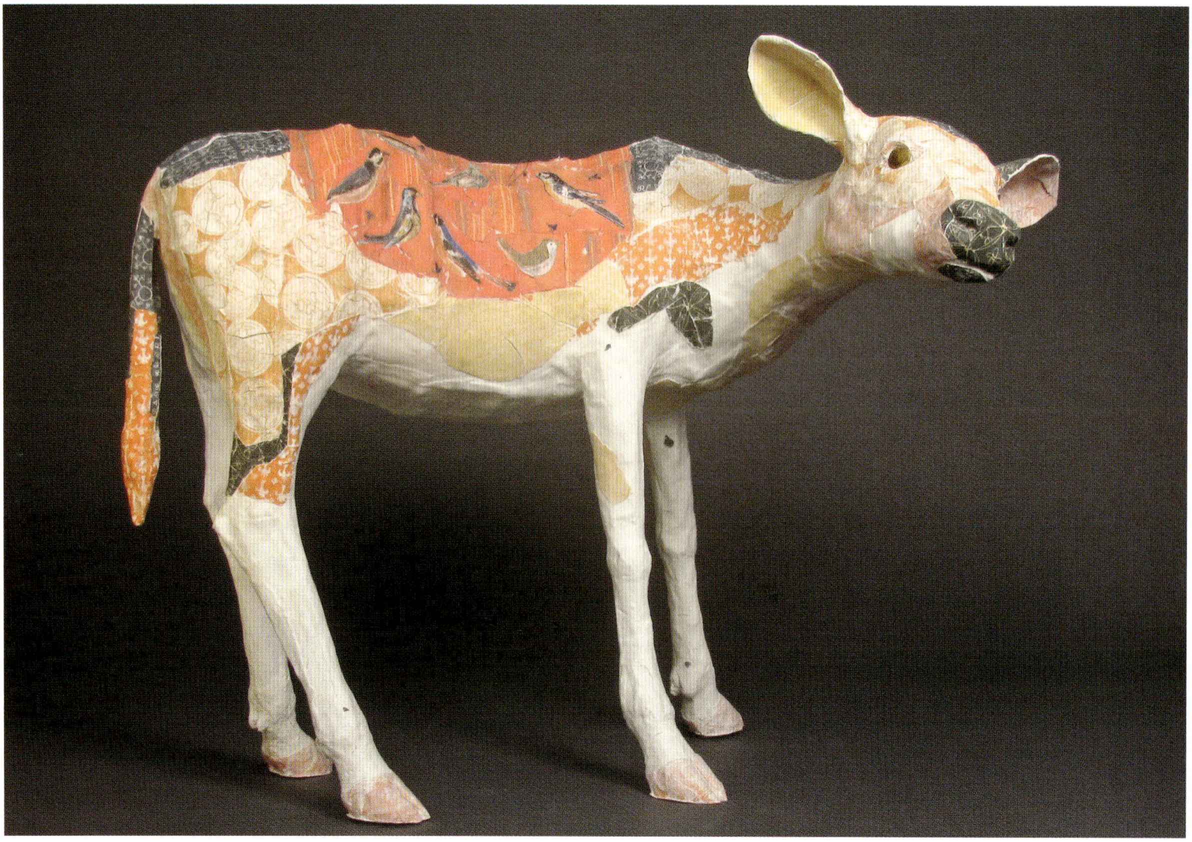

O'Byrne's large animals begin with a nichrome wire framework (wire that can withstand high kiln temperatures). Onto this framework she applies thin layers of stoneware paperclay. This helps to strengthen the work before the application of more fragile layers of porcelain paperclay. The final layers of clay are patterned and coloured using various printing, drawing and stencilling techniques. The thin sheets of clay are made by pouring slip onto plaster batts. Once decorated and dry enough, the clay is peeled from the plaster and collaged onto the animal.

Elements of chance, the natural twists and kinks of the wire, and the shrinkage of the clay around it during firing are allowed to contribute to the posture of the finished animal, a process which gives O'Byrne's animals an awkward vulnerability.

After graduating from Edinburgh College of Art, Irish-born O'Byrne set up her ceramic practice in Glasgow in 2002. She has exhibited widely, undertaken artist-in-residence posts both at home and abroad, and still manages to find time to lead many award-winning community art projects.

A curved framework of nichrome wire

'Organic, skeletal, fragile and vulnerable' are words used by **Leslie Risby** to describe her ceramics, which she makes in her small home-based workshop in north-west London. Her choice of words is apt: a nichrome wire frame is fashioned into a sinuous curve, covered with fabric and porcelain slip, and then subjected to intense heat that causes partial disintegration. She likens this process to the susceptibility of living organisms to environmental forces, whether natural or man-made.

Risby adds several additions to the porcelain casting slip: nichrome wire is an essential part of the form, aesthetically and structurally, and it fires to the high temperature required; finely chopped fabric (Domette, a soft, fleecy, acrylic wool) assists the slip to adhere to the wire; molochite 200 mesh (very fine) helps reduce shrinkage of the porcelain; silicon carbide gives texture; and oxides and stains add colour.

Making the porcelain/wire form

The initial design of the form is produced with a clay/wire maquette or a sketch. From this idea, a former or sitter is hand-built using crank, painted with batt wash and then fired to cone 7 in an electric kiln. It is now ready to use. The former/sitter is required to support the work during the firing, otherwise it would collapse.

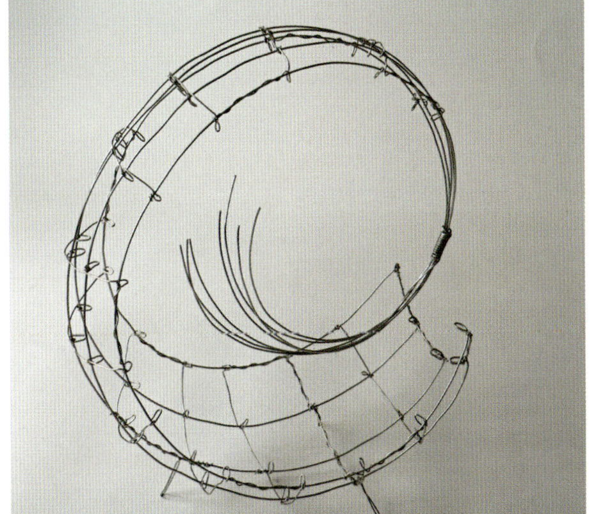

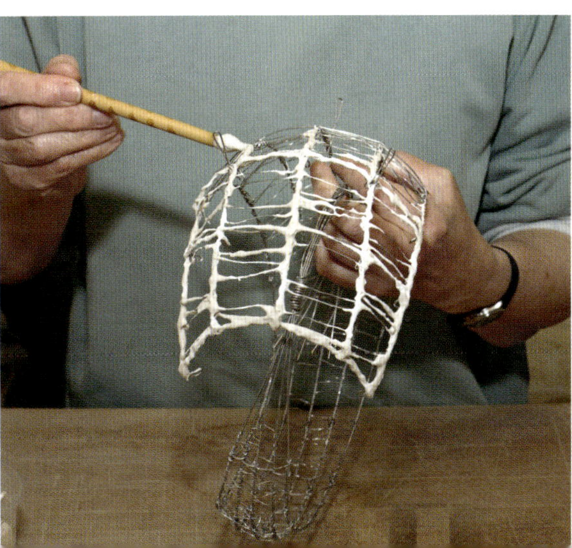

BELOW LEFT: Curved nichrome wire form showing the wire hooks.

BELOW RIGHT: Brushing on the porcelain casting slip containing fabric fibres. *Photos: Harry Baker.*

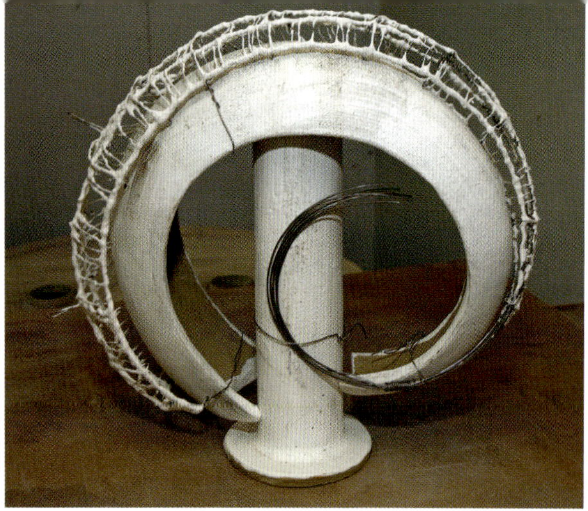

Completed piece wired onto the crank former/sitter, ready for a single firing to Cone 7.

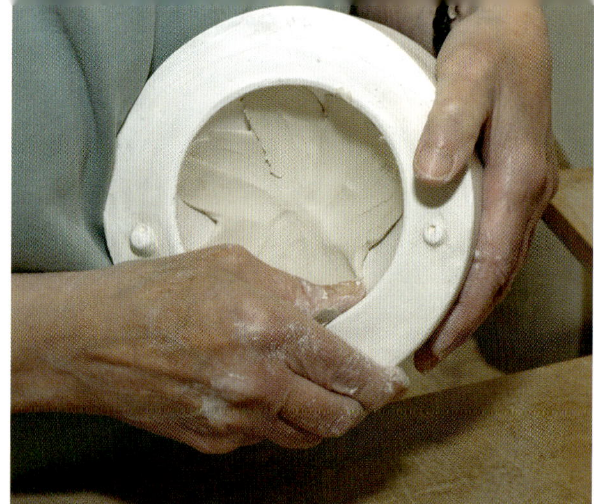

Smearing the soft porcelain from the base up the side of the cup mould, producing a thin and irregular edge.

A nichrome wire form is then woven to fit the former, using three gauges of wire (0.56, 0.9 and 1.2 mm). The wire hooks are an essential part of the interior surface of the form, because they prevent the glaze sticking to the former/sitter during the firing.

Porcelain casting slip (containing 5% fine molochite and fabric fibres) is brushed onto the wire form and built up as required. Additional coats of slip containing 3% black copper oxide and 3% silicon carbide are added for the black areas. Two or three coats of a brush-on, semi-transparent glaze are then applied. A heat gun is used to dry the coats of slip and glaze.

The finished piece is fixed onto the inverted sitter using nichrome wire and fired to 1220°C (2228°F) with a 30-minute soak. Crank clay barriers are used around the work to protect the kiln elements from the clay that spits off the wire during the cooling process.

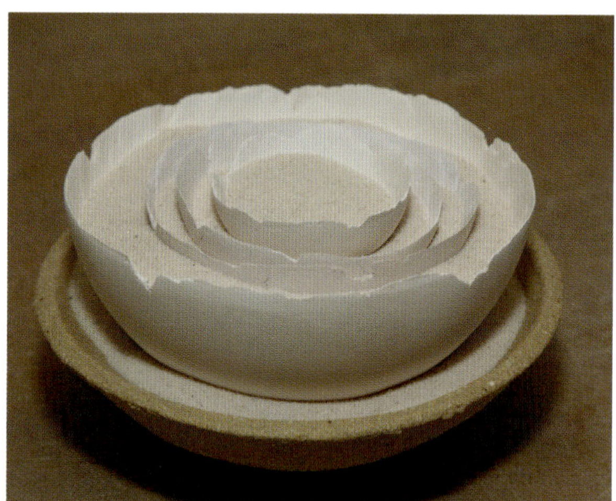

Groups of cups supported in silica sand, ready for firing; the work is bisque-fired to 1000°C (1832°F) and sanded smooth using wet and dry silicon carbide paper, before firing to 1220°C (2228°F) with a 30-minute soak. *Photos: Harry Baker.*

Making the cups

A specific weight of clay is used for each size of cup. The cups are press-moulded using soft natural or stained porcelain. A pad of porcelain is placed in the base of the mould and then smeared up the sides of the mould, producing a thin and irregular edge.

The dry cups are bisque-fired to 1000°C (1832°F), supported in silica sand within a clay bowl, one inside another. They are then sanded in water to a very smooth finish using 'wet and dry' (silicon carbide paper), before firing to 1220°C (2228°F) and sanding lightly again.

Support: steel wire and mesh

Deborah Sigel has combined her interest in mathematics and design in the creation of abstracted flower-like forms. Her choice of materials was guided by a desire to work sculpturally with colour and she quickly discovered the potential array of brilliant, candy-like colours that could be achieved using Egyptian paste. Other advantages are its single firing and low temperature properties, which are ideal, as she combines the paste with steel before firing. The use of a steel framework came out of an experimental need for a supporting structure when working with Egyptian paste.

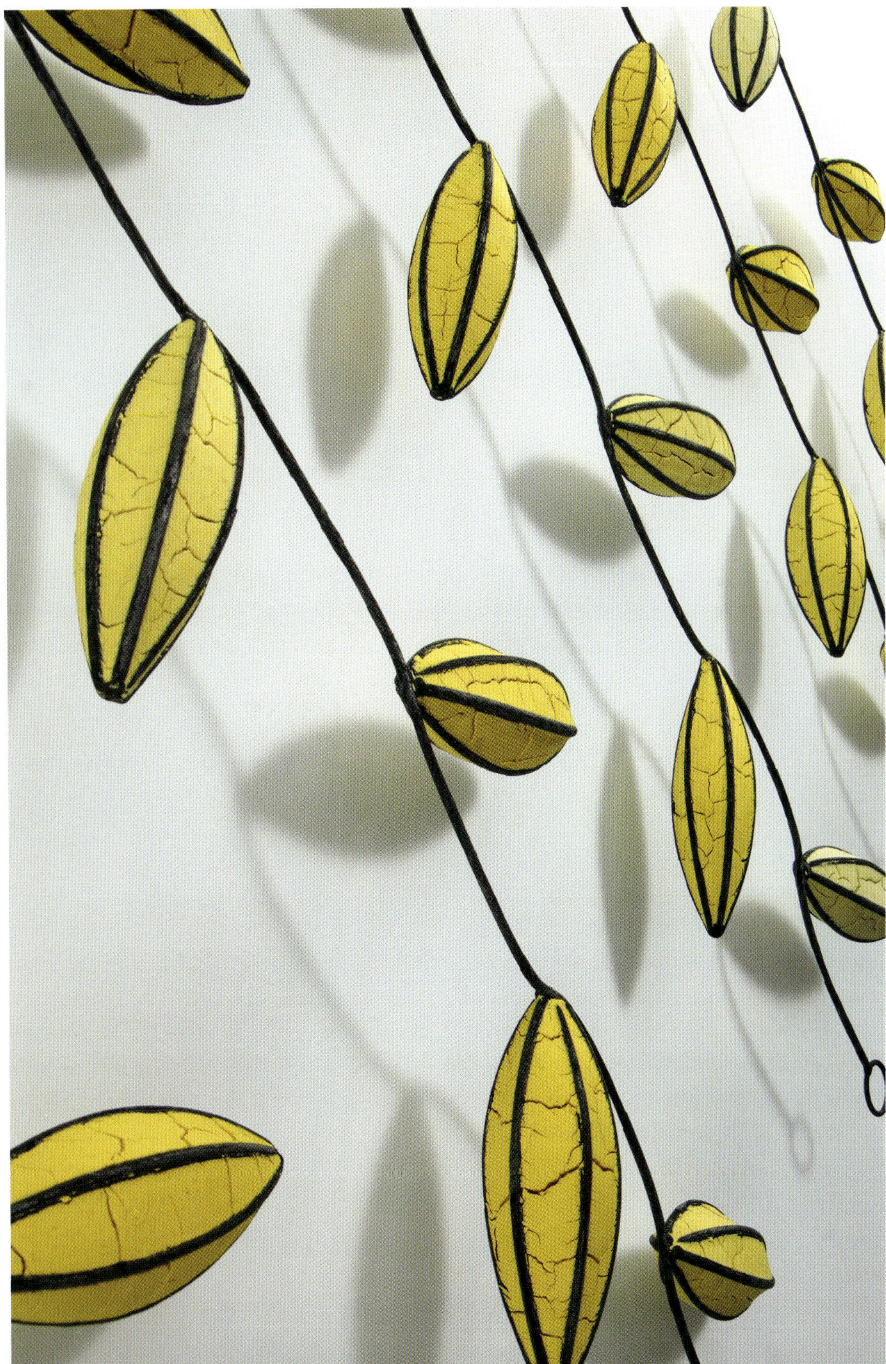

Deborah Sigel, *Wisp*, 2008. Egyptian paste and steel, suspended and fired to Cone 05, 68 x 33 x 5 cm (26¾ x 13 x 2 in). *Photo: Scott Gordon.*

Hot rolled mild steel is manipulated by bending and cutting all the pieces to size. The metal supporting structure is then created by welding these components together. Sigel advises that vinyl or latex gloves should be worn when handling Egyptian paste, because of the presence of metallic oxides and soluble salts that may be absorbed through the skin and cause irritation.

Using a fettling knife, rubber ribs and a sponge, she works on the Egyptian paste until a smooth surface, free from blemishes, has been created. It is important that there are no distractions on the surface to detract from the desired shrinking and cracking that occurs during the firing. Her 'wisps' are then suspended inside the kiln by threading them onto a steel pipe, which rests on brick columns. Sigel says that firing speed, temperature and gravity all affect the final outcome of her work.

The unpredictable nature of these two materials, steel and Egyptian paste, is part of the attraction of working with them. You can learn more about Sigel's work in Chapter 7 (p. 120)

An interest in the science of materials, how they behave both separately and in combinations with each other, is how **Linda Mau** describes her journey, culminating in her present work. She produces sculpture from her home studio in the San Francisco Bay area, California, where she also teaches at a local college.

As an artist living with an engineer in Silicon Valley, she was keen to make sense of the common quest to investigate and understand that leads to creativity. Experiments with three of her favourite materials followed: clay, handmade paper and metal. From layering paperclay slip onto a steel armature, to joining clay slabs using only steel nails or rods, the possibilities for Mau's work are endless.

Mau begins by drafting precise paper patterns of the design. Then, wearing leather gloves, she follows the patterns to cut half-inch (1.25 cm) sections of steel mesh with metal cutters. The seams are joined with wire, resulting in the finished shape in metal.

The next stage is to coat the wire armature, either by brushing or pouring, with paperclay slip. Each coat of slip is dried completely before the next layer is added, a process that can take several days. Mau chooses to use cotton linter because it lasts longer, with a reduced risk of it starting to rot and smell. She combines it with porcelain in proportions of 20% pulp to 80% porcelain. Knowing how many layers of slip to apply is gained by practice and experience: too few layers and the work lacks strength due to insufficient clay remaining when the fibre burns away.

Before firing, the steel mesh provides the form with strength, but after firing in an electric kiln to 1038°C (1900°F), the steel becomes brittle and it is the clay that gives strength to the form. The final slip layer is either white or red terra sigilatta. Further colour options are introduced by smoke firing the bisque pieces with newspaper in an open metal container, followed sometimes by an application of wax paste or shoe polish, and light buffing to encourage a sheen on the surface.

For her *Clay and Nails* series (opposite), Mau added vermiculite to stoneware clay. The resulting slabs were then textured by pressing in weathered wood, stones or seed pods. These slabs were joined using only steel nails to form various 'functional' objects, such as teapots. The juxtaposition of a familiar object that cannot function is part of the fun Mau derives from this work.

Linda Hansen Mau, *Memories of camping with Dad*, 2008. Porcelain paperclay over steel wire, blue terra sigilatta; fired at 1088°C (1990°F) in electric kiln; smoked with newspaper, 29 x 21 cm (11½ x 8¼ in). *Photo: by the artist.*

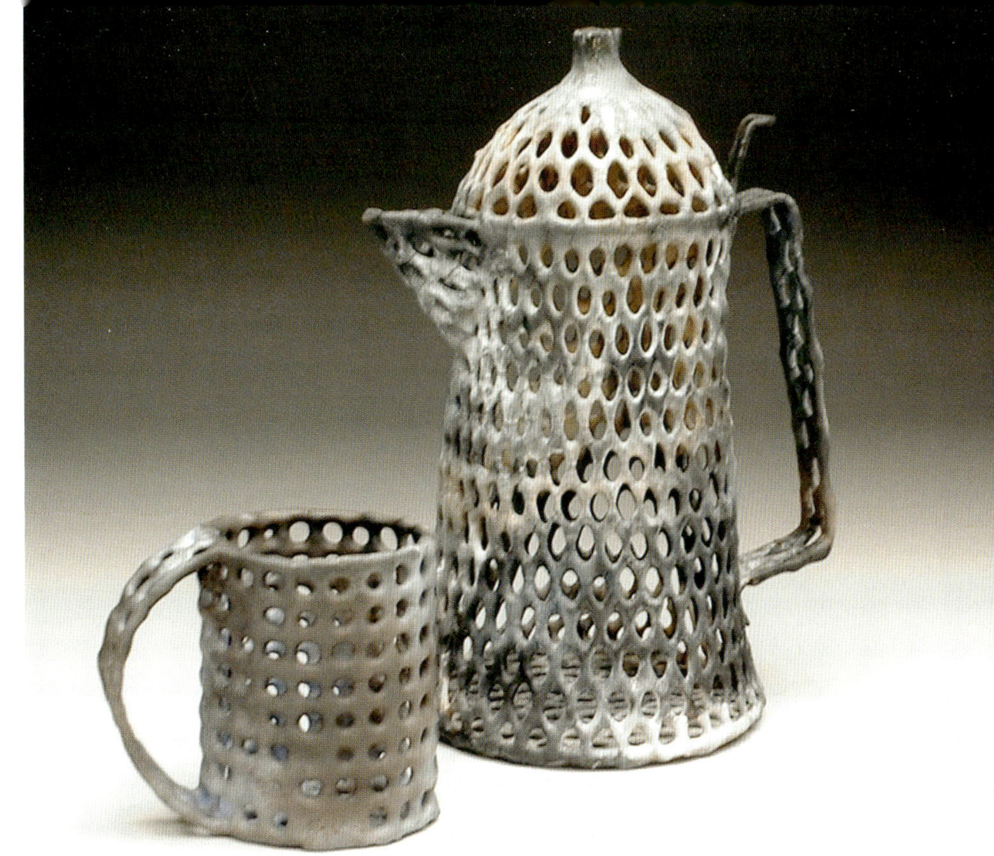

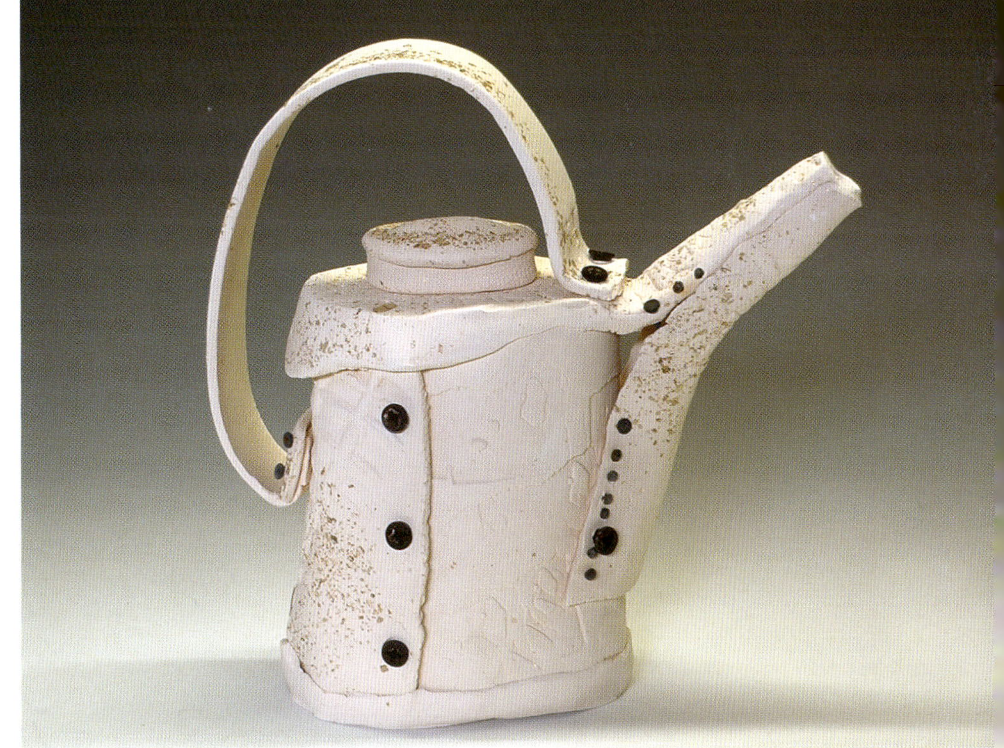

Linda Hansen Mau, *Clay and Nails Teapot*, 2011. Stoneware clay textured with found objects, vermiculite addition, and joined entirely with steel rods. Fired on a steel pipe to 1088°C (1990°F) in electric kiln, 24 x 22 cm (9½ x 8½ in). *Photo: courtesy of the artist.*

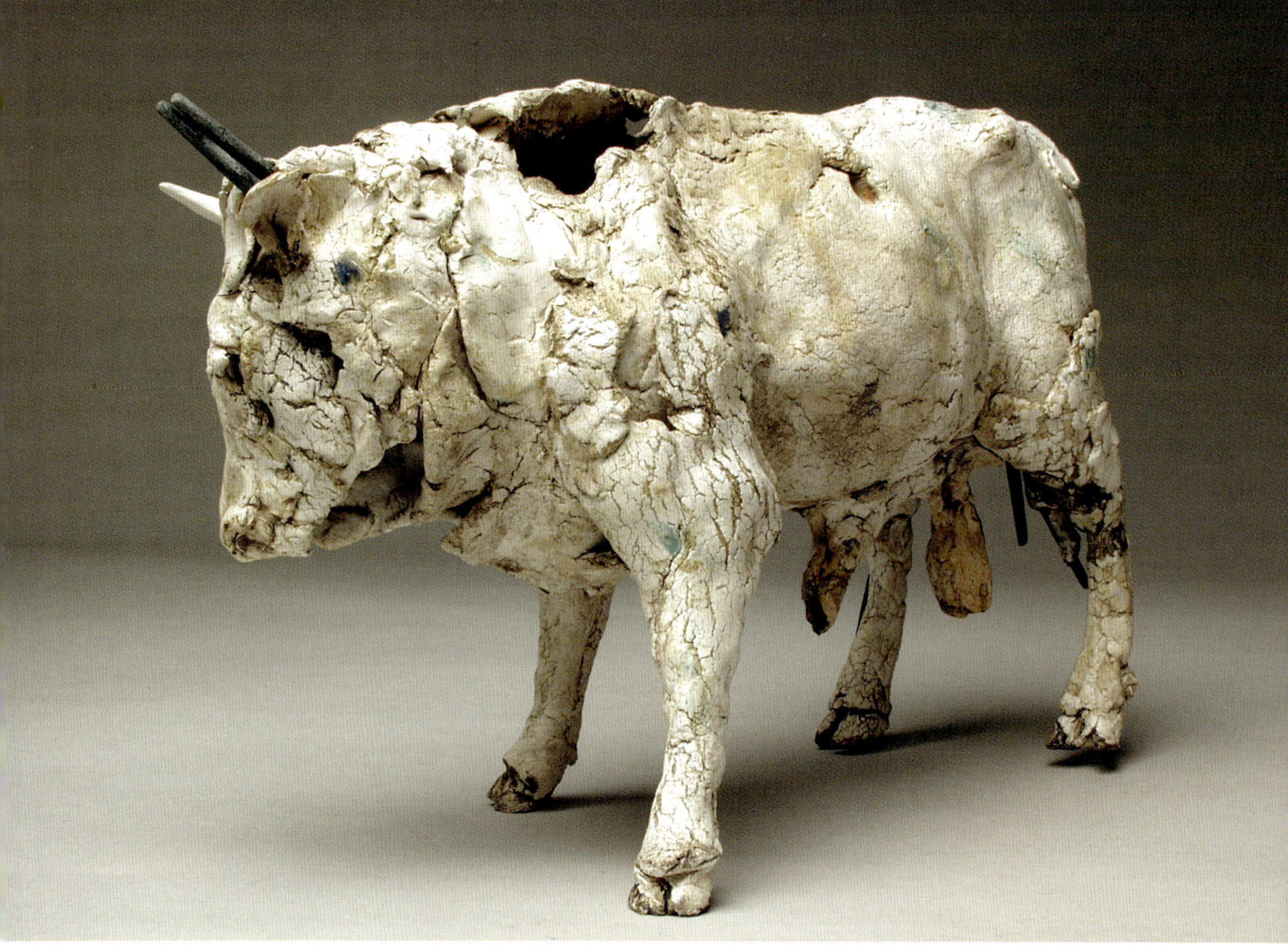

Emma Rodgers, *Bull*, 2010. Clay with metal nail additions, 40 x 25 cm (15¾ x 9¾ in). *Photo: Mills Media.*

Metal additions for interest

Nails, cogs from clocks, recycled kiln elements

Wild leaping hares, solitary doughty bulls, a decaying brace of pheasants, birds on the wing, performing monkeys: these are just a few of the extraordinary sculptural creations of one of Britain's leading sculptors, **Emma Rodgers**, whose imagination is captured in clay, glaze and found objects. From movement and tension to stillness and tenderness, she peels back the layers of existence, leaving just the essence of what it is to be alive or dead.

Rodgers' knowledge of her subjects is researched through close observational drawing, dissections of animal corpses, photography and travel. Her willingness to experiment has led to combinations of materials that don't easily fit into any well-established genre.

Some of her found materials are donated by friends, who recognise her penchant for the unusual: these include mattress coils, the innards of clocks, ancient-looking nails and broken china saucers, just to name a few.

Bull was made with porcelain clay (Audrey Blackman) mixed loosely with Earthstone clay, into which metal nails were inserted before firing. The nails add interest to the composition, representing horns and shin bones, and perhaps alluding to the sexuality of the beast. This sculpture, as with most of Rodgers' work, was fired to 1140°C (2084°F) with a 20-minute soak. The low temperature, combined with a soak of this length, conveys strength to the form, with a reduced risk of warping. A small gap was left around the metal insertion to allow for shrinkage of the clay, thereby avoiding unnecessary cracks.

Glazes or slips were applied before a second firing, again at 1140°C (2084°F) with a 20-minute soak. This procedure may be repeated a third time if adjustments to the final colour are required. A fourth lustre firing is carried out on some work. Rodgers emphasises that this repeat firing regime strengthens the work, in the same way that a higher firing would, but without distortion.

Rodgers' reputation is such that she has accepted invitations to exhibit in galleries in the UK, France, USA and the Far East. In addition, she finds time to run workshops in schools and colleges in the UK.

The Tower; *Forward 11*; *Orbit*: these are the titles of **Deirdre Hawthorne**'s trademark cylindrical beakers, which are as high as they are wide. But in this work they are pierced by metal tacks and staples, as well as imprinted with textures (see below). She acknowledges that these techniques push the clay almost to the point of destruction, making it fragile but revealing its inherent resilience. As with all her pots, they are fired in a sealed saggar to 1090°C (1994°F), and this time banana skins provided the combustible material.

You can find out more about Hawthorne's pots in Chapter 4 (p. 62–63).

Deirdre Hawthorne, *The Tower* and *Forward II*, 2010. Slab-built earthenware with tacks. Fired to 1090°C (1994°F) in an enclosed saggar with banana skins, 13 cm x 13 cm (5 x 5 in) and 11 x 10 cm (4¼ x 4 in). *Photo: Leon Coole.*

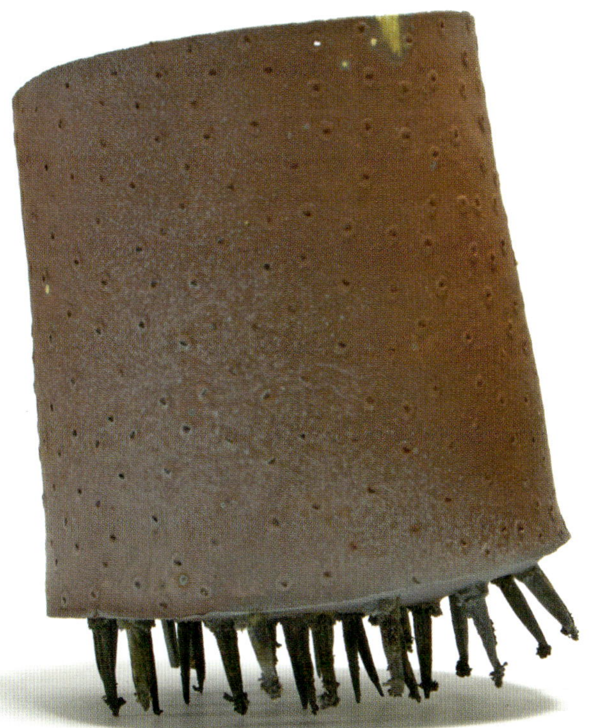

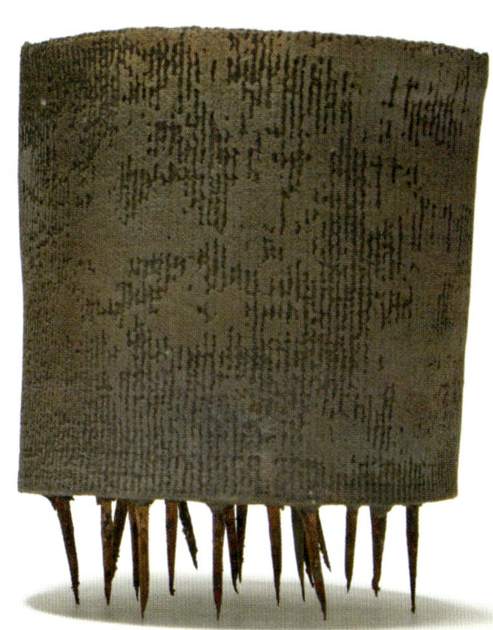

US artist **Todd Shanafelt** admits to a love–hate relationship with the ceramic medium. His 'solution' is to work fast: thrown vessels, metal armatures and extensions, and found objects are the components he frequently uses to construct his assemblages.

The creative process is often started by rummaging through his collection of metal objects in search of a suitable armature to support Egyptian paste, as shown in the piece titled *Cedure Tube* (opposite). Sometimes cutting and welding is employed until he has created an interesting volumetric form to fill.

These metals, including stainless steel rod, wire and mesh, do not burn away in kiln firings at 1177°C (2150°F). Shanafelt uses the wire as if it is a line drawing and enjoys the freedom it gives him to 'extend' the edges of his forms. To make sure the Egyptian paste doesn't ooze out, or fall out of the armatures, he will use some metal mesh inside the armatures to hold it in place until it dries and is fired.

The metal structures have a visual appeal as well as a practical one. 'I'm very attracted to the wire/metal mesh/screen pattern that is left after the firing on the Egyptian paste,' Shanafelt says, 'especially how it is reduced to just lines.'

Most vessels are thrown on a potters' wheel, which enables Shanafelt to make 'quick and intimate parts'. But to Shanafelt, the vessel, and its connection with a utilitarian function, provides him with a blank canvas to explore topics of interest to him: 'ongoing relationships found in everyday life, from environmental, political to societal shifts and changes occurring in our world today'. His complex work explores a complex world!

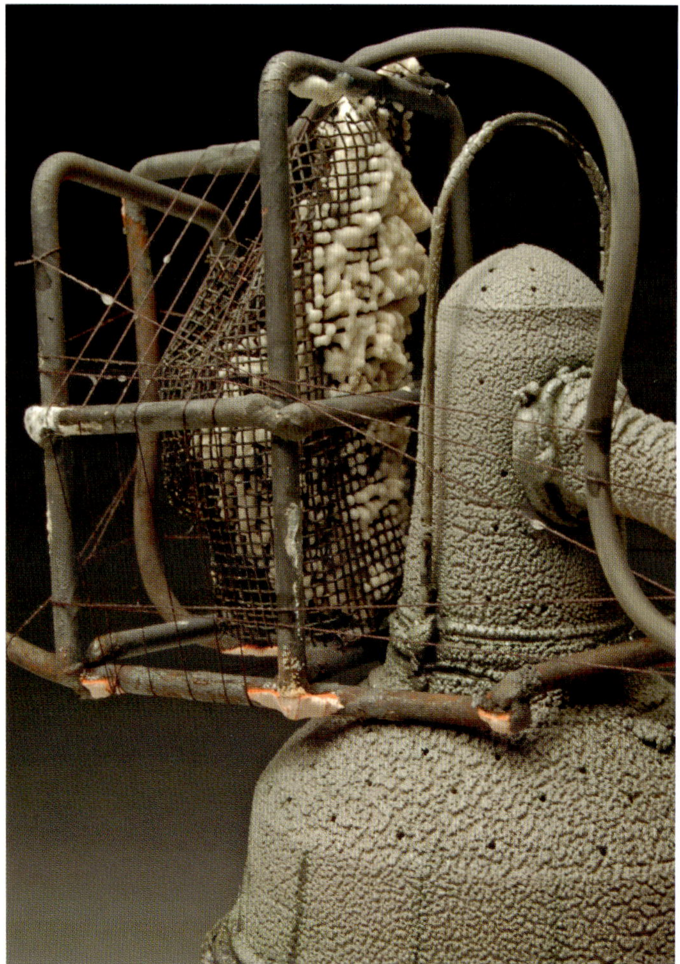

Todd Shanafelt, *Cedure Tube*, 2009. Thrown earthenware, metal, Egyptian paste, ceramic decal, found materials, rubber, tile, sprayed glaze, fired to 1177°C (2150°F), 22 x 30 x 17 cm (8½ x 11¾ x 6¾ in). *Photo: by the artist.*

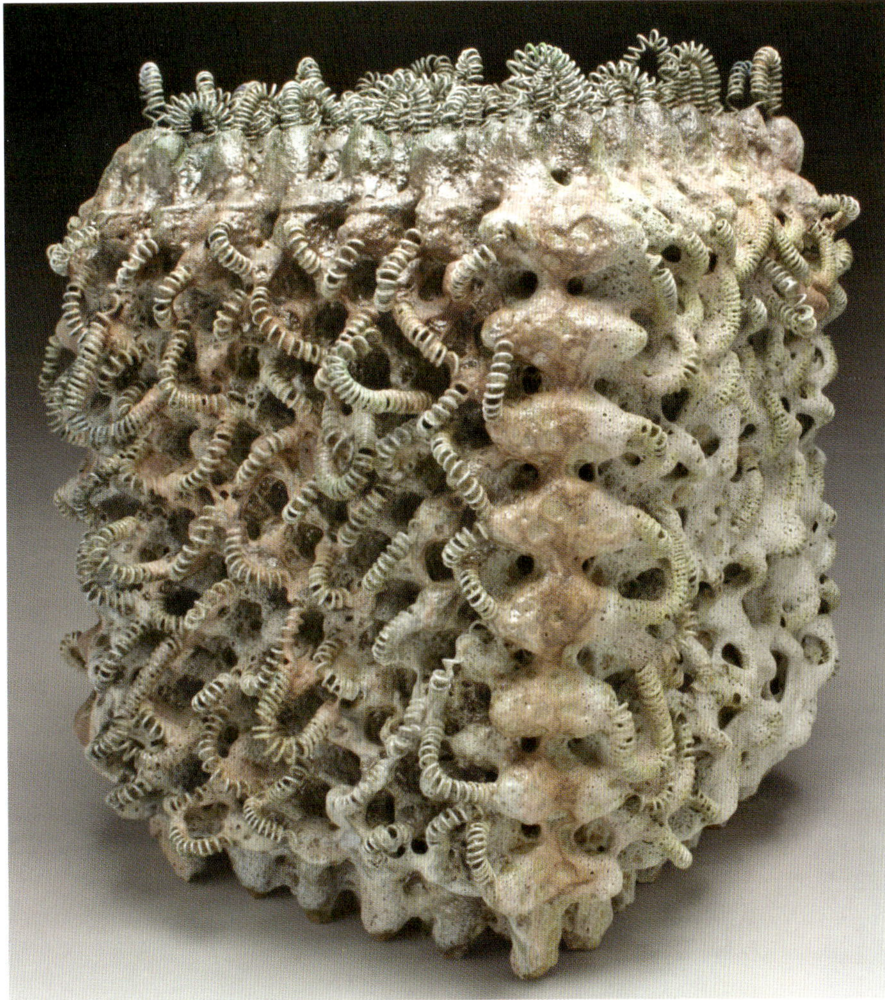

Todd Leech, *Hostile*, 2009. Press-moulded and slab-built, with drilled holes into which kiln elements are inserted. Silicon carbide glaze with stains, fired in reduction to 1282°C (2340°F), 43 x 40.5 cm (17 x 16 in). *Photo: by the artist.*

Todd Leech is another US artist who seeks to address universal themes: time, mortality and disintegration are the issues on his agenda.

The starting point for most forms is a geometric shape to represent the human body. Leech describes the next stages in metaphors: injuring the clay by drilling holes whilst leatherhard; inserting sutures in the form of recycled kiln elements; applying specially formulated glazes that reach and spread across these wounds, replicating human tissue regeneration. He says, 'I am endlessly fascinated and inspired by the body's ability to repair itself.'

Slab-built, press-moulded and sometimes wheel-thrown components are joined together to construct the chosen shapes. When the clay is leatherhard, Leech repeatedly punctures and cuts the surface and recycled kiln elements are inserted in some of the holes. Specially formulated foaming glazes are then applied, which cover clay and metal and seep into the cavities. Leech says that a reduction firing to 1282°C (2340°F) produces the best results, as the foaming of the glazes is most

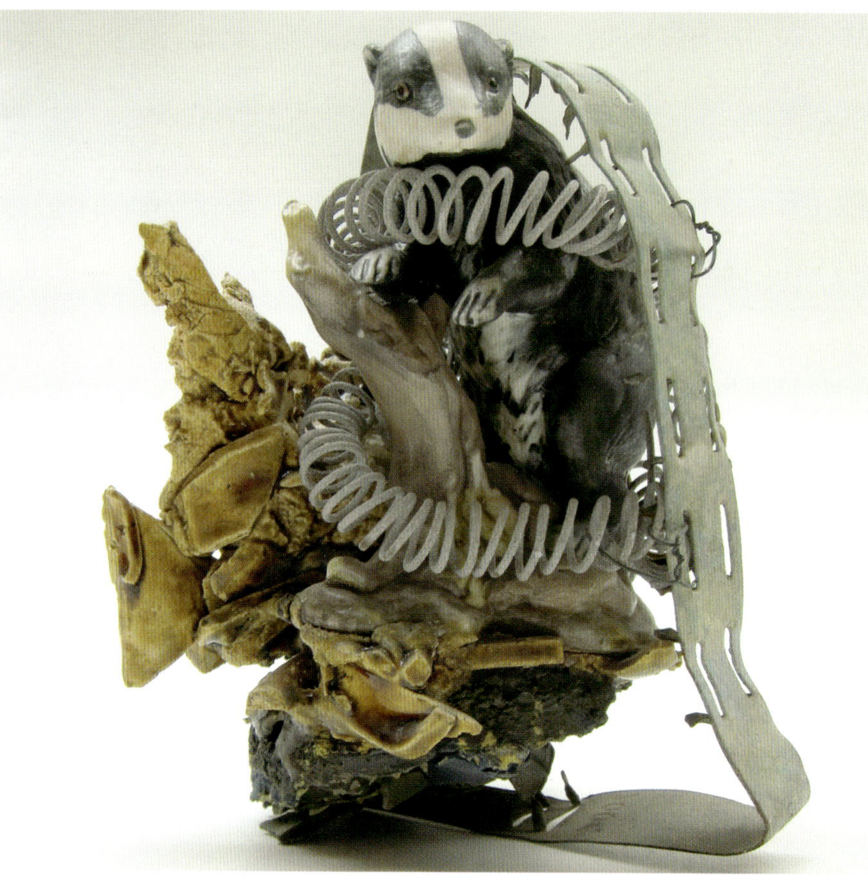

Robert Cooper, *Badgered*, 2011. Clay grog made from historical fragments put into the mix; glass bits balanced to melt, kiln elements fused in and glazed, 18 x 13 cm (7 x 5 in). In the collection of the Mint Museum, Charlotte, North Carolina. *Photo: by the artist.*

impressive. About 50 per cent of the work is also sand-blasted to reveal some of this underlying structure.

Leech works from his studio in Cleveland, Ohio, which is situated in a former meat-processing plant. There seems to be an interesting connection between this former use of the building and Leech's interest in mortality. His work is innovative and experimental, and demonstrates the many possibilities of metal additions.

Badgered is part of a series of sculptures about survival, created by UK artist **Robert Cooper**. He describes his work as being on the same track as that of Neil Brownsword, who gives new life to old industrial pottery elements.

These 'collages' consist of discards from other ceramic practices, used kiln elements, bric-a-brac pieces from charity shops and chance finds on beaches and estuaries. Clay, glaze and metal amalgamations are fired to stoneware temperatures, followed by multiple lower-temperature firings to fuse glass, glaze enamels and lustres. Parts that cannot be fired are wired on to complete the piece. Through Cooper's wonderful imagination, these components have a new life.

Cooper has inspired generations of students during his long teaching career (including me) and continues to teach at the City Lit Institute, London. He is also in demand as a visiting lecturer at several colleges in the UK, including the Royal College of Art, London.

Wiring up the clay – performance art

Ceramicists are not strangers to hazardous materials. Almost everything we use comes with a warning symbol, accompanied by a list of do's and don'ts. But **Andy Glass** takes risk to a different place altogether! As a qualified pyrotechnician (and electrician), Glass is suitably equipped to carry out 'live firings' in front of an invited audience. He advises that this is not something 'to have a go at' in your own studio!

During his firing events (which were part of the exhibition *Points in Time*), large coiled pots steamed like mini volcanoes; peeling layers of clay tumbled to the floor, and debris and detritus were scattered everywhere. Sadly I was not there to witness this performance, but he tells me with pride that the audience was transfixed.

Points in Time was the name of the exhibition hosted by the Bracknell Gallery at South Hill Park Arts Centre in November 2003. This event, together with other gallery works, was the culmination of a two-year residency at the centre.

So how did Glass come up with this notion of creating performance art by firing clay pots in situ and inviting an audience to watch? Test tiles of various mixtures of Egyptian paste, left sitting on a work bench, were the trigger. Over a couple of weeks, they started to fall apart (similar to lime spit) and this was the impetus for Glass to create work that disintegrated while he maintained control.

Construction and firing

The huge pots or sculptures were coiled by hand using basic school clay and 'quick match' fuse wire was placed in between the coils (coloured red in the image, see overleaf). This wire burns when it heats up.

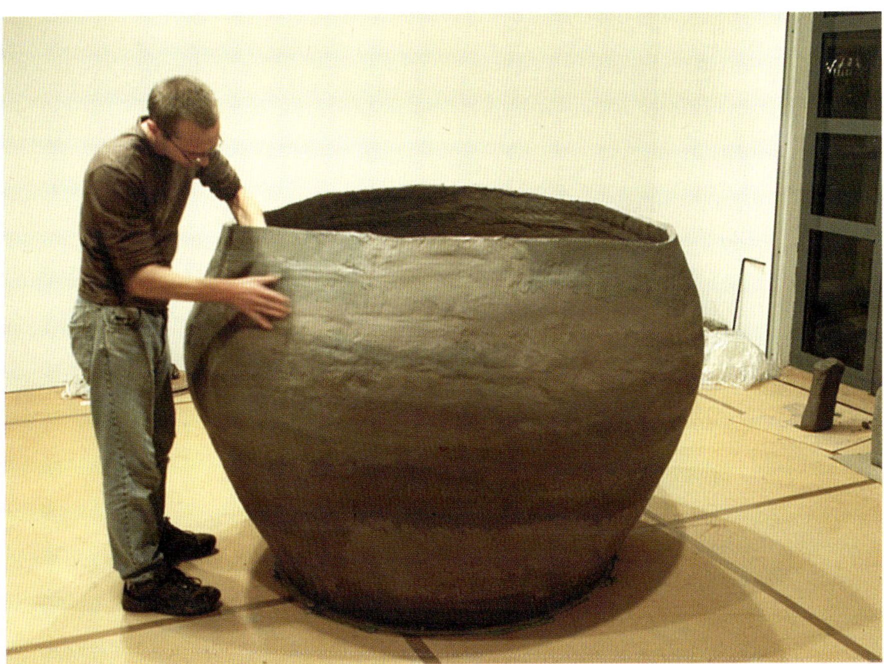

Andy Glass coiling the pots in the gallery. *Photo: by the artist.*

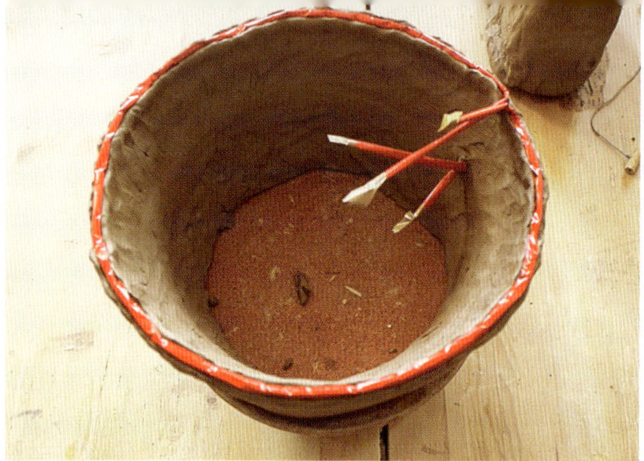

'Quick match' fuses (red) are buried between the coils.

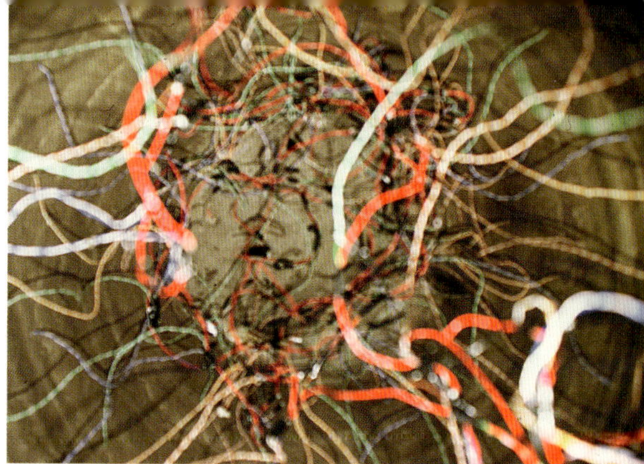

A network of igniter wires (recycled telephone wires) are connected up with the quick match fuses.

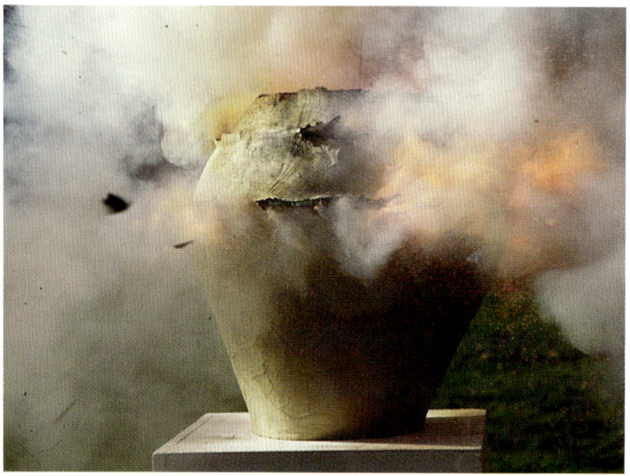

The pot is placed outside and the electricity switched on using a battery.

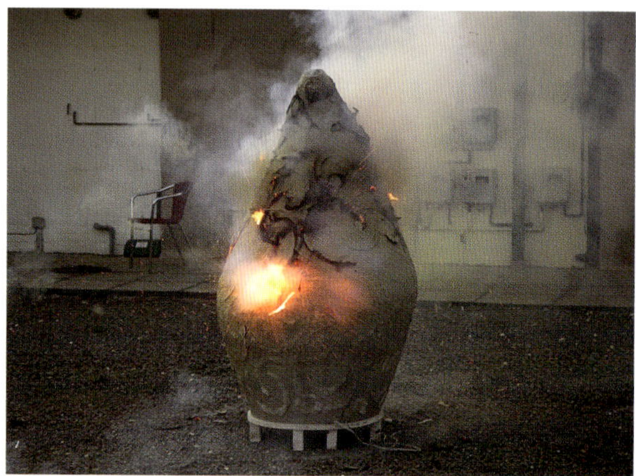

The fuses burn a pattern in the clay. *Photos: by the artist.*

The image showing wires inside the pot (above) illustrates the network of igniter wires (actually recycled telephone cable), each one leading to an area of 'quick match'. The igniter wires were then connected to a battery so that pots could be set off remotely in front of an audience. This decision was made for safety reasons.

The arrangement of wires enabled Glass to control the firing process, with different areas being ignited at different times, which in turn created a pattern on the surface of the pot. White slip was painted on the outside of each piece so that, when the pattern burnt through, it contrasted with the clay underneath (see opposite).

The pots were made in the gallery space during the exhibition and moved outside to be 'fired', then replaced in the gallery for the remainder of the exhibition. Several other performance events took place both inside and outside the gallery.

Glass calls himself a scientist and an artist, and informing the public about what he does with clay is a subject he pursues with passion. The alchemy of our chosen medium is one way of engaging people in art. Glass's early work involved throwing pots and firing them in a wood-fired anagama kiln. He says that trying to interest people in lumps of brown pottery was an uphill struggle, so he hopes to continue with live firings, this time using Egyptian paste.

RIGHT: The firing is complete and the pattern of buried wires revealed. *Photo: by the artist.*

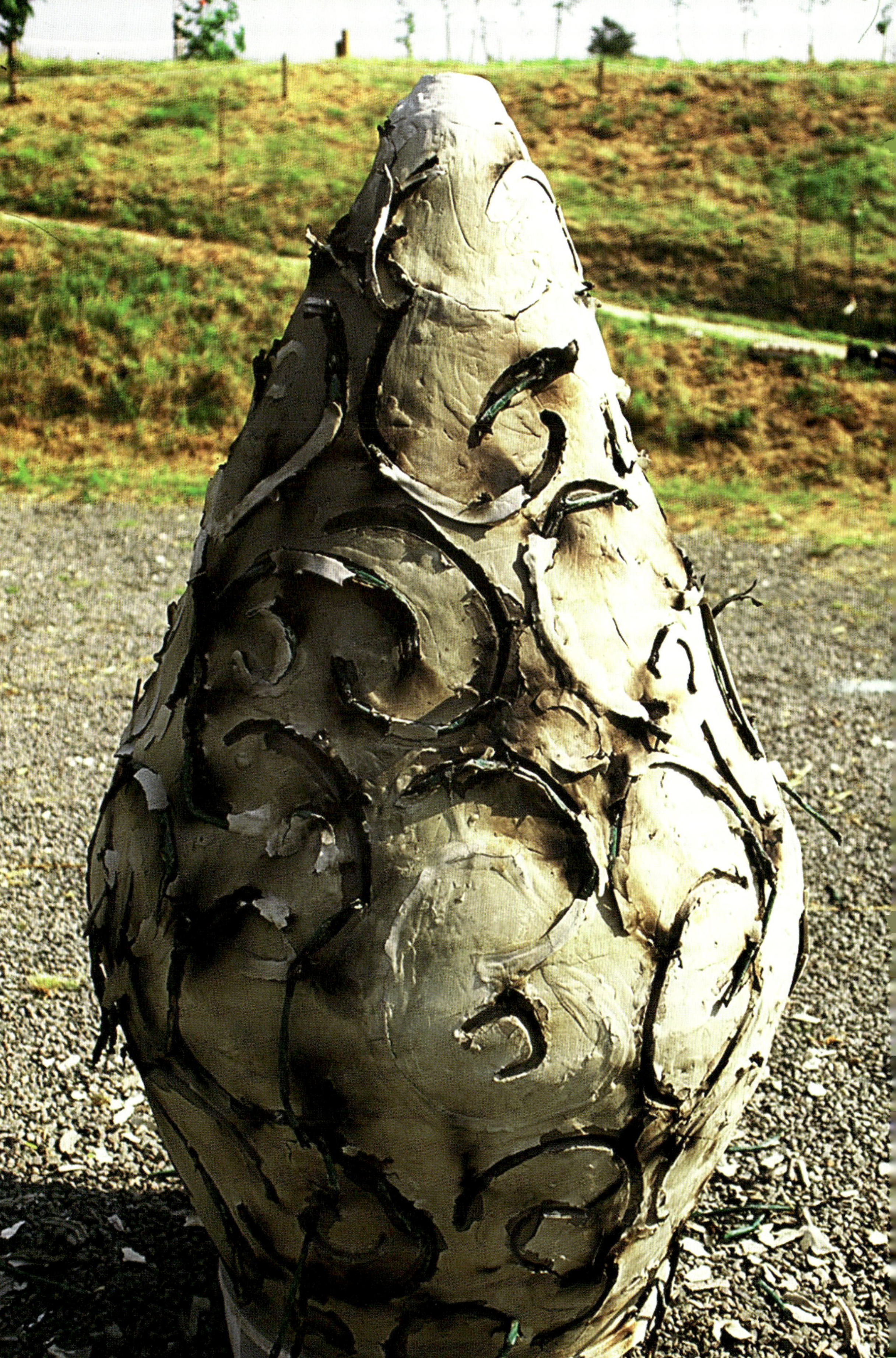

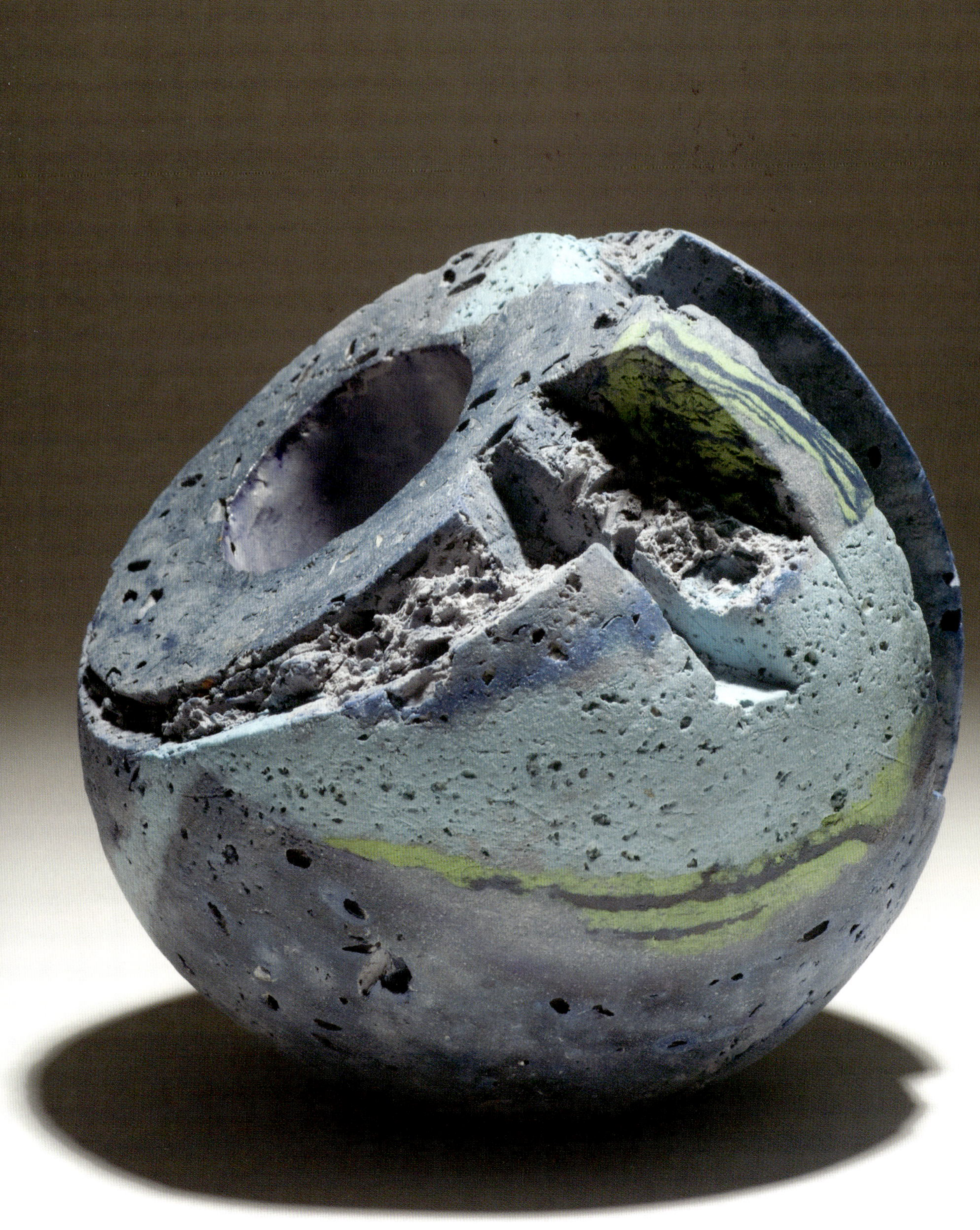

7 Colour

Many of the artists in this book add colour to their clay, as well as a variety of other additions. I asked six of them to describe the procedures they follow and the colouring materials they use.

A broad range of techniques is covered: I measure and mix all my materials in the dry state, as does Barbro Åberg, whereas Fred Gatley makes a wet, coloured slip that he adds to the plastic body; Liz Emtage and Paul Payne use colour sparingly, ensuring that translucency of the clay body is maintained; and American artists Deborah Sigel and Todd Shanafelt both make low-firing Egyptian paste in several colours.

Of course, clay has its own distinctive colour, which in turn is related to the temperature to which it is fired. Whilst looking through the clay section of a pottery supplier's website or catalogue, you will come across a wide range of clay bodies. Each one will contain technical information but also a description of the colour and usually an image of a fired sample. Typically, the colour range will include white, cream, buff, grey, many reds and browns, and black. But there are times when a different colour palette is desired and that is the situation I found myself in. One test has led to another and over a period of time I have collected an exciting array of coloured clays.

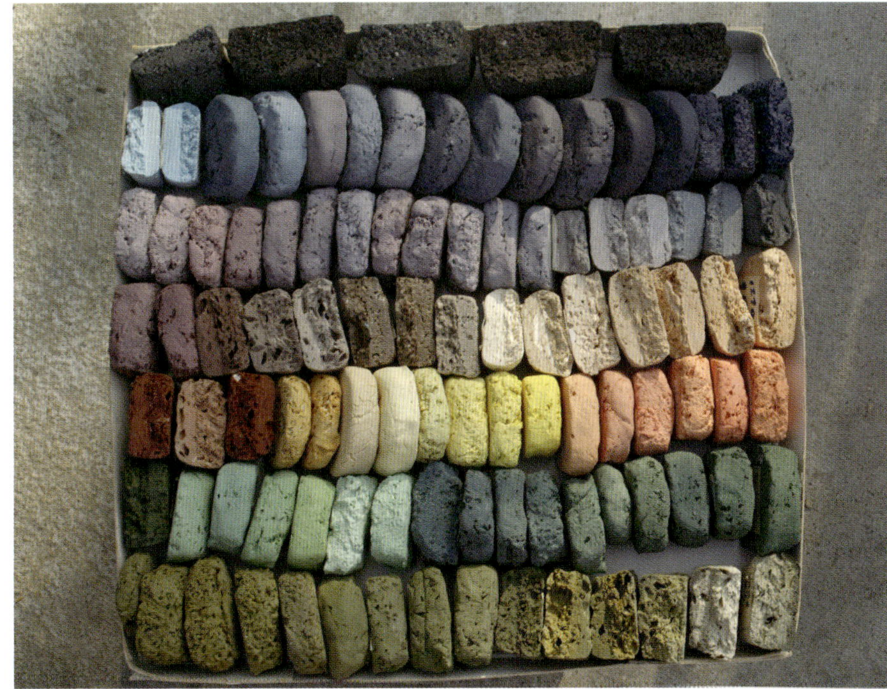

LEFT: Kathleen Standen, *Two Blues Rock Pool*, 2009. Porcelain clay body, organic additions, body stains and oxides, glaze, 15 x 16 cm (6 x 6¼ in). *Photo: Roland Paschhoff.*

RIGHT: A selection of colour testers fired to 1220°C (2228°F). *Photo: Kathleen Standen.*

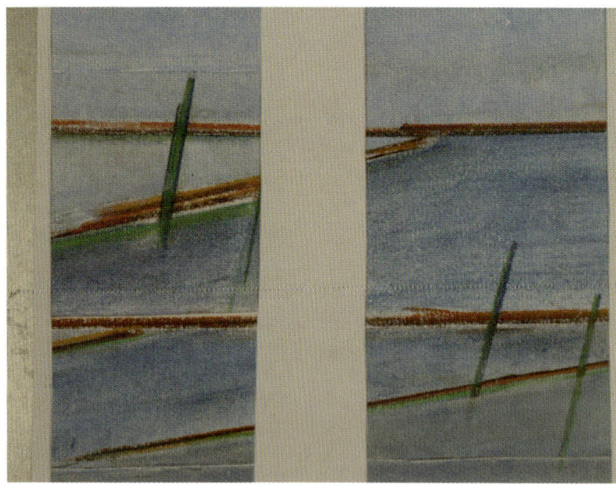

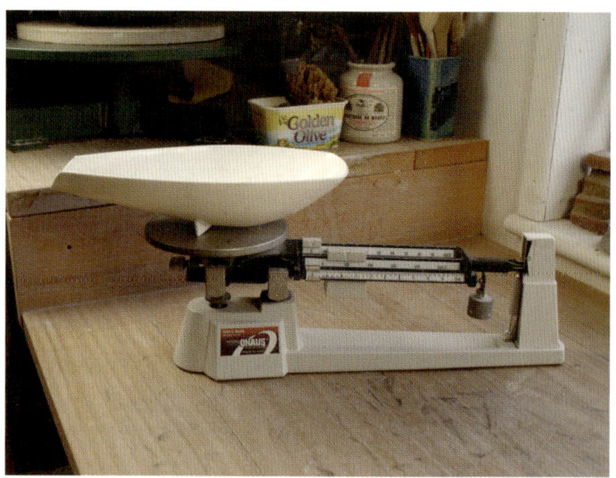

ABOVE, LEFT: Explorations of colour and pattern.

ABOVE RIGHT: I use a beam balance because it allows me to weigh small amounts very accurately, which is very useful if you test glazes and colours for clay making. *Photos: Kathleen Standen.*

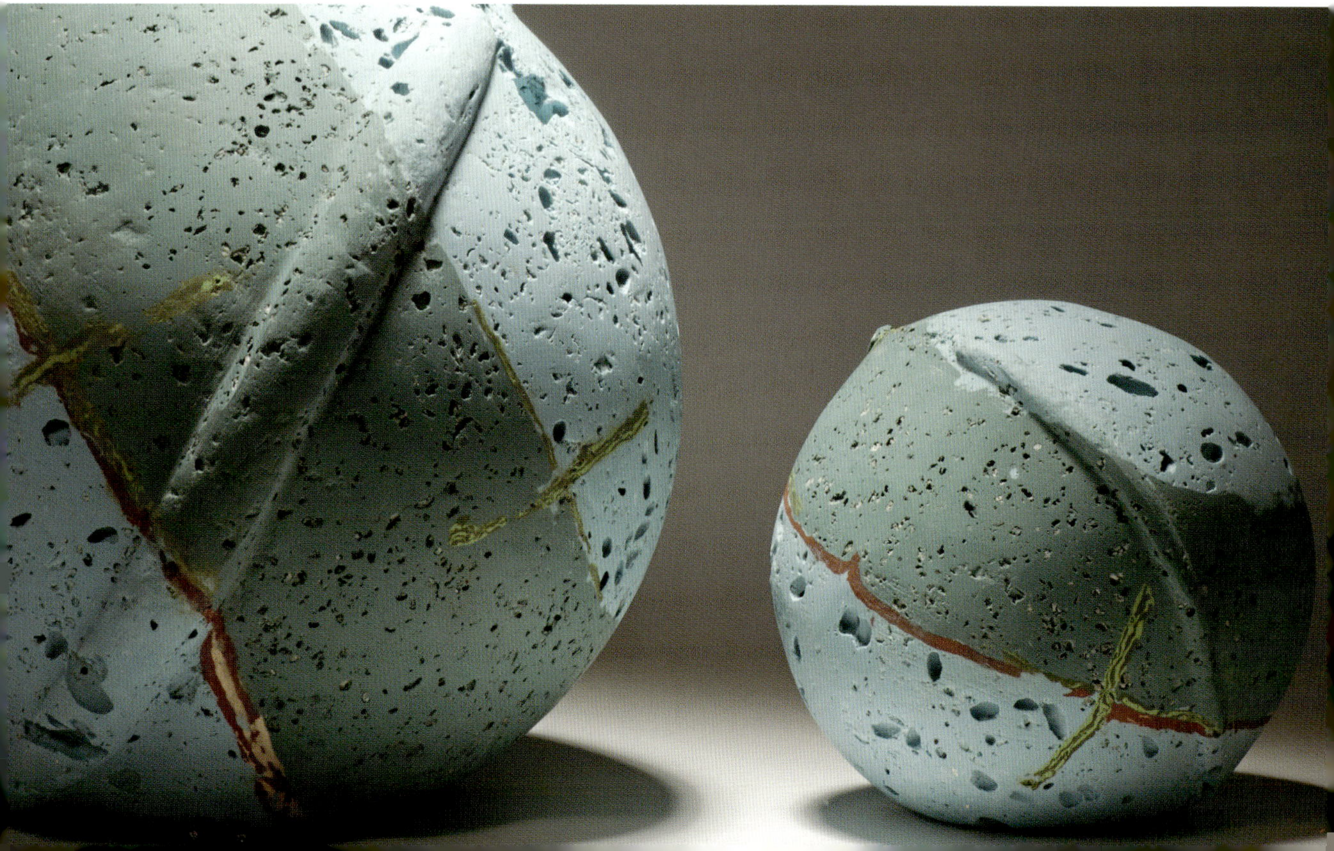

The search for colours to represent the experience of living by the coast of Ireland has been the driving force behind my colour tests. Before I carry out tests in the studio, I thoroughly research the colours that interest me: for example, I frequently take photographs of the same view, capturing variations in light and charting the changing seasons, and on visits to art galleries I can research artists and 'see' through their eyes. Colour and pattern are then explored in my sketch book. There are more examples of colour studies in Chapter 3 (p. 54).

All my colouring additions are added as dry weight to the base clay mixture. The details of how I do this are described in Chapter 1 (p. 22). I always wear gloves and a mask when handling dry materials.

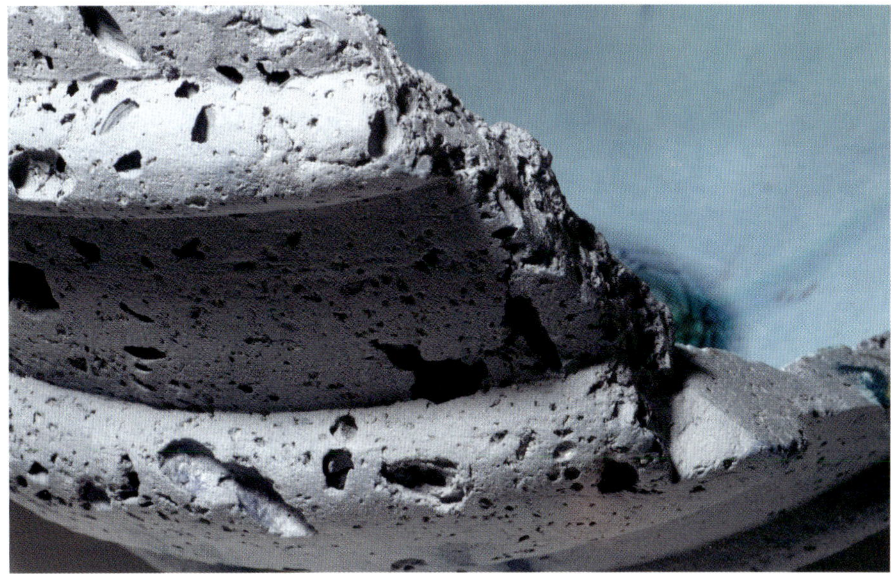

Detail of *Haze*: this colour was made by mixing cobalt oxide with red body stain. *Photo: Roland Paschhoff.*

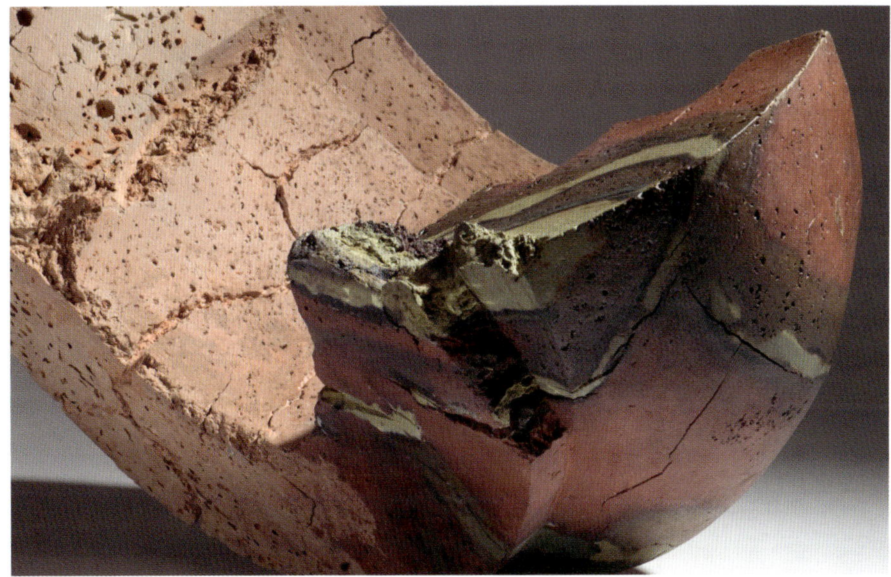

RIGHT: Kathleen Standen, *Earthform I*, 2008. Porcelain clay with organic additions and oxides: iron oxide, vanadium pentoxide, rutile, chromium dioxide. Also yellow body stain and black clay, 36 x 54 x 37 cm (14¼ x 21¼ x 14½ in). *Photo: Roland Paschhoff.*

LEFT: Kathleen Standen, *Shoreline 1 and 2*, 2011. Porcelain clay, organic materials, body stains and oxides: blended blue and green for blues; blended blue and yellow for green; iron oxide for brown; rutile for cream; chromium for green, 21 x 21 cm (8¼ x 8¼ in) and 12 x 12 cm (4¾ x 4¾ in). *Photo: Roland Paschhoff.*

I test varying percentages of body stains and oxides. I also blend one or more combinations of colouring materials: red and yellow body stains to achieve oranges; red body stain with cobalt oxide for purples; manganese dioxide, cobalt oxide and copper carbonate for blues. Several tests involve quite small differences in percentages. Each set of tests acts as a springboard for the next batch.

One essential tool is my weighing scales, which allow me to measure very small percentages of colouring materials with great accuracy. Digital weighing scales cannot do this, so larger samples must be weighed and then divided up by eye rather than weight.

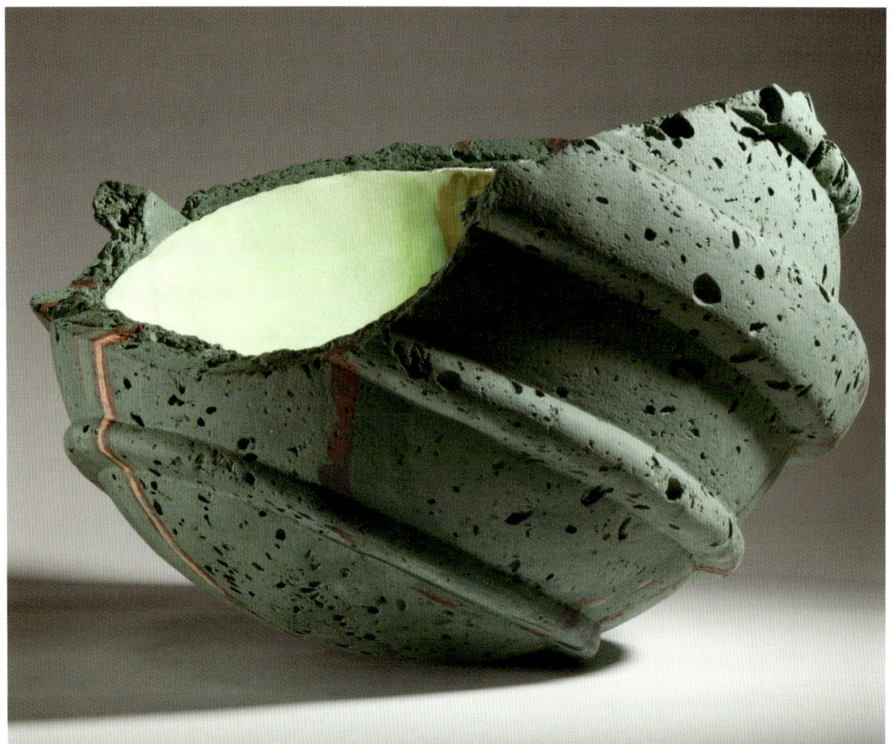

Kathleen Standen, *Landfall*, 2011. Porcelain clay body, organic additions, oxides and body stains, glaze, 40 x 36 cm (15¾ x 14¼ in). *Photo: Roland Paschhoff.*

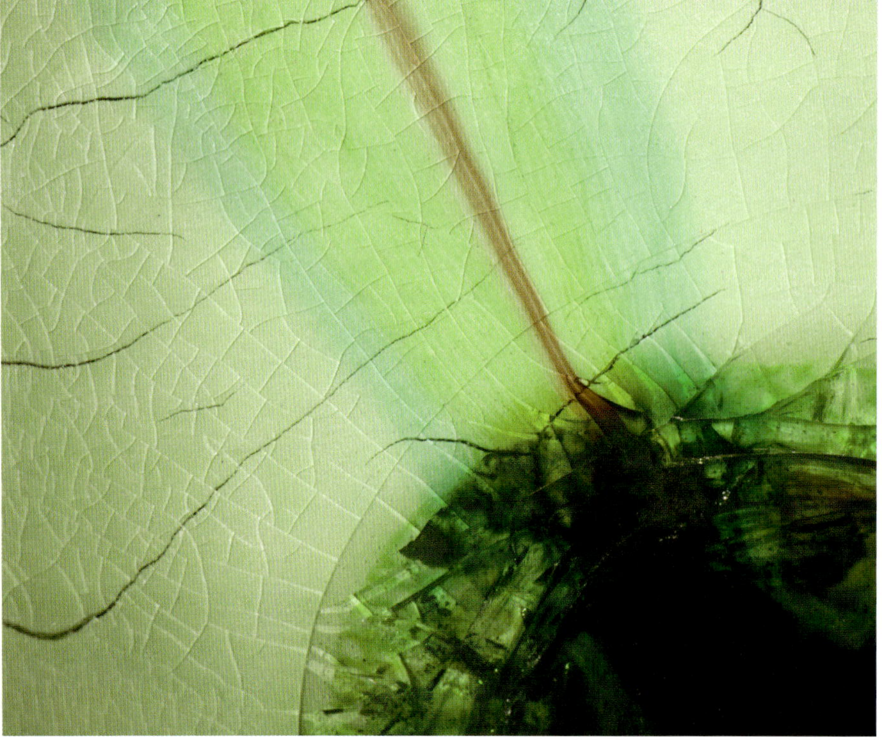

Kathleen Standen, *Landfall* (detail), 2011. Porcelain clay body, organic additions, oxides and body stains, glaze, 40 x 36 cm (15¾ x 14¼ in). *Photo: Roland Paschhoff.*

Barbro Åberg – monochromatic sculptures

White is the predominant colour of Barbro Åberg's work (see also Chapter 5, pp. 77–78). She finds that making work in monochrome enables her to focus on form and expression and the resulting work is simpler and stronger. Even when she deviates from white, as in *Organic Brown Vessel* (below), the use of a single colour demonstrates this principle successfully.

Iron oxide and clay are measured and mixed in a dry state, before adding sufficient water to form a thick slip. Additions such as perlite and paper fibres are then added and the resulting clay mix is allowed to firm up. Åberg models the form by hand on top of a plaster mould, then turns it over and continues the process. Adjustments to the colour are also made by brushing on iron oxide and sometimes body stains. All work is fired at approximately 1140°C (2084°F).

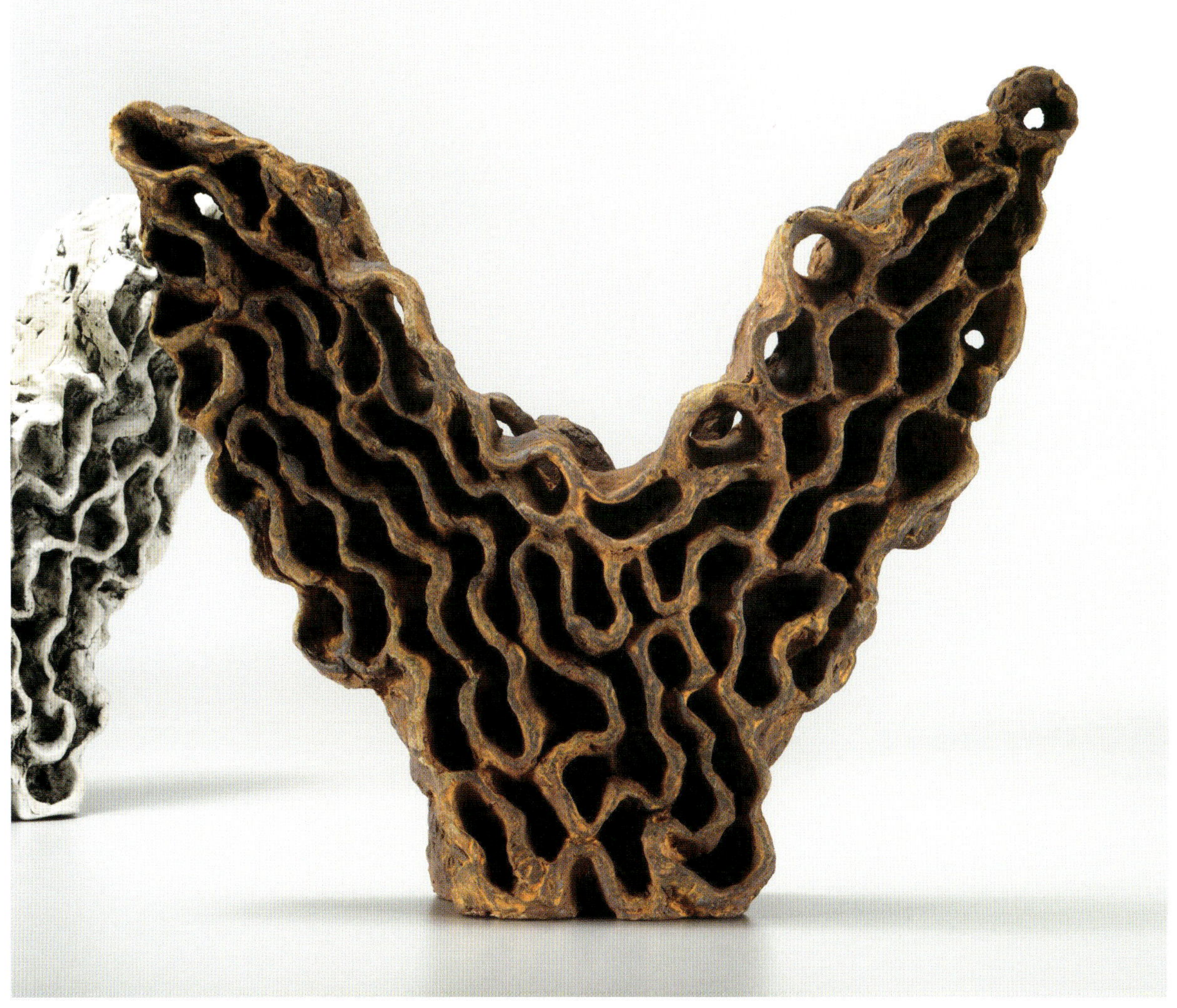

Barbro Åberg, *Brown Organic Vessel*, 2010. Clay with perlite, paper fibres and iron oxide, 23 x 27 x 7 cm (9 x 10½ x 2¾ in). *Photo: Lars Henrik Mardahl.*

Fred Gatley – earth colours, with one exception

Fred Gatley's ceramics typically display a subtle range of earth colours, together with black and white. Most of his vessels are white with subtle earth colour inclusions. But occasionally Gatley departs from his colour range, as shown in this blue porcelain bowl, made especially for his wife Lizzy.

Mixing in the colour

The method used by Gatley is to add colour to the plastic clay. He makes the assumption that 40% of the clay body is water, so 140g (5 oz) weighed out should be 100g (3½ oz) dry clay and 40g (1½ oz) water. The water percentage is only a guideline and will vary slightly for specific batches of body and different manufacturers.

His technique is to measure out the appropriate amount of both stain and clay by weight, then mix the stain in a small amount of water, sufficient to make it as liquid as milk. A small amount of the clay body is added to this slurry and the two are thoroughly mixed. This mix may be further thinned to the consistency of thin single cream and then passed first through a 100-mesh sieve and finally a 200-mesh sieve. If you have access to a liquidiser or hand mixer, it may help at this point.

If the stained body isn't needed in liquid form, this mixture can be poured onto a clean plaster slab to absorb most of the water. As this is happening, the remaining clay can be introduced and the two thoroughly wedged together. If you require a stained slip, simply add all the clay and blend together with sufficient water to form a liquid.

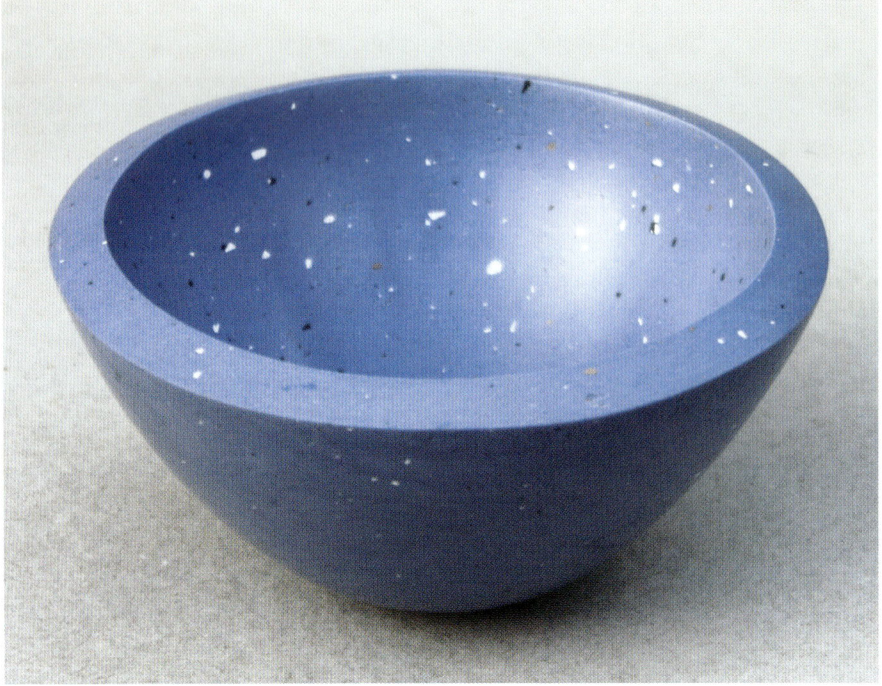

Fred Gatley, *Blue Bowl*, 2004. Polished blue porcelain bowl with black, dark blue and pink grogs. Formed by jiggering and fired to 1220°C (2228°F), 9 x 12 cm (3½ x 4¾ in). *Photo: by the artist.*

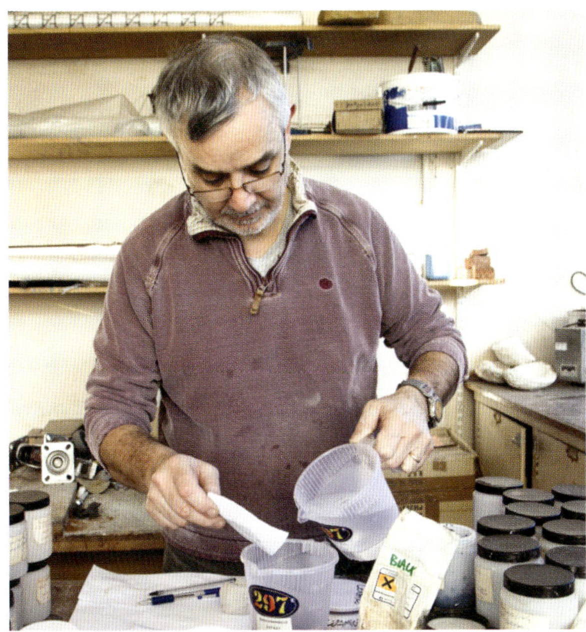

Combining the weighed body stain with the water and a small amount of the clay body.

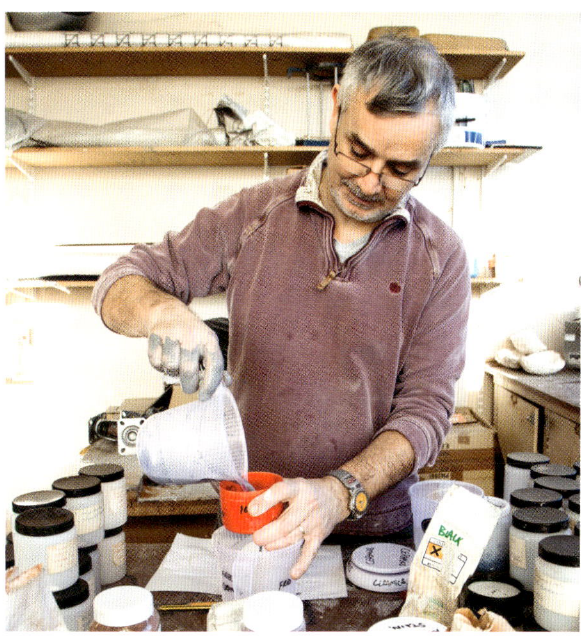

After mixing with a blending wand or by hand, this concentrated slurry is pushed through the first 100-mesh sieve. This is repeated with a 200-mesh sieve.

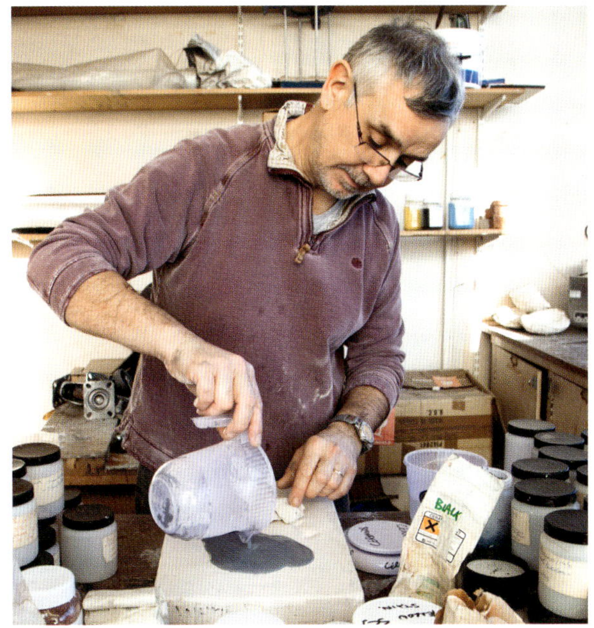

Pouring the concentrate onto a clean plaster slab.

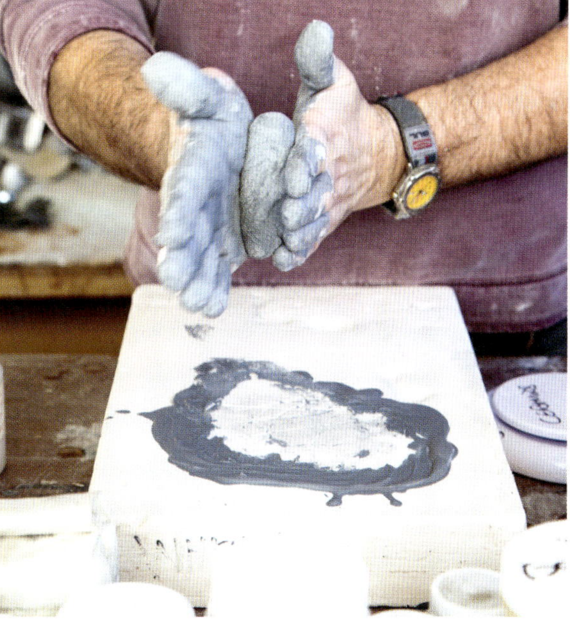

Combining the main body with the concentrate. This is a 6% mix, which is 6g of black body stain added to 140g (5 oz) of plastic bone china. (140g/5 oz plastic clay is approx. 100g/3½ oz dry weight clay). *Photos: Lisa Rigolli.*

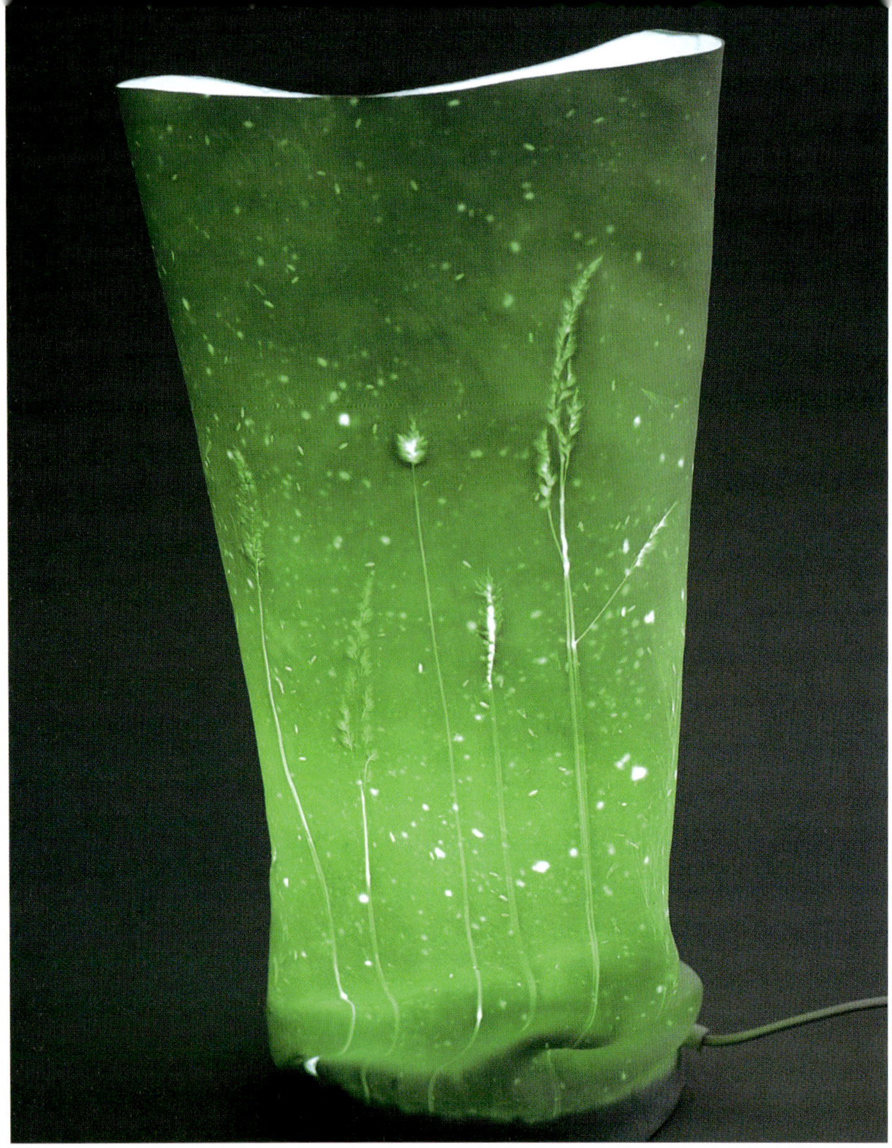

Liz Emtage, *Extra-large Aqua Grasses lamp*, 2005. Extra-large porcelain lamp inlaid with grasses, green body stain mixed into the clay, 54 x 20 cm (21¼ x 7¾ in). *Photo: Sussie Ahlburg.*

Liz Emtage – body stains and paperclay

The intense green colour of Liz Emtage's *Aqua lamp* comes alive when it is switched on, although it is still subtly discernible when switched off. Green body stain was mixed into porcelain paperclay. Emtage carries out tests using different percentages of colour until the right shade is obtained.

Her *Extra-large Aqua Grasses lamp* is just that, at a height of 54 cm (21¼ in). It has been inlaid with different grasses, which have burned out in the firing. You can see more of Emtage's work in Chapters 3 (p. 50) and 5 (pp. 81–83).

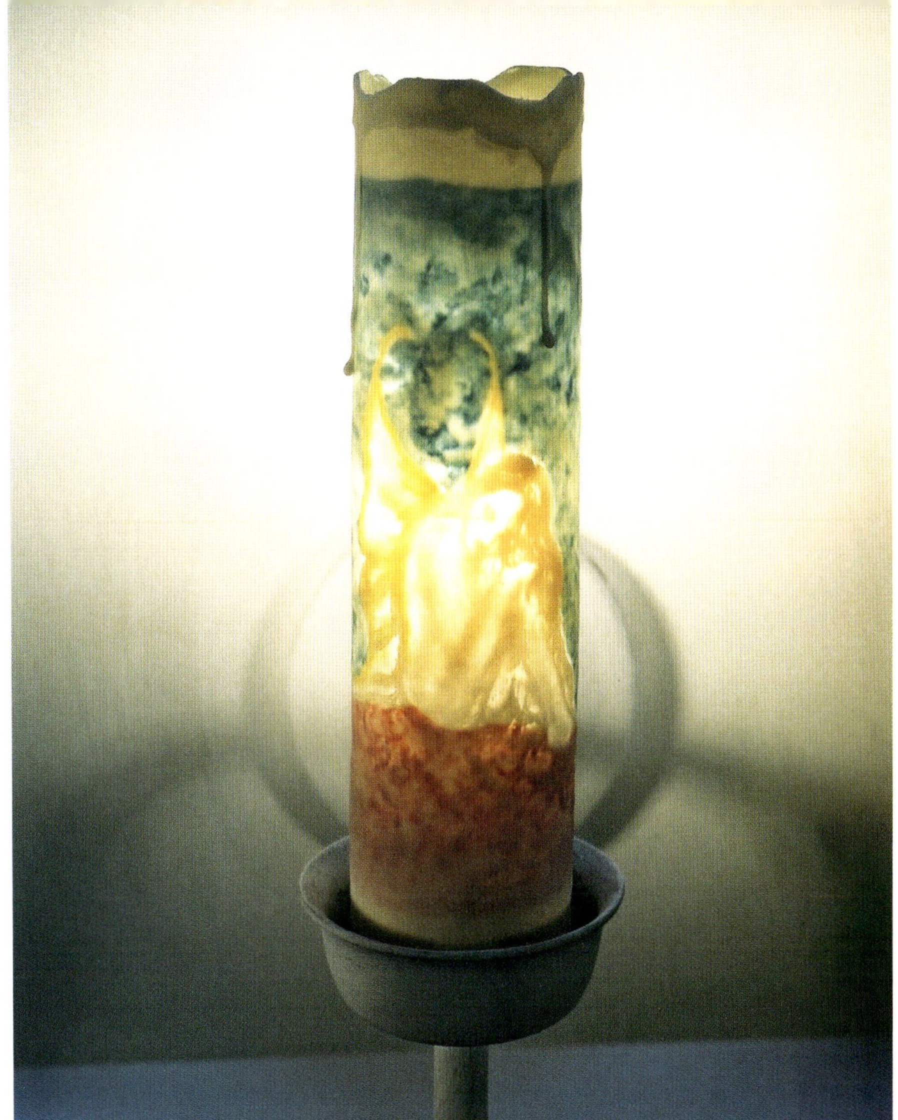

Paul Payne, coloured lamp, 2010. Porcelain casting slip, fibreglass and oxides, 12.5 x 4.5 cm (5 x 1¾ in). *Photo: by the artist.*

Paul Payne – oxides with porcelain and glass fibre

Paul Payne's coloured lamp, shown above, is a good example of a coloured translucent light. Payne created the piece using laminates of porcelain casting slip, glass fibre and oxides. A wash of oxide was selectively brushed onto one laminated layer of glass fibre and slip, before the next one was added and the process repeated using contrasting colours.

Once the different elements of form and colour have been incorporated into four or five layers and laminated together, they are biscuit-fired to 1000°C (1832°F). A semi-matt glaze is brushed onto the structure before a final firing at 1260°C (2300°F).

Payne says that he mainly learns from trial and error how much of each oxide to use. Too much and the porcelain loses its translucency, but too little and the colours are insipid. He has experienced other problems when using certain oxides, such as bloating and blistering, and was advised by Nigel Wood at the Royal College of Art in

London that the likely cause was a reaction between the colouring oxide and silica in the glass fibre, due to excessive fluxing. Experience has helped him to select the safer oxides. You can read more about Payne's work in Chapter 5 (pp. 87–91).

Deborah Sigel – large sculptures of coloured Egyptian paste

Deborah Sigel has been using Egyptian paste for over 20 years. She still uses one of the original recipes she got her hands on as a young artist to create large sculptures of colourful flower forms. Over the years she has made small adjustments to the formula to address problems with post-firing surface **scumming**. This was corrected by decreasing the amount of soluble salts in the recipe.

The process starts with dry weighing everything, followed by dry mixing, then adding enough water so that it can be wedged together well. Cobalt carbonate and chrome oxide are added to the basic recipe to make blue and green. Body stains are also used to extend the colour range. The amount of stain varies depending on the intensity of the desired colour and even in some cases the melting point of the colourant or stain.

Sigel is known for her large-scale sculptures, comprising several flower forms. 'For years I mixed everything by hand, even sixty-pound quantities for larger pieces,' she says. 'I now have a baby Bluebird mixer, which has made the process much less laborious.'

Deborah Sigel, *Flowers*, 2009. Egyptian paste and steel, fired to Cone 05. Each flower is 48 x 12 cm (19 x 4¾ in). This is part of a large wall display measuring 1.27 x 7.56 x 0.12 m (4.16 x 24 x 2.5 ft). *Photo: Otto.*

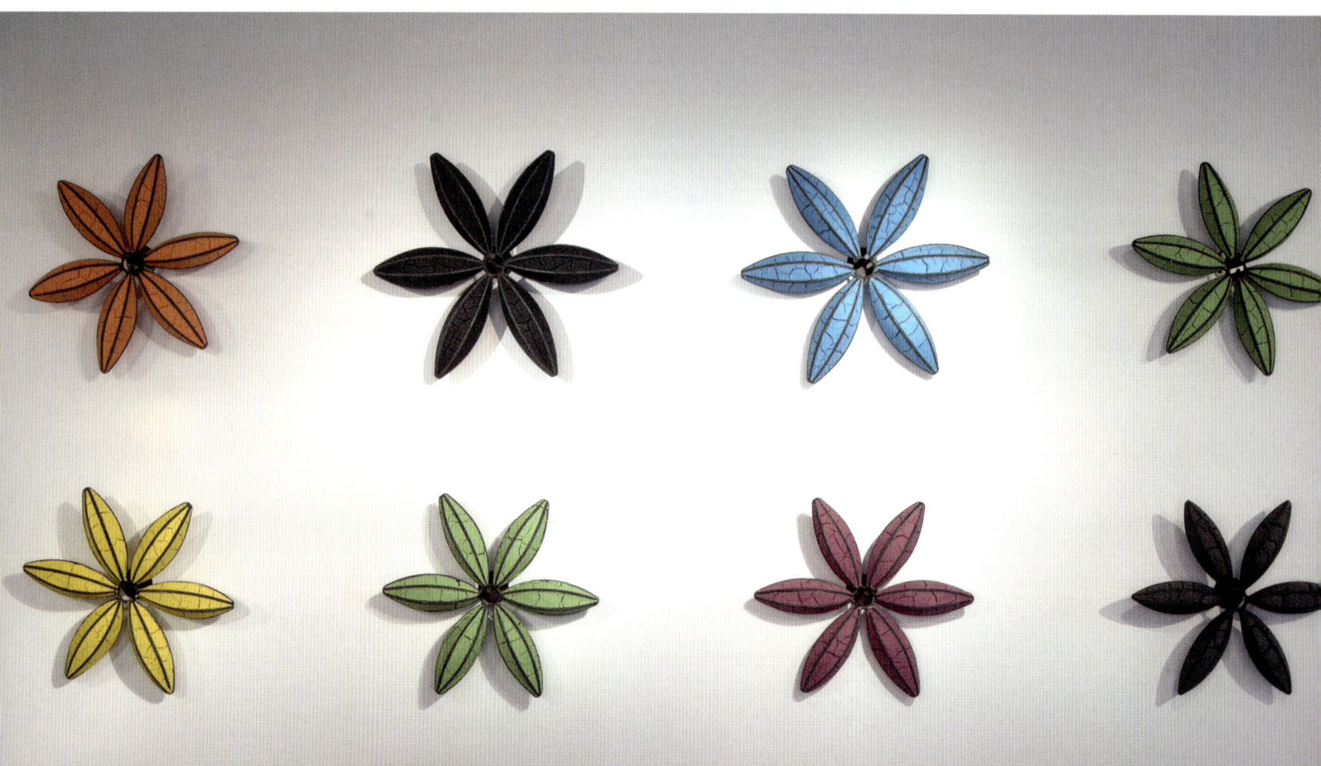

Todd Shanafelt – coloured Egyptian paste

Todd Shanafelt used coloured Egyptian paste in the piece *Fiets sap.* He says that the colour makes it look somewhat like an edible item, as well as industrial: 'I liked the contradiction and juxtaposition that happened through all the materials employed.'

Process

Waterproof gloves are used for making the paste and filling the armature. Shanafelt mixes the Egyptian paste with very little water in a bucket until it is slightly thicker than thick yoghurt. Colour is introduced in the form of stains or oxides in varying percentages, adding up to 10% for a bold colour or as little as 2% to the Egyptian paste base if softer tones are needed. This mixture is then spread onto a plaster batt to firm it up slightly (allowing the plaster to absorb some of the water). The coloured mix is then packed into the armature structure. The work is fired in an electric kiln to Cone 03.

Shanafelt is also excited about post-firing changes in Egyptian paste. He describes it as the development of 'faded, fuzzy, salty surfaces'. This is what Deborah Sigel calls 'scumming', and has taken steps to avoid. It is always interesting that each artist seeks a different and particular outcome.

Once fired, the piece was attached to a ceramic tile that, in turn, was mounted onto the wall. The 'feet' attached to the bottom of the tile are actually metal legs from an old, worn out electric kiln. 'I was interested in having the piece protrude out from the wall,' says Shanafelt, 'and those were just the things I was looking for – however, a bit of a challenge to install.'

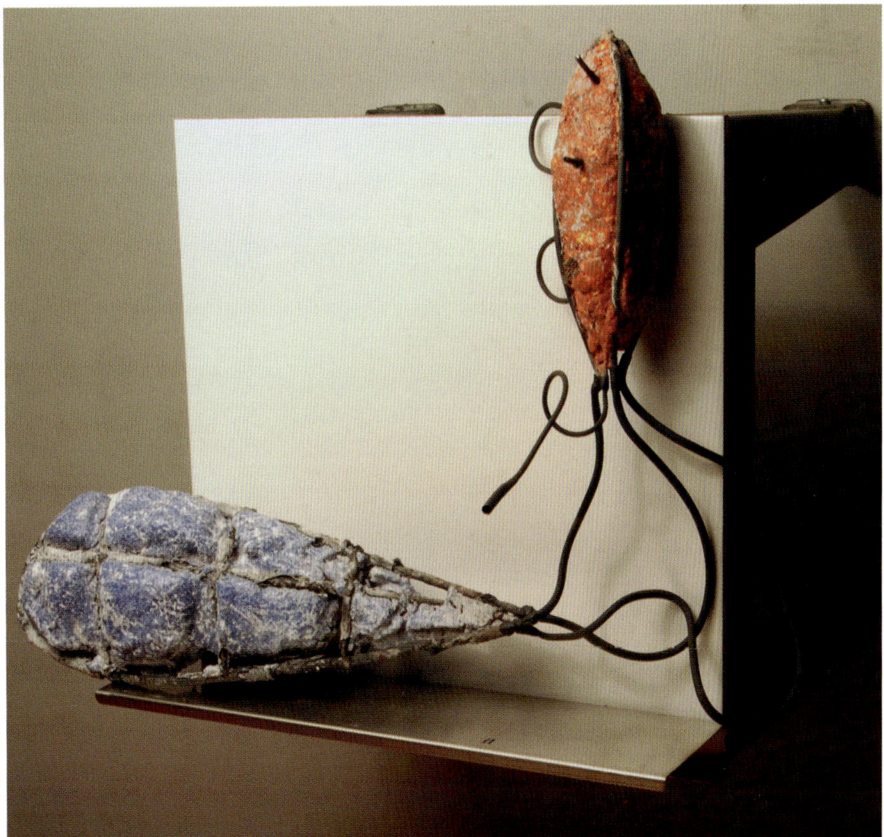

Todd Shanafelt, *Fiets sap*, 2009. Metal wire, Egyptian paste, tile, metal legs, fired to Cone 03 in electric kiln, 30 x 30 x 24 cm (11¾ x 11¾ x 9½ in). *Photo: by the artist.*

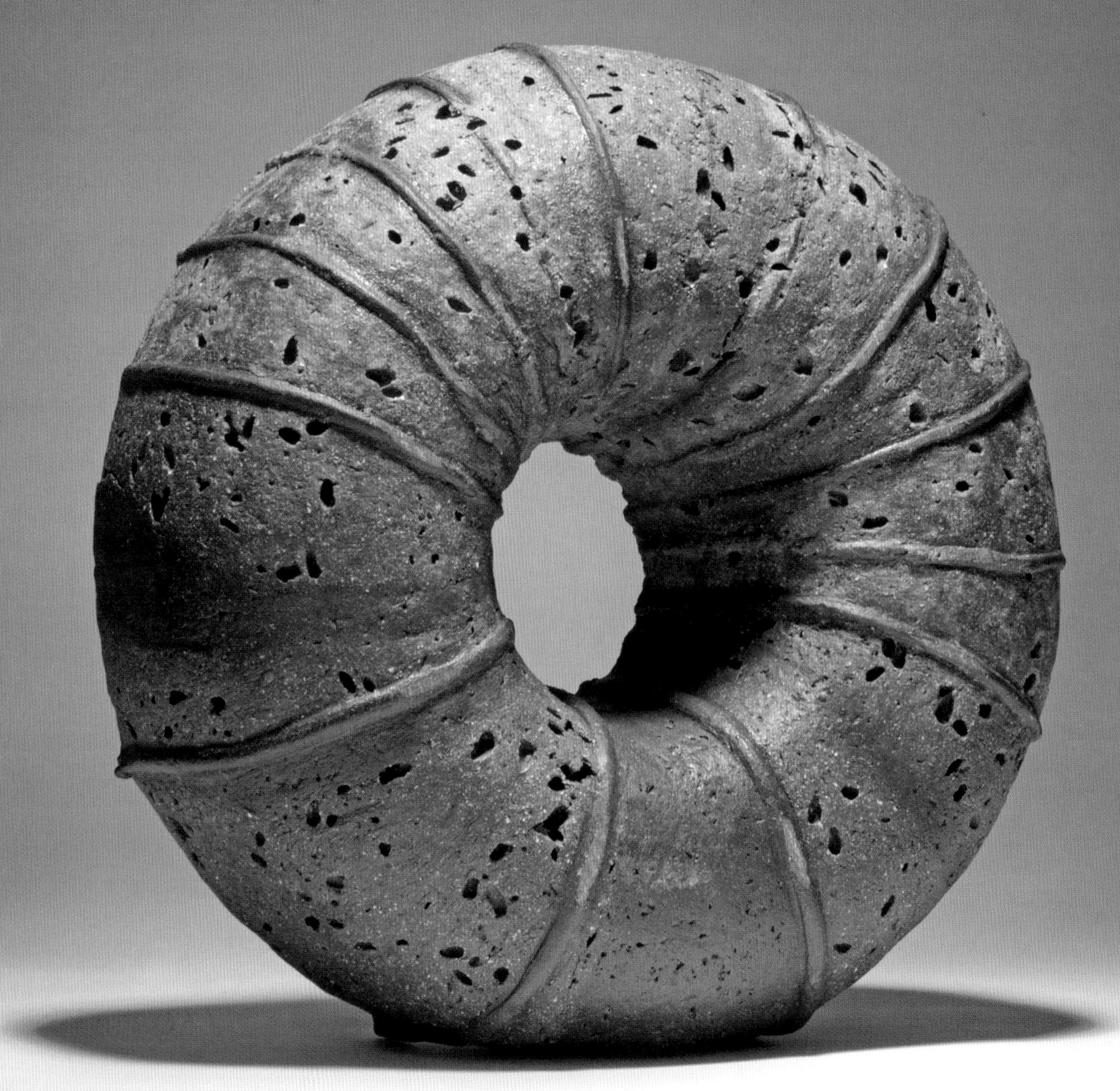

Glossary

anagama A type of wood-fired kiln.

batt wash A glaze-resistant material sold in powdered form, made from alumina and china clay. Mixed with water and painted onto kiln shelves, it prevents the glazed ware from sticking during firing.

bentonite A highly plastic clay that will improve the plasticity of a clay body; additions of 1% or less will keep a glaze slop in suspension.

biscuit or **bisque** A first firing, usually to 1000°C (1832°F), which precedes glazing.

cellulose Organic plant material used to make paper products and mainly sourced from wood pulp and cotton.

china clay or **kaolin** A pure, natural clay, which is an essential ingredient in porcelain and bone china bodies.

cotton linter Cotton fibre sold in sheets and used for making paperclay.

crank baffles Slabs of fired clay that are positioned inside the kiln to protect kiln elements from damage, for example, from spots of glaze.

deflocculated slip Contains an additive that reduces the amount of water required for fluidity. Sodium silicate or soda ash are commonly used for this purpose.

Egyptian paste A very old type of prepared clay body that creates its own glaze during firing.

greenware Unfired pottery.

LEFT: Kathleen Standen, *Horizon III* (view 1), 2011. Porcelain clay body, porcelain paperclay impressions, organic additions, oxides, 27 x 27 x 10 cm (10½ x 10½ x 4 in). *Photo: Roland Paschhoff.*

grog Ground, fired material added to clays for texture and to reduce shrinkage.

jolleying A process of forming a pot using a spinning mould.

lithophane A moulded or etched porcelain form which reveals a three-dimensional image when back-lit.

lustre A type of glaze in which a metallic surface is formed by the reduction of precious metallic compounds.

maquette A small model.

molochite Calcined china clay, used as grog in white bodies.

nichrome wire A wire that can withstand high temperatures.

plaster batt A flat surface of plaster, used for drying clay.

saggar A heat-resistant container, usually of clay, into which unfired ware is placed in the kiln.

scumming Marks left by soluble salts crystallising on the surface, which occurs in some bodies, such as Egyptian paste.

slip A homogeneous mixture of clay and water.

soak Maintaining the same temperature for a given period as part of a kiln firing schedule.

strath A Scottish term for a wide, flat valley, through which a river runs.

terra sigillata A slip made of very fine clay, which is usually coloured and burnished after firing.

thermal shock Stress created within a ceramic body by a sudden temperature change.

vermiculite A natural mineral sold in garden centres and added to clay for decorative purposes.

wax resist A waxy substance used to prevent slips, engobes or glazes from adhering onto the clay body.

Suppliers

UK

CLAYS AND RAW MATERIALS

Alisdair Kettles Pottery Supplies
Arlary Farm Cottage
Milnathort by Kinross
Fife KY13 9SJ
Tel: 01577 862 551
www.alisdairkettlespotterysupplies.com

Bath Potters' Supplies
Unit 18, Fourth Avenue
Westfield Trading Estate
Radstock, Nr Bath BA3 4XE
Tel: 01761 411077
www.bathpotters.co.uk

Ceramatech
Units 16 & 17, Frontier Works
33 Queen Street
London N17 8JA
Tel: 0208 885 4492
www.ceramatech.co.uk

Clayman Pottery Supplies
Morells Barn, Park Lane
Lower Bognor Road
Lagness, Chichester
West Sussex PO20 1LR
Tel: 01243 265845
www.claymansupplies.co.uk

Commercial Clay Ltd
Sandbach Road
Cobridge
Stoke-on-Trent
ST4 2DR
Tel: 01782 274448
www.commercialclay.co.uk

DBI
Blackrock Road
Cork
Ireland
Tel: +353 2142 92888

Global Ceramic Materials Ltd
Milton Works
Diamond Crescent, Off Leek New Road
Milton, Stoke-on-Trent
Staffordshire ST2 7PX
Tel: 01782 537297
www.globalcm.co.uk

Hesketh Potters' Supplies
14 Micklefield Way
Seaford
East Sussex BN25 4EU
Tel: 01323 896 444
www.heskethps.co.uk

Potclays
Brickkiln Lane
Stoke-on-Trent
Staffordshire ST4 7BP
Tel: 01782 219816
www.potclays.co.uk

Potterycrafts
Campbell Road
Stoke-on-Trent
Staffordshire ST4 4ET
Tel: 01782 745000
www.potterycrafts.co.uk

Scarva Pottery Supplies
Unit 20, Scarva Road Industrial Estate
Banbridge, County Down
Northern Ireland, BT32 3QD
Tel: 028 406 69699
www.scarvapottery.com

Valentine Clays Ltd
The Sliphouse, 18-20 Chell Street
Hanley, Stoke-on-Trent
Staffordshire ST1 6BA
Tel: 01782 271200
www.valentineclays.co.uk

SPECIALIST EQUIPMENT AND ADDITIONS

Alec Tiranti
Sculpture supplies
3 Pipers Court, Berkshire Drive
Thatcham
Berkshire RG19 4ER
Tel: 0845 123 2100
www.tiranti.co.uk

DK Holdings
Stone polishers and diamond abrasives
Station Approach
Staplehurst
Kent TN12 0QN
Tel: 01580 891662
www.dk-holdings.co.uk

Encore Diamond
Diamond cutting, grinding and polishing materials
Encore House, Main Street

Endmoor
Cumbria LA8 0EU
Tel: 015395 67957
www.encorediamond.co.uk

Glasplies
Glass fibre tissue
2 Crowland Street
Southport
Merseyside PR9 7RZ
Tel: 01704 540626
www.glasplies.co.uk

John Purcell Paper
Cotton linter
15 Rumsey Road
London SW9 0TR
Tel: 0207 737 5199
www.johnpurcell.net

Norwich Sheet Metal Co Ltd
Metal
11 Hurricane Way
Norwich
Norfolk NR6 6EZ
Tel: 01603 416266
www.norwichsheetmetalcoltd.co.uk

Sheffield Refractories Ltd
Refractory castable cement and aggregates
113 Laughton Road
Dinnington
Sheffield S25 2PP
Tel: 01909 568444
www.sheffield-refractories.co.uk

Wires.co.uk
Nichrome wire
18 Raven Road,
London E18 1HW
Tel: 0208 505 0002
www.wires.co.uk

USA

AMACO/brent
6060 Guion Road
Indianapolis, IN 46254
Tel: 317-248-9300
www.amaco.com

Aardvark Clay
1400 E. Pomona Street
Santa Ana, CA 92705
Tel: 714-541-4157
www.aardvarkclay.com

Bailey Pottery Equipment
PO Box 1577
Kingston, NY 12402
Tel: 845-339-5530
www.baileypottery.com

FreeForm
1912 Cleveland
National City, CA 91950-5510
Tel: 619-477-1004
www.freeformclay.com

Highwater Clays
P.O. Box 18284
600 Riverside Drive
Asheville, NC 28814
Tel: 704-252-6033
www.highwaterclays.com

HyperGlaze
6354 Lorca Drive
San Diego, CA 92115-5509
Tel: 619-286-1836
hyperglaze.com

Laguna Clay Co.
14400 Lomitas Avenue
City of Industry, CA 91746
Tel: 800-452-4862
www.lagunaclay.com

Olympia Enterprises
PO Box 321
715 McCartney Rd
Youngstown, OH 44405
Tel: 330-746-2726
www.olympiadecals.com

Mason Color
PO Box 76
East Liverpool, OH 43920
Tel: 330-385-4400
www.masoncolor.com

Seattle Pottery Supply
35 S. Hanford Street
Seattle, WA 98134
Tel: 800-522-1975
www.seattlepotterysupply.com

Standard Ceramic Supply Co.
One Walnut Street
Carnegie, PA 15106
Tel: 412-489-5240
www.standardceramic.com

Standard Ceramics
24 Chestnut Street
Carnegie, PA 15106
Tel: 412-276-6333
www.standardceramic.com

US Pigment
815 Schneider Drive
South Elgin, IL 60177
Tel: 630-893-9217
www.uspigment.com

Ward Burner Systems
P.O. Box 1086
Dandridge, TN 37725
Tel: 865-397-2914
www.wardburner.com

Bibliography

Arefhaghi, M, *Traditional Adobe in Iran*, www.greenhomebuilding.com, viewed 22 June 2012.

Binns, D 'Aggregates in Ceramic Bodies: A Research Project', *Ceramics Technical*, Issue No. 23, 2006.

Christian, J 2007, Aneta Regal Deleu website, www.anetaregel.com, viewed 1 June 2012.

Cooper, E 2010, 'Gillian Lowndes: Potter and sculptor noted for incorporating a wide variety of materials into her work', *The Independent*, 20 October.

Munck Jørgensen, U 2006, 'Barbro Åberg', *Ceramics Monthly*, March issue, pp. 51–54.

Philp, R, *Fired Clay: The Ceramic Work of Paul Philp*, design and production by Ashted Daster, London.

Rhodes, D 1988, *Clay and Glazes for the Potter*, A&C Black, London.

White, S 2003, 'Light and Shade', *Ceramic Review*, July/August issue.

Roberts, G 2004, 'Filling the Silence: Toward an Understanding of Claudi Casanovas' Blocks', *Interpreting Ceramics*, Issue 5.

The Hollies 2010, Centre for Practical Sustainability, Enniskean, Cork, Ireland, www.thehollies.ie, viewed 30 May 2012.

Tolstrup, L 2004, 'Barbro Åberg – Ceramic Sculpture', *Kerameiki Techni*, no. 46, pp. 4–7.

Tudball, R 2004, 'Points in Time', *Ceramic Review*, May/June issue.

Whiting, D 2010, *Emma Rodgers*, written for the Bluecoat Display Centre, Liverpool.

Index